My Lesbian Husband

ALSO BY BARRIE JEAN BORICH

Restoring the Color of Roses

My Lesbian Husband

~

Landscapes of a Marriage

Barrie Jean Borich

Graywolf Press

Saint Paul, Minnesota

Some portions of this book have appeared in the *Evergreen Chronicles*, the *Gettysburg Review*, and *Gravity's Loophole*, the 1997 McKnight Award anthology published by The Loft Literary Center.

Being Alive—Music and Lyrics by Stephen Sondheim
© 1970—Range Road Music Inc., Quartet Music Inc. and Rilting Music, Inc.
Copyright renewed.
All rights administered by Herald Square Music Inc.
Used by permission. All rights reserved.

Publication of this volume is made possible in part by a grant provided by the Minnesota State Arts Board through an appropriation by the Minnesota State Legislature, and by a grant from the National Endowment for the Arts. Significant support has also been provided by Dayton's, Mervyn's, and Target stores through the Dayton Hudson Foundation, the Bush Foundation, the McKnight Foundation, the General Mills Foundation, the St. Paul Companies, and other generous contributions from foundations, corporations, and individuals. To these organizations and individuals we offer our heartfelt thanks.

Published by Graywolf Press
2402 University Avenue, Suite 203
Saint Paul, Minnesota 55114
All rights reserved.

www.graywolfpress.org

Published in the United States of America

ISBN 1-55597-292-6 (cloth)
ISBN 1-55597-310-8 (paperback)

2   4   6   8   9   7   5   3   1

Library of Congress Catalog Card Number: 99-60733

Cover design: A N D

Cover art: Karen Platt

AUTHOR'S NOTE

This is a book of creative nonfiction in which I have mingled the sensory facts of memoir and personal essay with some degree of poetic license. Aside from changing many (but not all) of the names, I have worked to write within the bounds of the actual, as I perceive it. That others may perceive shared events differently is unavoidable. When I have intentionally strayed into speculation and imagination I have tried to make that shift obvious.

Contents

for
Portland Avenue

Somebody hold me too close,
Somebody hurt me too deep,
Somebody sit in my chair
And ruin my sleep
And make me aware
Of being alive,
Being alive.

Stephen Sondheim

My Lesbian Husband

When I Call Her My Husband

Linnea and I have been lovers for all these years, and I wonder—are we married?

I ask her as we sit at our red kitchen table, in our South Minneapolis corner duplex with peeling walls and crumbling Victorian trim. Outside, the stoplight on Portland Avenue sends a shallow green, yellow, red wash in through the front windows as gearhead cars and accessorized Caddies with dark-tinted glass shriek through the intersection. As downtown commuters in tidy Hondas plod home south after work. As Harley guys rumble past with pipes clattering. As red Isuzu Troopers with big speakers in the back cruise by slow, bellowing with low bass, hip-hop, thump-da-thumps. As another family of kids we haven't seen before careens around the corner on bikes, the little ones on Big Wheels, pumping to keep up with tires growling and buckling over loose stones and broken glass.

Inside, our three cats lounge beneath the ceiling fan. Our dog digs through her basket of bones and toys. We are surrounded by the clutter of ourselves. Snapshots of friends and nieces. Funny postcards of women in vintage drag. Homemade valentines too sweet to throw away. Herb tinctures, and big bottles of vitamins. Big bottles of olive oil and every kind of tea. Glossy urbane magazines and mail-order catalogues for things we never order—books on tape, or down comforters, or loose-fitting casual clothing. Piles of clippings from the *Village Voice* that we don't have time to read. City newspapers and poetry books or volumes of lesbian and gay theory or books about quantum physics or *Star Trek* or dogs. Our moderate collection of plastic dinosaurs, including the five-foot-long, blowup pteranodon hanging from the kitchen ceiling. Our large and varied collection of holy statues and candles, Catholic and Orthodox, mostly the Madonna, along with a few other saints and goddesses: Saint Lucy with her eyes on a plate, Kannon with her many arms, Marilyn in plunging black décolletage, shell ladies from ocean-beach resorts, and a piñata rendition of Madonna (the pop star) we made a few years back for a party. All this is seven years of us. So are we married?

I ask her in the summer as we ride in her Chevy Blazer truck on our way to a week in a one-room cabin on the shore of blue-gray and un-blinking Lake Superior, the dog's head hanging between us from her spot in the back as the forests along the northern highway grow more blue-green and needled.

I ask her in the winter over big bowls of steaming seafood soup at our usual table, between bright white walls and abstract prints of fish, in the nonsmoking section of our favorite restaurant, run by a Chinese family emigrated here from Vietnam. Mostly daughters, black-haired and half our size, one-by-one they interrupt us to admire the silver jewelry Linnea buys me at gem shows, to ask us questions about our relationship, to describe how *their* lives are changing—a wedding engagement, a new baby, a college acceptance on the East Coast.

In all these spots, public and private, I ask Linnea, "Are we married?"

Her response is always to move closer, pull me closer if she can. Let's say we're at home, lying side-by-side in the king-sized bed that we bought with our only joint charge card (Slumberland). The bed is one of just three joint purchases we've made in our first seven years. The others were a TV and a queen-sized water bed that we sold later when we started waking up aching, my back, her knees. The water bed was our first joint purchase, and I cried when we bought it in our second year to-gether because it was so complicated. There were enough boards and rubber and cords to fill up the back of a pickup truck. "I moved my whole life to Minnesota in a Pinto," I sobbed. "And now just the bed takes up a whole truck." Now we lie on our king-sized King Koil on a plain steel base, big enough for both of us, the dog, and a cat or two if there isn't any roughhousing. We're still waiting to be able to afford a frame for this extravagant mattress. We want something showy and romantic, like a

Victorian sleigh bed, to match our feeling for each other. But our dreams surpass our credit limits. If the state of marriage is determined by property, we may not have enough to qualify.

So we're lying in this bed on a Sunday evening, the dog curled up just under my stocking feet, one of the cats annoying me by obsessively kneading at my chest, and I ask her, "Do you think we're married?"

Linnea rolls over, shooing away the cat, resting her belly alongside my hip as her chin nuzzles my shoulder. "I think you're my wife," she says.

I laugh and squeeze in closer, turn so I can kiss the soft exposed flesh below her ear. She is completely serious and not serious at all, in that queer way we learn to roll with a language we are at once completely a part of and completely excluded from.

"Yes, honey," I say. "You are my wife, too." But this is not the right word for it. I can feel the vague tensing in her limbs as she holds me, the structure of her embrace still solid as something deeper steps away. What is it in her that is compromised, knocked off its feet, when I call her wife? A sort of manhood? But this is not the right word either. "I don't know the word," she would say. "But I'm not a man."

So I press myself even closer, sliding my thigh up to rest between her legs, sliding my hip up against her hip so I can feel our bones touch. The evening sun falling through the lace we have hung on our bedroom window scatters bright, sun-colored roses across her face and chest.

"Not your wife," she says.

"My handsome wife?" I try.

"I don't like wife."

It's true, it doesn't fit her. But who does the word wife fit? Fishwife. Housewife. I don't like it either. But when Linnea calls me her wife all that falls away. Then it is a word filled with all the attention she gives me, plump with kisses on the neck as my thighs part to her hands. We can only use this word if we steal it. Hidden in our laps it's better.

Better for me. When I say, wife, her jaw muscles stiffen. She becomes strange, unknowable to me while the sun outside falls behind clouds, while there is no light dappling our bare arms and faces, while the surface of our skin chills.

"OK," I say. "How about husband?"

· 5 ·

With this word, husband, I feel her relax, the flow between us return-ing. Can I call her my husband without meaning a man? Without mean-ing a woman who wants to be a man? Without even meaning a woman who acts like a man? Even now, over thirteen years a lesbian, I still meet men I am attracted to, but just from the surface layers of my skin. No man can touch my face, my lips, and cause everything in me to drop, bones to water, as Linnea can, as women like her, butch lesbians, do. Who in the world can fly you to the moon, set you to swoon, send you down with that old black magic in a Tony Bennett ballad kind of love fever? For me it's a woman who would rather be a husband than a wife.

When I call Linnea my husband I mean that she's a woman who has to lead when we slow dance, who is compelled to try to dip and twirl me, no matter that I have rarely been able to relax on a dance floor since I stopped drinking. She leads me between the black walls of a gay bar, our faces streaked with neon and silver disco light, the air so dark Linnea's black leather belt and both pairs of our black boots seem to vanish, leav-ing parts of us afloat in the heavy smell of booze and cigarettes. She leads me slipping under streamers and lavender balloons, in the center of the light cast by several dozen candles, on some friend's polished oak dining-room floor cleared for party dancing. She leads me across a Sunday morning, sun streaming into our living room through southern exposed windows, so bright it sets the dust spinning. We dance clumsily on the purple oriental rug we bought cheap at a garage sale, the worn wool covered with cat and dog hair, the dog barking and nipping at our heels, me in stocking feet, Linnea wearing athletic shoes because the arches of her feet went bad a few years back.

When I call her my husband I mean that she's a woman I saw dressed seriously in a skirt and heels just once, early on, when she still tried to cross over for job interviews. Her head, shoulders, hands looked too large, her gait too long, an inelegant drag queen. This is a woman who's happiest straddling a motorcycle, who wears a black leather jacket and square-toed biking boots even when she's not riding. For years I've been telling her that her thick, curly hair would look fantastic long, wild with its own life like the hair of Botticelli's Venus or Arlo Guthrie's hair in the *Alice's Restaurant* days, but she will always be a woman who wears her hair short, cut to look slicked back at the sides, a grease-free DA. She's a woman who does not look like a man, yet is often mistaken for one, a woman who meets a clamor of gasps when she enters into the pale green light of shopping-mall rest rooms. The other women are caught with their naked hands motionless over the bright white sinks. The boldest and least observant among them checks her own reflection in the mirror, straightens her back, breaks from the pack to protect the others, points to some unseeable place on the other side of the cloister wall—"*This* is the *women's* room."

I mean Linnea is a woman who once stood at the center of the Gay Nineties Saturday-night throb, her Levi's tight across the ass, her black leather boots and black leather jacket absorbing the speckled silver light refracting from the spangled curtains of the drag stage. She was caught in a fast second of instinct when she swung around and decked a drunk flat in the nose. He had reached between her legs from behind to grab what he thought was her dick. "He got two surprises that night," is what Linnea says about it.

I mean Linnea is a woman who is a woman because she was born with a woman's body. The large breasts and tender nipples. The monthly swelling, cramps, and blood. The opening up into her that she will do anything to protect, even break a man's nose in the glittering dark of a bar where drag queens sway on a sequined stage in sequined gowns and sequined eyelashes, *their* breasts made of foam rubber or silicone, *their* dicks taped up safe between their buttocks, as they smile like pop stars before paparazzi and mouth the words of Whitney Houston songs.

When I say husband I mean the woman lying beside me on a cool spring Sunday evening while the thinning light streaked over our bed from the west turns rose-colored. "You are my husband," I whisper to her, and we both laugh a little under our breaths, as we kiss, as she rocks me until I am nearly asleep, as the light flickers and sinks into night, as we listen to Luis outside in the yard behind ours crooning in Spanish to his four little dogs while his pet parrots shriek, as our dog pants alongside our bed, waiting for her supper, as the cat kneads my chest, using her claws, and I shoo her off to the floor. "But does that mean we're married?" I whisper to Linnea. But she is drifting off into a nap. We won't solve this today. The rose light flickers and I drift off with her.

The World in Our Bed

It has been in these wordless moments as we fall off into sleep, or as we arrive back to the light, awake, still together, that I have wondered. Before it was the birds, our neighbor Luis's chattering pets, that filled in the background of my endless questioning, or it was the honk and rattle of Portland Avenue, or the heavy steps and laughter of our upstairs neighbors, their sounds creaking down through the weakening walls of that crumbling duplex. Now, as I look at our lives together, I see some things have changed. Linnea and I have new windows that look out onto a different side of the neighborhood. Another gaggle of voices screeches and coughs in the alley. Different splays of light form across the bed-clothes. Still, the same questions inhabit me.

I am not the type who can disappear easily into the music of a moment, although I've learned to try, learned a little bit of the deep breathing, the mind-release of meditation, learned to master at least a momentary physical dissolve that allows me to meld my usually frac-tured consciousness with the particular tree rustle and traffic rumble of the city's sunny or thundering afternoons.

Still, most of my moments overflow with other moments. I rest against Linnea's breasts and stomach in a room where the sharp edge of afternoon light slowly dulls to matte and grainy dusk. The hot summer water spirits that had been writhing up from the sidewalks vanish as the evening cools. The voices of children thin as some are called home. Even in these hovering moments where I touch my lips lightly against Linnea's lips, run one finger along the curve of my lover's encircling arm just to feel her skin against my fingertip, even here I have to work to stay in just this one place. I have to sing in low whispers, *breathe, now now,* to keep myself out of daydream. This is one fact of our marriage. I am too easily distracted. Linnea sees just the one she loves but I'm always lost in a wide lens. I watch the muscled body of the world push between us and obscure the face of our body's love with its wide slice of cheekbone, its glimmering and familiar slopes of skin.

The question is simple. Who are we, the two of us, together? If we could look down on ourselves from above, what would we see? A married couple, like any married couple, linked through our coupling by history and tradition, literature and song, to the great pitch and roll? Or huddled refugees, expatriated by our aberrations, grabbing on and flying off again, but at home in the sweet wildflower ditches we find along the side of a the road?

I would like to stop worrying about it. I would like to just lie here, inside this moment, with Linnea, in our rumpled bed, on the grimy and gardened south side of a Midwestern city where I was not born. I would like to touch Linnea's lips against my own, and let my lover fill all my open spaces. I would like to let us, just us, drown out the other populations, the music of people and places that surround us even when we aren't looking out our windows. But then I am overcome with long-finished minutes. I might recollect a dinner with our friends, a cackling chorus made up of women who wear a tumult of natural black hair or green and copper weaves of imitation braids or maybe a stiff blond brush cut, and men with gray beards or homegrown dreadlocks or a sandy jazz dot on the chin, gathered around platters of organic turkey or homemade lasagna or walleye with black bean sauce.

Or maybe it's the face of my brother's wife I see, in the years before their marriage, in Chicago, the first time I meet this woman who will be my sister-in-law. Her long black hair hangs loose down the back of a rumpled T-shirt. Her smile is easy, from the side of her that likes this moment of her life in a big American city, speaking a language she was not born to and completely unafraid of her boyfriend's lesbian sister. Mitsuko's feet are slightly pigeon-toed, and she holds a glass of something cold in her hand, something she has been drinking as she sits up in Paulie's bed, watching television with her lover in the moments before Linnea and I arrive at the old apartment near the center of the city, the one with the doorman and the view of all those brick and tar rooftops, just a block from Lake Michigan.

This moment opens in my mind, dissolves into focus suddenly, without bidding. I can keep it to myself, or I can tell Linnea about it, but either way the moment is fuller and more fractured than it was before, and the world, welcome or not, is here in bed with us.

The Laws of the Game

My little brother Paulie was breathless. Even over the phone I could tell that his chest was pounding, his thoughts racing.

"I've got news," he said. "We're engaged."

The room where we stood trembled red. Every December on Portland Avenue Linnea hung Christmas lights, the flickering kind, usually an unbroken line of red or gold or blue, because she knew I liked the solid strings, the unbroken impact of just one shade, better than the random tones of the multicolored strands. She hung them while I was out, working or shopping for groceries. Then she waited for me to return, laughed when I gasped at the transformation, the center of our home rinsed in new color. This year she taped them up in the front window in the shape of a top-heavy star. They blinked out at empty Portland Avenue as Linnea and I leaned over the phone.

"You are?" I said. "Engaged?" And then I was breathless, too.

It was a usual New Year's Day in Minneapolis, strangely quiet. Everyone in the city seemed to be home. Nursing hangovers. Watching football. Linnea and I were not hungover, but there was a football game droning from the TV in the next room. I didn't know which teams. When I tried to pay attention to the game the players blurred, and I thought of the electric football set my brothers Paulie and Benny shared when we were kids. Little plastic quarterbacks and linebackers buzzing along on a rattling electric field—a mass of tiny men who all looked the same, jumbled up in a ridiculous, toppling mass. It's not because I'm the only girl child in my family that I grew up hating football. My mother is the biggest football fan of all, with closets of Illinois colors, blue-and-orange sweat-shirts and caps and windbreakers that could almost double for both the Fighting Illini and the Bears if not for the grand embroidered logos—a snarling mammal, a fake Indian. But early on, I was compelled to distin-guish myself from the rest of the family, from my mother especially. What I liked was different from what they liked. Whether it was my dif-ference that influenced my preferences or my preferences that defined my difference, I never have been certain. What I can say definitely is that I have always hated football.

"It's New Year's Day," Linnea said. "I have to watch football." It meant something to her, so I tried not to complain, even though this sounded a lot like something one of my brothers would say, even though I was an-noyed by the constant shouts and banter of the announcers and the cam-era shots of male fans with their bare chests painted the clashing colors of some team they adored beyond all reason. The game itself has always mystified me, even though I've tried to follow Linnea's careful explana-tions. But the questions I ask defy easy answers. Is the hollering coach with the scrunched face a happy man? Is the boxy guy in the middle of the field married to someone he loves beyond all reason? Does he think about his love when ten guys try to crush him with the entire weight of their hurled bodies?

"It's just a game," Linnea said.

Just a game, which aside from the grunting and body bashing, is pre-cisely why I don't understand. How do people feel such physiological al-legiance to something as separate from their own bodies as a team of beefy guys whose faces they can't even see, whose hearts they will never know? Even in high school I had a problem with team spirit. My high school was enormous, over a thousand in each graduating class. I knew one, maybe two, football players. A couple more I recognized from those Saturday-night bacchanals advertised by word of mouth when some rich kid's parents were out of town. There was usually a hard-jawed sports hero or two reeling and barfing on the front lawn from all that free keg beer. The few times I actually went to a football game, the fun for me was getting stoned and watching the cheerleaders. Were they really so much prettier than everyone else? Did they deserve their nearly holy status?

When their arms flew up over their heads and their feet rose up off the ground, levitated by a long physical wail of joy (what was going on down there, on that painted grass) were they sincere? Did they really love their team beyond all physical law, beyond all rational explanation? And what was the point, on those gusty, late October Saturday mornings, of clapping with mittens on?

But it was New Year's Day and Linnea and I were still working out the concessions we would make for the sake of each other's marital bliss. So I put up with the football game, and Linnea put up with my bitching about the football game. It was a million years since high school and my brother was on the phone from Chicago. The same game that pulsed and shouted in our living room echoed long-distance through the speaker phone, as my little brother told me he was getting married.

~

It was not a shock, this news. Paulie had been involved with Mitsuko for a while. For the past year they had lived together in the apartment where Mitsuko used to live alone, in a high-rise near downtown Chicago. They shared the wide, white walls hung with matted posters of French photographs, the *Little House on the Prairie* quilt Mitsuko made by hand, and a collection of plastic Godzilla figures Paulie brought back from the trip they took together to visit Mitsuko's family in Japan. They had even bought a good department-store mattress and box spring. Still, my mom wouldn't let them sleep in the same room when they stayed over at her house in the near south suburbs, because they weren't married.

"Ma, that's so silly," I said to her once, in her blue-tiled kitchen, while handing her a stack of dirty dishes I carried upstairs after some holiday dinner. "They sleep together at home."

"Not in my house," she said, lifting her head out of the dishwasher to look at me; her face looked to be screwed on too tight like a jar I'd never be able to open.

My mother and I have always had a bickering relationship. I have friends who have studied the subject, friends who tell me their theories: that mothers and daughters can never get along, that mothers see the girls that emerged from their bellies as the bodies they didn't get a chance to finish living in, and so they will not, cannot, abdicate what they feel in their bones is their right to choose for us. Perhaps this is the case between my mother and me, and it's worsened by the fact that her oldest, her only daughter, not only moved away but came back a lesbian. An underground creature. My mother has stopped saying to me, "When are you going to be normal. Get married. Have children," because I always cry when she says it, and then I don't surface again for a year or so.

It's not that I think she doesn't love me. She cries, too, every time I leave, and in her dissolving face I see what she has never been able to tell me, that she loves me as a woman can only love the one who was the first to inhabit her, share her blood. It's a bond neither of us can shrug off even though she has told me many times that she wasn't ready, when I was conceived, to leave her first good teaching job to raise a child. When I do come back, I can still see her strain to recognize her blond, banana-curled baby, and her squint of disapproval at who I have become. But she's not like me. She doesn't think too hard about these things. She's like a cat who has burnt her whiskers on the gas jet enough times to know she has to take another route to the top of the refrigerator. Why ask questions about the nature of fire, of heat? Just avoid it.

So when she makes these pronouncements that I find ridiculous, I can't stop myself from challenging her, even though I know I might start it all in motion again—the high unpunctuated sentences, the tears I can't stop, the words that hurl me back across Wisconsin to my remade home in Minnesota.

"You let Linnea and me sleep together here," I countered. "We're not married."

My mother was silent for a moment at this. She used both hands to pat down her hair that I noticed was straighter than it used to be, and longer, almost to her shoulders, a change from the tight perm she had begun to wear sometime in the 1970s to free herself from those Friday after-work trips to the beauty parlor to get her bouffant washed and ratted. Now I watched her, the newly loose hair, the narrowing eyes. I expected the worst, but instead she surprised me. She laughed.

"Well, if I didn't let you, then you wouldn't come home," she said. She was right about that.

Later I went down to the bedroom in the basement that used to be my brother Benny's room, when he moved back for law school. Mitsuko was putting a pillow in a fresh case so she could go to bed. Paulie and Benny, hypnotized by the gray glow of late-night TV, were sprawled on the sofa in the next room. I sat down on the bed next to Mitsuko and told her what my mother had said, about her and Paulie, about me not coming home. She sat back on the bed laughing. Her narrow body made barely a ripple in the bedclothes, her long black hair fell into her face. She knew I was the only one in the family who would tell her such a story.

∾

I asked Paulie about marriage once, as we walked down Rush Street in Chicago, past a strip of rowdy sports bars with sliding-glass doors that opened up out onto the sidewalk. I used to frequent those bars when I was nineteen, but walking by again at thirty-three I couldn't remember what I liked about them. Years back, Rush Street was more of a disco scene, subterraneanly lit, full of straight men in quiana shirts wearing three gold chains, their hair tucked behind their ears. Now that the 1970s have come in and out of style again this memory feels made up, a deliberate embellishment, but this is really what I remember, in as much as I can be expected to recall the sights of a time when I wasn't seeing too clearly. This is what grown-up life is like, I must have thought, how real living feels inside my bones, as I drove forty minutes up from the South Side just to drink. Paulie and Mitsuko ended up living just a couple blocks away from this street where the disco beat is gone, where the bars are raucous and well-lit, where televisions hover from every corner, and where most nights you're likely to see some former high-school hero in a Bears jersey puking over the curb. But the Saturday afternoon I walked by with Paulie the racket was just a fraction of what it would be later that evening. Paulie led me past the wide open doors of the sports bar where he had met Mitsuko. There was a rough ripple of laughter from some full tables in the back, and the sloshing pitchers of grain-colored brew caught the late afternoon light. "I saw her sitting alone under the basket-ball net," Paulie said, rosy with his recollection of it. "I thought she was really pretty."

The wafting smell of beer pulled me from that moment and into an-other, a fifteen-year-old memory of how I drank in those Rush Street bars until that awful disco mono-beat throbbed through my bloodstream, until I was transfixed by the liquid staccato light of the disco ball as it slid and shimmered off the surface of those slippery shirts, until I was willing to dance with whatever man approached me. I couldn't talk without sinking into wet laughter, then I drank some more until I couldn't remember how I got away from those *Saturday Night Fever* wannabes, could barely remember driving back south to the family house, stone drunk at dawn, careening around the steep turns of the S-curve, a double hair pin that used to be just north of the Loop on Lake Shore Drive.

"Oh, great place," I said to Paulie, feeling mean about the street, as if it had been the geography that made me who I was at nineteen. I saw too late on Paulie's face that he had been trying to give me something, a memory of falling in love. I stumbled trying to make it up to him.

"So do you and Mitsuko ever think about getting married?" I asked.

He didn't answer, just scowled, pretended not to hear. The din of cock-rock videos and basketball games subsided as we turned off Rush Street, down a block of brown brick walk-ups, toward his thirty-story high-rise with the computerized door locks and the surly night doorman. We rode up the elevator in silence, and I didn't ask again, afraid there was too much want in my voice. I didn't understand why I cared about my little brother's marital status. I didn't even know yet if I would take the long walk down the aisle with Linnea, if we had that to choose.

≈

The whole family had been waiting to see if Paulie and Mitsuko would get married. Linnea and I had been waiting, too. We both loved Mitsuko and had been hoping she would stick around. Paulie was not like me, not the type to spit at convention. Eventually it would either be marriage or nothing. I had been waiting to see if my love had been wasted on someone who would disappear, become part of Paulie's past. I was afraid Mitsuko would go back to Japan and forget how she accepted Linnea and me right away, forget about how she said to me once, "I like it when you are in Chicago. Then I don't feel so strange in your family."

The summer before they were engaged Mitsuko and Paulie came to Minneapolis to visit us. It was a holiday weekend, the Fourth of July, and Linnea's mother was visiting, too. Linnea's mom, Toni, was barely fifty then, long divorced from Linnea's dad, and with her incandescent hair, the peacock tattoo on her upper back, her Long Island Italian accent, and her stories about her ex-drunk, ex-biker, ex-boyfriend, she seemed more like an older sibling, or a wild young aunt than anybody's mother. Toni was fighting a slight summer bronchitis. She stretched out on our vinyl sofa and blew her nose, then dropped her billowing red head back and laughed. What a jerk that guy was—throwing her over for a pale young woman who smoked pot with him and didn't care when he snuck away for another swig of cough syrup with codeine.

Mitsuko and Toni bonded like old school friends. Throughout that crowded afternoon our porch off Portland Avenue was filled with lesbian friends barbecuing chicken or tofu dogs and exclaiming over the egg-rolls Mitsuko had made that morning. When I was in chem dep treatment we called these sorts of parties "sober fun," and there was a time when sober was the only part of that I understood. But that had changed for me. Now the most fun I could even conceive of was an afternoon like this one. Our makeshift yard was overflowing with every kind of dog pack-wrestling in celebration of our dog Patsy's fifth birthday. When another neighbor kid set off a firecracker or bottle rocket in the alley, the dogs whined and burrowed together under the porch, in and around the mildewed wood scraps, rusty nails, and discarded chunks of the house exterior, until Linnea and I could cajole them out again with bacon treats or special ice-cream snacks designed just for dogs. Paulie, who can talk to anyone, even Japanese uncles, even lesbian ex-lovers, even a porch full of people who used to get high, mingled outside. He sprawled in a lawn chair and hung with the gay girls, genially offering his opinion in various discussions of the heart.

Mitsuko sat in the living room with Toni, the two straight women the only ones who didn't feel like blending. When I stepped in to see what they were doing, Toni had moved to the zebra-print chair and Mitsuko was sitting at the edge of our turquoise wagon-wheel couch, sipping tea out of a zebra-patterned mug. They both looked strangely at home in our living room where almost nothing matched. I didn't know what they'd been talking about, but it was as if Mitsuko had heard my thoughts, the question I had been wearing just under my skin all weekend. "You know Paulie and me," Mitsuko said to both of us, "we're just boyfriend and girlfriend."

Toni nodded. Enjoy yourself, no commitments, she seemed to be saying as her red-crowned and coughing head bobbed in complete sympathy. Outwardly I nodded, too, wanting everyone to keep getting along. But inside I felt myself moving too fast, ready to clean up the kitchen in three minutes flat, or pull out the big noise-sucking vacuum, things my mother would do if she heard something she didn't want to know.

It's not that marriage would lock her in, assure me of other Fourth of Julys, other crowded moments where my family and Linnea's family and my grown life formed one varied and continuous wash of translucent light. I had been waiting for a while now to hear the good news that would pitch me into a long wail of happiness. I wanted Mitsuko to join my family. But why? I was shocked by what I was thinking. This was me, the one so suspicious of all convention, the one who had always savored the right to leave my family at any time, my choice, whenever my shoulders tensed and the back of my eyeballs began to ache. How unfair of me to expect Mitsuko to promise anything.

Already my parents treated Mitsuko as the long-lost daughter I would never be. My mother's voice rose in wonder when she told me about buying gifts for Mitsuko, a jacket for instance, a size six, *too big*, as if Mitsuko's willow body, normal in Japan, was something she had achieved through hard work and tenacity, earning an advanced degree in waist and hips. I am as tall and big-limbed as my brothers, and I no longer believe in starving myself skinny. When my mother tells me these things I know she wishes it were me who were so slender, so girlish.

Throughout my childhood, I felt cornered by my mother's fantasy of a docile daughter, a princess myth from a Disney cartoon, that cheerleader who, through her sheer love of the game, could actually feel her feet float up off the gravel. Maybe my mother wanted what all the other women she knew seemed to have in their daughters—a friend for herself, a confidant who shared her head for math, her love of repetitive exercise, her compulsion to keep things clean, and her refusal to dwell on the past. She would have expected a natural barrier between herself and her sons, but not from her daughter.

My differences, however propagated, had to have been organic. The things I was drawn to as an adolescent—tragic Russian novels, Joni

Mitchell's white-wine blues, yoga classes at the community college, the sloppy introspection brought on by marijuana—all felt physically necessary to me, essential food for my negative photosynthesis. I didn't want my arms to rise toward heaven, didn't want my wails of joy to helicopter me over the ground. If anything, what I craved was under the crust, below the city's surface. I wanted to tunnel my way to a new home. And so, for better or worse, I did, but I had always felt I was less than I should be, a disappointing daughter. This is not a feeling I wished on Mitsuko. Yet since she had been around, a neutral patch of dirt had opened up for me in my family territory. I could dig or I could hover. I had ceased to be the only daughter. I liked having a straight-girl sister.

But my mother was wrong if she thought Mitsuko was Cinderella, even if she came a lot closer than I did. Although Mitsuko was slight, spoke softly, looked like she needed protection, came from a country where women rarely lived alone, she had left her own family, worked as a travel agent thousands of miles from her home, and at twenty-seven had already traveled to Hawaii, China, Egypt, England, and Chicago by herself. She always had money in the bank and could book her own flight to anywhere. Neither my mother nor I could push Mitsuko into doing anything she didn't want to do.

I knew all this, and understood it. I wanted to lay back my head and laugh for Mitsuko's freedom along with redheaded Toni, but now that I had surfaced, stable and sober and trying to flower above ground, now that I found myself squinting in the afternoon light, I had to admit I was a bossy older sister, more like my mother than I liked to believe. My desire to manage Mitsuko's destiny was not too deeply buried. Stay together. Get married. Have my nieces and nephews. Don't leave my family. I had been hopeful now for more than a year, ever since Mitsuko's work visa expired and she needed to either win the green-card lottery or go back to Japan. But Paulie said that was no reason to get married, and it turned out she didn't need to get married to stay. According to the Department of Immigration, she won the lottery twice, once as Mitsuko Minoru and again as Minoru Mitsuko. So it was simply a matter of choice. Of course, my feet stayed on the ground. I didn't sink, didn't shout out anything stupid, didn't make any demands on my brother's behalf. I knew it was not me or my mother that Mitsuko would be marrying, if it came to that. Still, I had been worried ever since I heard her say it. Just boyfriend and girlfriend.

~

"We announced to everyone, the whole family, on Christmas Eve," Paulie told us.

"You announced it to everyone at once," I shouted back. Linnea stood behind me, peering down, as if we could see him there, the shape of his face emerging out of the speaker phone like a genie. Our bent bodies were reflected in the front glass of our apartment, turning red and then pale again in the center of Linnea's Christmas star. Outside I could see more lights blinking. They hung unevenly from the unsteady eves of a ragged Victorian, kitty-corner across the street from us. It was a house I hated walking by in the winter because the public sidewalk in front was never shoveled. Where my parents lived, where Paulie was making this call, the lights were neatly hung, the walks always shoveled. I preferred the sloppiness here, this mixed-up and ramshackle neighborhood, the same world but more visibly out of control. But there were moments when my vision blurred and our block of bohemians and unleashed kids, of drug dealers and yuppie renovators, seemed sad compared to the swept-up place I came from, a place where Paulie announced his engagement to everyone but me. I am years gone from my home, and sometimes I don't even go back there for Christmas.

"I thought it would be fun to make a big formal announcement," Paulie said.

"Was it?"

"Oh yeah, it was great."

I already knew some of this story, had known it my whole life. Christmas was at Aunt Cecilia and Uncle Tony's that year. Paulie picked a grand stage, an old South Side house I had always loved with high ceilings, tall windows, and a flagstone fireplace Uncle Tony built himself, thirty years ago. They lived in a hilly neighborhood in the neatly segregated part of Chicago, full of spacious brick homes and brick-laid streets. Mitsuko was probably one of very few to have crossed the color line into Cecilia's living room.

Paulie's voice on the telephone was tinny and distant. I couldn't tell if this was because of the crummy speaker, or if it was something about the weird way I wasn't quite residing inside my body as I listened. "I waited until everyone was sitting down for dinner," he said, "but made my move before Aunt Cecilia started bringing out the food. That's when I picked up the wine bottle and stood up."

I could see the dinner table Paulie was describing. I could hear it. I could smell it. I knew Aunt Cecilia's house almost as well as the houses I grew up in, and Cecilia meant for her home to be unforgettable. My father's sister believed in decorating. With a little bit more ambition and a WASP name she could have been a home-crafts diva the likes of Martha Stewart. She and her middle son, my cousin Dino, both had a passion for transcendent presentation. It seemed to me their homes were the proof they needed. Look, we belong here, too, in the middle class in my aunt's case, who remembered when Croatians were called bohunks, to the territory called normal in Dino's case, who had been called a faggot since grammar school. I don't know if Cecilia influenced Dino or the other way around, but either of their home interiors could be the set of a Saturday-morning home-decorating show—the antique copper cookware hanging in Cecilia's kitchen, the gallery of black-and-white photographs matted under glass in Dino's center hallway. I often wondered if Cecilia, who I heard took to her bed for a week when Dino told her he was gay, knew how much her home was the sort of place an older, professional gay man might live.

Aunt Cecilia's perfect table, her clean, cream settings were nothing like my mother's Christmas Eve dinners. My mother, who had always worked full-time, had no fire for turning homemaking into an expressive form. Her house was clean, serviceable, full of pictures and mementos that marked her family's passage, full of objects dear to her. She had no patience for artful arrangement. Dusting had always been my household chore, and I used to try, when I was a teenager, to put things in some kind of order. I shoved loose envelopes and stray snapshots left on the bookcase into a drawer. I organized my mother's pottery statuettes and china cups into formations based on color or height. But in a day or two it all fell back to how it had been, dust-free but endlessly cluttered.

My mother's holiday dinner would be set up in the panel and linoleum basement full of mismatched chairs and couches that used to be upstairs. No design theme, just the things my parents liked. Black-and-white photo collages my father took of Paulie, Benny, and me when we were in high school. Matted prints of Mexican landscapes that my father photographed on family camping vacations hung in carved wooden frames he bought at Mexican tourist markets. A bookcase of my father's old books—Hemingway, Fitzgerald, Arthur Miller—and his old jazz albums—Brubek, Nancy Wilson, Charlie Parker. A shellacked porcupine fish we'd picked up on another family vacation, hanging from a fishing line over a varnished oak wet bar my father built twenty years ago when he bought this three-bedroom ranch in the about-to-be integrated near south suburbs. The smell of my mother's dinner would permeate both floors on Christmas Eve. There was the sweet meat of turkey with sausage stuffing. There was the sharp sugar of sweet potatoes cooked with marshmallow. There was the fruity shiver of Jell-O. Dinner would be served around a Santa candle, on a red-plaid tablecloth thrown over the old round kitchen table and with a folding table beside it. Paulie and Mitsuko would have broken the news here, at my mother's table, if it had been my mother's turn to give Christmas Eve. It wouldn't have changed their lives together, the new version of our family they were about to begin, but it might have changed the story a little, at least the way I heard it.

Growing up I was always a little short of breath when Aunt Cecilia gave Christmas Eve. There was a promise inside her presentations. It's the same feeling I get today if I flip through a home-decorating magazine or watch Martha Stewart on television making perfect holiday topiaries out of a Styrofoam cone and a bowl of cranberries, making gift wrap with a rubber stamp and plain brown package paper. I like the idea that one might find happiness in such detail. I can see the design principles. I can even modify them. I too would like to transcend. If grown-up living is not getting drunk on Rush Street, I think I should find something else to do. I have a friend today, in Minneapolis, who is so good at this, although his is an anti-Martha Stewart aesthetic. Cy spends Saturdays in baggy paint-stained trousers, painting his walls blood red, his ceilings a churchy velvet purple, and even making his own woodwork with corkscrew corners and sprayed with gold leaf. For him this work is a sort of prayer and I would like to practice such devotion. What I lack is the physical focus. I just can't hold my hand steady enough. The pigment I used to touch up my walls stains my favorite shirt. The ink from the stamps I used to make gift wrap smears and leaks through the paper onto the dining-room table. Still I try, hoping to find something holy in these worked-over surfaces, but it seems I am more like my mother than Aunt Cecilia. I get too annoyed at my mistakes, lose interest fast and snap at Linnea whenever she walks past to see what has me so rattled.

What Cecilia presented on Christmas Eve was not just the faint fragrance of seasonal potpourri, not just an antique white tablecloth with matching napkins gathered into wooden napkin rings carved with a festive but subtle holly-wreath design, but also the agility to pull it off, and so to appear happier than the rest of us. Her table was set around a fluted-glass vase filled with deep burgundy dried flowers mingled with evergreen sprigs. Cecilia would whisk it away just before she served a dinner red enough to ruin her entire place setting—lasagna, homemade raviolis, linguini with clam, manicotti, all with heavy homemade sauce that she learned to cook thirty-five years ago for her Italian husband, all smelling of tomatoes, cheese, and basil, all served in lovely patterned bowls she made in her basement ceramic studio, or on glass platters Dino brought back from his travels in South America or Greece. What a stage for Paulie. It's as if this place were just waiting for the *ching ching* of a fork against a glass, the obvious clearing of a throat.

So there it was, Frank Sinatra crooning softly from the stereo at Grandma Rose's request, the ice in the cocktail glasses clinking. The whole thing might have had exactly the cocktail-party ambiance of an old Sinatra movie, if you weren't the type to notice shadows. If you didn't know that this lovely house sat in one of the all-white enclaves on Chicago's South Side, in a school district known in the old high-school race-riot days of the 1970s as one of the most violent in the city. If you didn't notice there was a Japanese woman sitting at the table not letting on how she felt when Cecilia said, "You should have been at Frankie's wedding. You could have translated for that Chinese photographer." If you didn't pay attention to what Dino left out of his animated monologues about his latest trip to Greece with his "roommate," who was, in fact, a man named Danny, sitting silently beside him. Danny was so male-model handsome that my mother kept snapping photos of him. If you didn't know that Dino's little brother Frankie was a good guy about it when Dino told him he was gay, but that his older brother Antony lit up, hot as a welder's torch. I heard that Antony threatened to beat the crap out of Dino and Danny both before he finally calmed down and got used to the idea of having a faggot brother. As long as you didn't notice how Antony slouched at the table, divorced again, exhausted from too much work, too many cocktails. But why break the spell?

Paulie must have timed it just right. After cocktails. Before the pasta. Definitely before our brother Benny began his annual performance of Sinatra's "My Way," as Dino accompanied him on the piano. Benny's crescendo was always delivered from down on one knee on Aunt Cecilia's cream shag carpet. Paulie would have built his announcement perfectly into the arc of this evening.

"Everyone was noisy and talking, of course," Paulie told us. "Benny got Antony going with one of his weird jokes, and you know how Antony won't stop laughing once he's out of control."

Paulie paused. I heard a gust of voices from the TV in the other room. The football game. I noticed Linnea's eyes had wandered toward the set, and I nudged her. I wanted to hear the rest of the story, even though I could already taste it in the back of my throat. "So it's noisy . . ."

"Yeah, so I had to tell Benny to shut up and stop egging Antony on, and I had to tell everyone else to shut up, too, and I pulled Mitsuko up beside me and I finally got to say it."

"What? How did you say it?"

"I said, 'Mitsuko and I have decided there's going to be a wedding.'"

I closed my eyes. I could see every movement, could smell the mist of wine on the newly popped cork.

"Then everyone hooted and clapped and crowded around to look at Mitsuko's ring, and I passed around the wine and they all toasted us."

And I wasn't there to see it, wasn't there to hear my father's booming "Bravo!" the delighted clink of Aunt Cecilia's glass, no matter what she really thought about this dark woman marrying her nephew, Uncle Tony's loving "Hurrah," Dino's theatrical clapping, Antony's yelp as his wineglass sloshed, Benny's nodding applause, our mother's wet eyes. I started to feel my body stretch upward at the thought of this scene, ready at last to wail, to really participate, when I felt a new crush, the heft of hurled bodies. Why did I feel so squashed by this moment? Right then, my family felt like a big smile, and I was smiling, too. But I had missed it, this big event. I wasn't there to toast, wasn't there to unobtrusively lean against Linnea so she could read my thoughts through my skin, wasn't there winking at Mitsuko who was sure to have curled her usually bone-straight hair for the occasion, wasn't there to feel happy or relieved or cheated or hungry or hollow or all mixed-up. That's when I understood it wasn't Cecilia's place settings that mattered, or the chime of the wine flutes meeting over the tabletop, or even the swell of music that must have rolled in around all of their heads thick as the mist from a stage-show smoke machine. All that fell away when I realized what I should have already known—this wedding business was the core, the center weight.

"Everyone clapped?" I asked, quieter now.

"Everyone but Mom. She was mad we didn't tell her ahead of time."

"So Mom isn't glad?"

"Oh yeah, she's thrilled, but you know how she gets. Since it happened at Cecilia's, she thinks she was gypped, that she was the last to know, that we like it better over there. But I just wanted to tell everyone at once."

"We need to clap, too," Linnea said, and we serenaded him over the speaker phone. "Bravo! Hurrah! Paulie and Mitsuko are getting married." It wasn't a long levitating holler, but it was sincere.

"Congratulations my friend," Linnea said, and I watched her lean over the phone. Her wide back was as familiar to me as any of my family's faces, any memory of Christmas Eve dinner. Linnea has changed my family, too, I thought. The blinking star in the window just beyond her head looked as if it had two legs, as if it were dancing. The Doral dancing star, I remembered, a TV ad from when I was very young, where glittering cardboard stars with skinny legs sticking out the bottom formed a Rockettes' kick line. "Join our team. Buy our cigarettes," those grown-up cheerleaders seem to have been saying. On the phone Linnea was teasing Paulie. "So, you're going to make an honest women of her?" She talked to him in a guy-to-guy way that was part jokey, part natural, her normal style with straight men, which Paulie has always accepted as nothing out of the ordinary.

I wondered if Paulie thought of Linnea as his sister-in-law, or maybe his brother-in-law. I wondered if some sort of lesbian wedding, a phrase I couldn't imagine saying to my mother, would make any difference. This news had me feeling light-headed. *Now I will have a sister.* It felt safer to love Mitsuko now. But I had to remember she was just Mitsuko, herself, not my mother's new daughter, not even Paulie's wife, yet. Then I remembered Linnea, how she taped up that Christmas star, how she must have stood on a chair to reach the high spots. I looked at her leaning over to talk to my little brother and I finally did let loose a long sound. Silent. Buried. A luscious caterwaul of love at a register well below the laws of the game. Our Christmas Eve dinner had been seafood pasta. It's what we always had on the night before Christmas if we stayed in Minneapolis, because December 24th was Linnea's birthday, because she was Italian, too, on her mother's side, and seafood pasta is what she has always had on Christmas Eve. I thought of the time Linnea was with me at Cecilia's on Christmas Eve. How everyone sang her a tipsy happy birthday. How Antony ran out of the kitchen bent over laughing at Benny's latest joke of balancing a whole grapefruit on a half-full highball glass. "Look—vodka and grapefruit." How Cecilia and Linnea chatted in the kitchen about the best way to make raviolis. Yet no one had ever said that Linnea had joined this family, too.

Oh how I had disappointed my mother. Her blond, banana-curled daughter had never brought home the right kind of husband to toast on Christmas Eve. Of the three of us, Paulie, Benny, and me, the only one to do it so far had been Paulie, the baby, and even he was already thirty years old. The truth about his story is that I didn't know about the last scene, the cheering and toasting. I am the one without team spirit, the one who has never wanted the family bond, the hoopla. At least I never thought so.

I heard the distant love chants of the football fans billowing from the TV, and our red Doral dancing star was high-kicking out on Portland Avenue. As happy as I was, I couldn't find my next breath.

Long, Painted Echo

I was shopping one summer evening, wandering through a three-story mall full of corporate clothes and ruffled knickknacks, in search of a gift for another new sister-in-law's wedding shower, when I came across a glass-shelved store filled from ceiling to floor with hand-painted nesting dolls from Eastern Europe. Some were slight enough to carry on a key chain, others were long trains of diminishing bodies in which the lead doll was as large as my head, the smallest no bigger than the nail on my pinkie finger. All of them, more than 1,000 dolls, were brush-stroked and polished, down to a dot of eyelash on the tiniest painted face.

I'm certain I played with dolls like these then I was a child, although neither my mother nor my grandmother remember giving them to me. Today when I ask myself what my place is at the weddings of my brothers and their wives, among family that has no suitable words for the life that Linnea and I share, I remember separating the halves of the big outer doll, wide as my hand, and opening it like a plastic egg, wondering what kind of jelly beans or silver charms might be hidden inside, only to find another doll, the same doll. My questions cradle inside of questions. Twist open one and there is another, sometimes an identical pattern, sometimes completely new, with a different expression, another color dress, a new sweep of hair. So much is contained in so little, the dolls grow smaller and smaller, the subtle detail is harder and harder to make out. Each narrow eyelash, each painted rose petal shrinks and becomes more delicate as time disappears.

My middle brother Benny announced his engagement the same month that Linnea and I celebrated ten years together. My youngest brother Paulie and his wife Mitsuko had been married for almost three years and had a child. My parents were retired from teaching high school and thinking of leaving Chicago for Florida. Linnea and I had just moved our common household to a new block on the same south side of Minneapolis where we had both lived for so many years, away from our families. I found out about Benny's engagement the same way I found out about Paulie's, by phone. Benny proposed under the Marshall Field's clock on State Street in the Chicago Loop, on a brisk day a month before Christmas. (Did he get down on one knee, as Linnea did for me? I haven't asked.) His girlfriend had already picked out the ring. They hoped for a Labor Day wedding.

This time I didn't really know the woman my brother was marrying, but after years of single Chicago Symphony tickets and no one but our family to groan at his jokes, he seemed happier. There have been times when I've loved living alone. I was once sure I could never want to share every night's sleep with another breathing body, but my brothers had always planned to marry. Benny's getting married seemed a good thing, but I envied him the sacraments and family blessings, the toasts and toppling towers of gifts. Yet I lost my breath again this time when I heard the news. I lost it twice, a breath caught inside another breath. I had done a little reading since the last engagement announcement. I hated the way Linnea and I faded to shadow in the bright light of another impending family marriage, yet it was also the very idea of marriage that unsettled me.

Under the heading *marriage*, the Oxford English Dictionary quotes the old politicians and philosophers. *The two pillars upon which God has founded the edifice of civilized society are, after all, property and marriage.* Pillars and owners. Property and God. Each of these notions is a wall, closing in, stealing my breathing space. Traditions, laws of culture, are such inspired creations, the repeated acts of human ingenuity engineered to control, to contain, that which will otherwise bend, for better or worse, toward what feels best. And yet, the act of repeating, of echoing, of emerging from a tumble of song and rhyme and a sweet familiar taste is part of what defines any individual. I want to reject tradition. I want to embrace it. I open one doll and the doll inside her is smiling. I open the next and the doll inside has a curious expression, as if she wonders why she is caught in this long, painted echo.

As I wonder. Should we, Linnea and I, want to marry? In order to claim our place? In order to recreate history's wide mural? One of the Oxford definitions of the word *marry* is *to join for life as husband and wife according to the laws and customs of a nation.* According to the laws and customs of our nation, marriage cannot exist between two women, between lesbians. Our love may be permanent, as far as we can tell. It may be an emotional union. We may form a common household. We may be acknowledged, at least among our friends, as together, as linguistically joined, *barrieandlinnea*, one long roll of soft consonants and vowels. And yet the very first definition of the word *marriage* is *the social institution under which a man and a woman establish their decision to live as man and wife.* The very words exclude Linnea and me, who are by law two women, no matter how we choose our clothes or cut our hair.

Which is the same argument the ones who hate us use when they write letters to the editor, or call into radio talk shows. They heave the heft of dictionaries over the airwaves. *One man. One woman.* They are as rigid in their defense of language as a Mack truck in a thunderstorm. But look at the detail of the next doll down, how her eyes have a curious green glint. Language is more like painted wood. It's porous. It wears away in weather. And even the dictionary allows for metaphor. Toward the bottom of the page there are other words for it. *Intimate union. Any close or intimate association. To splice together like strands of two ropes for use as a single line.*

So two become one. This notion has not always been reserved for one man and one woman. Plato, in "The Speech of Aristophones," created another definition. He wrote that we humans began existence as two halves of one whole. This one thing was either man and man, woman and woman, or woman and man, but as punishment for human foolishness the gods split us in two. We ache to remarry our missing half. *Then the two of you would share one life as long as you lived, because you would be one being, and by the same token, when you died you would be one and not two in Hades, having died a single death. Look at your love and see if this is what you desire.*

If the next doll is the doll of my desire, I cannot quite see enough of her facial detail. I wish to share one life with Linnea, and I ache for her when she is gone. And yet I do not wish to be swallowed, do not hope to become just a hint of former flavor in a whole new soup. In a world where the homosexual body is rarely seen as moral, do Linnea and I really want to embrace a notion that would seem to dissolve away our separateness, our hard-earned, distinct identities as individual humans who choose—with our instincts, our bodies, all our ideas of God—to live together for as long as we both shall desire to live together?

These are not the things my brothers think about when they tell me they are getting married. They are in love. *She is the one*, they say. So Linnea and I will travel to Chicago for the wedding shower, will stand aside and watch as the aunts and female cousins embrace this pretty stranger, offer her finely wrapped packages, say, "Welcome to our family." The unmarried older sister of the groom is not important to this ritual. She is the tiny doll at the end of the line. Her features are indistinguishable, except to herself and the unmarriageable stranger she has chosen.

The Oasis

I learned how to marry the ketchup when I was sixteen, a bus girl at the Lincoln Oasis. Oasis is a fancy word for truck stop, but this was a time when Maria Muldaur's bittersweet voice ached through the radio waves singing "Midnight at the Oasis"—camels sleeping under a desert moon, love among the dunes. So my oasis was more than just hard work that left my upper arms and lower calves aching. More than just the smell, not traceable to any one source, that lingered in my hair and in the creases of my palms—stale macaroni and cheese, overcooked coffee, dried condiment splots, sludgy brown meat sauce. More than just the stickiness of my hands, my elbows, my shoes, after eight hours of mopping up spilled cola, wiping down the crummy fake-grain tables, wiping up the condiment jars. More than just the grinning dishwasher who offered to give me a hickey on a regular basis. It was my first job, an oasis from school, family, all the places where I was still a child. It was my life beginning.

"Midnight at the Oasis" was a hallucinatory refuge, made up by my love-song notions of life, made up by stock-image songwriters who knew as little about deserts and camels and escape as I did. Yet I was driven by a hunger to grow up to an adulthood that would be, I thought, just like Maria Muldaur's voice, full of humid embraces in the hot starlight, full of longing expressed straight from the spot between my breasts, full of me deciding how to live. But at any hour my oasis was no desert view. Headlights and taillights were the predominant scenery. The Lincoln Oasis was a glass-encased bridge built over the toll road, one of several just outside the Chicago city limits—the Hinsdale Oasis, the Belvidere Oasis, the Lake Forest Oasis—all of them spanning a Chicago-area tollway, all of them exactly the same.

The oasis was a bank of pay phones that smelled faintly of gasoline. The oasis was a gift shop of highway souvenirs. Salt-water taffy. Stuffed bears wearing White Sox caps, the same bears that wore Cardinals T-shirts in the truck stops outside of St. Louis. Big pencils and felt flags with cartoon maps of the state and Illinois spelled out in orange block letters. The oasis was rest rooms, always gritty with freeway dust, and a Howard Johnson's cafeteria, my favorite restaurant when I was little, where I discovered that almost everything served there was made out of some kind of powder.

But this was my first job, my chance to touch and breathe in the world, even as it sped away under my feet. I heard it in the muscles of my limbs when Maria Muldaur sang, beckoned, with her chesty, dark vanilla pleas. I knew she was singing about sex, and I wanted to fling my body at someone, anyone, just to feel that way, flung out and falling. But not into sex. Not really. I wanted to fling my body at life itself, at a grown life with no ties. I wanted to fall out of my adolescence as heavy and fast as a rock would fall from this frantic view, straight down into the rush and blur of the highway. I was sure that once I started falling I would keep falling forever in a constant state of ecstatic plummet. No crash landing. No problem avoiding the oncoming wheels. That is what I thought it was to be grown. No constraining arms. No safety ropes. For I never intended to be attached and was certain I would never marry.

Standing before the glass, I could see out over the headlight-spotted world, and I could see myself, reflected. Pale orange HoJo dress, wide white waitress shoes, apron stained yellowish. I touched the window with my fingers, imagined my body's particles sparser than air, imagined that I could slide right through. I could almost hear the wind howling on the other side. I could almost feel myself step into the dirty column of air settled over the freeway.

But meanwhile I had work to do, a big aluminum cart to push. The bus cart was as long as a motorcycle and nearly as heavy once it was loaded with sticky ceramic dishes, hard plastic coffee mugs and soda glasses, knives and forks and soiled paper place mats with this month's maze or crossword puzzle, all left behind by busloads of senior citizens enroute back to central Indiana from their day at the city museums or zoos, or by station wagons full of families with carsick kids, or by truckers who came up behind me to ask if I'd ride with them to Canada or Arkansas. I shoved that cart through the look-like-wood dining room, between the orange vinyl booths as freeway traffic streamed in two directions beneath me. I laughed at the truckers, their smiling invitations. I would not have gone with them, would not have known what to say if we really did hit the road, but I did wonder how it would feel to fall away from my childhood in the front seat of a semi.

But meanwhile there was work. Load garbage into the big stinking bins in the back. Load the dishes into the huge industrial dishwasher with a conveyor belt and steam that fogged-in the tiny chrome kitchen. I laughed at the guy (a boy my age) whose job it was to unload and stack the clean glasses and plates. He asked me to lay myself down on the conveyor, he would get me clean. I laughed at the manager when he told me to marry the ketchup. What did he mean? Something nasty I was sure. Some kind of Rod Stewart sex-with-a-bottle joke.

But it was a real thing to marry the ketchup. Sweet Mary Fran, who worked the food line, showed me how. Mary Fran was from a Catholic family so large she had been an aunt since she was eleven. Mary Fran went to Mass every day before school. I had to believe she told me the truth. You balance the open mouth of one bottle over the open mouth of the one below, and the ketchup from the top bottle rides down, a mud slide into the lower one. In the end you have one full bottle where you had two half-empty before.

"There you are. Man and wife," Mary Fran said.

One lies over the other. Two become one. The empty bottle is thrown away. Lose yourself. Become someone different, a compound person, joined and lost. No way out, I thought. No way.

I quit the oasis before that winter's snow melted clear of the outer parking lots. They had stopped playing Maria Muldaur's song on the car radio, and anyway I had started listening to the FM art-rock programs that aired after 10:00 P.M. in Chicago which made the AM hits sound hollow. And I was tired of wiping fingerprint smudge off the big glass doors that looked out over fuel pumps, hazy with gasoline mist in the waning afternoon light, and of how the bus cart left my hair stinking. I was tired of the pranks kids play in places like that, tired of wiping out the sticky soup of mustard, mayo, ketchup, pepper, and cigarette butts they left for me in the ashtrays, and tired of sopping the front of my dress when I tried to pick up a quarter tip left cupped under what *looked* like an *empty* water glass. I was tired of so many of the people who worked there, too. Tired of the bus girl with the bully cackle who purposely knocked the bus cart against my shins. Tired of the food-line girl not as sweet as Mary Fran, who disappeared with the boy who was supposed to be stacking dishes to make out in the mop closet, leaving the blank-eyed, hair-netted lifers to dole out the mashed potatoes and macaroni alone. Tired of the pissy-mouthed manager always yelling at me to hurry up, a bus was coming in.

I left for a ground-level job as a coffee girl at Geno's Supper Club. More money. Less of a view. Geno's was dim lit, upholstered, too interior. But the kids there partied hard and more often. I got stoned to feel that pull from between my breasts—free-fall from behind the wheel of my dad's old Chevy. I didn't know yet how many restaurants I would work in before I turned twenty-five, didn't get it that I wasn't free-falling, I was just falling down. In the meantime I had work to do. I stocked glasses and coffee cups in the waitress stations, filled baskets with crackers, breadsticks and square, puffy, white-bread rolls, and I sliced cheese-cake, married the ketchup, and poured water and coffee for married men who pinched me from beneath the folds of the white linen tablecloth while their wives with tinny voices snapped at the waitresses. I thought, those wives are gone, lost in the hollow oasis of married life, dissolved into the immovable mud of their husbands' booming voices and stupid jokes. I thought about inhaling deep and dissolving slow, about the toll roads between this place and the wide open beds of my soon-to-come life, and about how, wherever I went, I wouldn't promise to stay. I thought, I will never get married.

Up All Night

So are we married? If we aren't, it's not because she never asked me.

The first time was in her pearly blue-tiled kitchen, cluttered with the dinner and breakfast plates from six sloppy housemates. Linnea was wearing her black leather jacket, the old one that doesn't fit her any-more, and the same gray wide-brimmed hat she wore on our first date. Her scratched leather briefcase was set on the muddy floor, she wore her old brown buffed cowboy boots, and she was laughing, as she had been constantly the first six weeks we had been lovers.

She was laughing because she was in love with me. She was laughing because she was exhausted. For weeks we had made love all night through, had seen the first yellow streaks of dawn squeak in from high windows over her bed, had whispered, "Shit, it's getting light," and had laughed because we were so in love. So full of the need to keep touching each other. So tired.

I had no place to be in the morning, but Linnea had students waiting every day at 8:00 A.M. I already had a key. I didn't have to get up. But sometimes I did anyway, just to stand in the shower with her, stare at her big gorgeous breasts, full and tumbling as a landslide. I would kiss her mouth under the steaming hot stream that mashed her thick curly hair flat against her head. She was all face and stupendous breasts and endless torrents of laughing.

What was so funny?

There was her black-and-white frowning angel fish, circling its tank in her bedroom, a few feet from our heads, that I swore stared at me all through the night because I was stealing Linnea away from her.

There were the silly names, Bundra and Hundra, and some joke I never understood about a ride 'em vacuum cleaner that made her laugh so hard her face opened like a box of holy light, and I had to laugh along to be closer to her.

There was the candle on her bookcase that melted down past its wick while I was trying to suck both her nipples at once, because I had the idea it was her fantasy. When she cried out, "It's burning, it's burning," I thought she meant the hot ball of our love. I wasn't thinking about her books, didn't see her F. Scott Fitzgerald collection catch fire and start to blacken at the corners.

To be so attracted to a lover, to have it be new, to have it be clean, not a sneak thing, no others to lie to, to fall in love with a woman so wide-shouldered and awake and so attracted to me that she rolled me down on the bed two, three, four times a night until the morning sky started to laugh with its very first light, this was much better than dreaming. What makes it possible, this total absence of sleep for weeks on end? Now sex relaxes, calms me. Even if I come to her, my thighs spread over her face, my back arched, my lungs bellowing release, later on I sleep, dreaming deeply of small details from my distant past. But at the start we stayed up all night, one night, ten nights, and during the day it was the same pump of blood rushing to the highest points behind my cheeks that kept me awake and caused people in stores to flirt and wonder why they found me so pretty.

A morning after one of these nights, we stood laughing among the mist blue tiles and Linnea asked me, are you my girlfriend, and I laughed and said, oh yes, I am your girlfriend, and she laughed and sang the girl-friend song, *you are my girlfriend, you are my girlfriend,* and we both laughed when a housemate walked through rolling her eyes because there we were, caught in a private bubble in a too-blue kitchen, stupider and happier than usual humans, and the best part was we didn't care what the housemates thought. We floated, angel fish in a cool blue sea as the cold blue sky steamed in through the frosty kitchen window and she said, my girlfriend, will you marry me, and I laughed and said, but what does that mean? She laughed and said, I don't know, I love you, and we kissed for longer than she had time for. Then I watched her step down her icy back steps with bouquets of blue-white frost blooming out of her mouth, and

I watched her climb into the cold cab of her truck, swinging her battered briefcase in over her lap, and I watched her pull down the driveway, her truck exhaust bellowing cold blue smoke, and I laughed a deep blue laugh that rose from my chest to my shoulders to my face and said to myself, "I'm serious about her."

PRESENT TENSE

Opposite Attractions

For as long as I've been in love with Linnea she has been a watcher of birds. I am not. When we walk the dog together, sludging through the soggy overgrowth around Cedar Lake or dodging bicyclists on the black-topped paths of the Mississippi, or kicking through the bottle-strewn sidewalks across two busy avenues into the big green bowl of Powderhorn Park, Linnea will stop short, not even noticing that I am still walking. When I see that she's not with me, I look behind to see her shoulders slack, her face rapt and gazing skyward, as she peers into what is to me just another flutter of leafy rustling.

Linnea's fascination with birds is just one of so many things that she loves and I don't. Not that I have anything against their little beaked faces and the paintbox of feathers Linnea points out to me when we page through one of the bird guides I've given her for her birthday or Christmas. It's just that I don't think to notice them most of the time, not in the trees around my house nor rising and falling out of the shrubs around the park lagoon. If they do catch my eye, my first thought is that it's something to tell Linnea about when I get home.

I don't know what those who don't know us well think about our relative sameness or difference. Some people I'm sure just see two lesbians, or even just two nondescript women on their way into the thicket of middle age, without noticing what distinguishes us. Others, like our seventy-five-year-old Norwegian widow next-door neighbor, the first person we met on the block the day we moved into our new house, reverses our names, calling me, the one who must seem a little more female, by the long soft syllables of my lover's name, Linnea, and calling

Linnea by my name, Barrie, the name most people assume ought to belong to a boy.

In our first year together, Linnea and I posed for an artist's sketch. The artist was a friend of ours who was playing around with ways to draw two women's bodies together, and since it was just an experiment, she let us keep the drawing. We have it still, framed and hanging in our bedroom, and it's one of our only visible records of that time when we were in our twenties, still a little bit strange to each other, both so thin and willing to try anything. Looking at the drawing now, I see the sloped shoulders, the unbound breasts of two women touching, my leg around Linnea's waist, her arm resting on my thigh and her hand on my ass. Even then the frame of Linnea's body was boxier than mine. Her head, torso, and thighs were shaped around a rectangle while mine seemed more based on an oval. If we embraced this way today, naked before that same artist's eye, the picture would show the long oval from my shoulders to my hips grown into a fleshy figure eight and Linnea's rectangles widened into soft-cornered squares. We are not opposite the way a man and a woman are supposed to be, and yet neither are we congruent. And like anyone, our attraction is bigger than our bodies. We can't claim to have stayed together all these years simply because we both have breasts or both have a sheltered opening between our thighs, any more than we can blame our continued attraction on the fact that her toes are longer than mine, my thighs longer than hers, her breasts bigger, my pinkie finger more crooked. From a distance, it might seem there are more things alike than different in our two bodies and so it must be the way we have always fit together that describes why we are together still. But when I look closer, I see it's the differences that stand out.

At the beginning, I wasn't always sure Linnea and I would survive our many differences. If we do not experience that fabled electromagnetic current of biological oppositeness, which is supposed to constitute marriage, then shouldn't it be our sameness that that holds us together? If we insist on snubbing the conventions of romance, persevere as lesbians, then aren't we at least supposed to be some kind of carbon of each other? There is a tricky aspect to homosexual desire. One might assume by the prefix *homo* that we're looking only for sameness, not difference. Common understandings of the ways of the world suggest that hetero couples, one woman, one man, are composed of essentially contrary beings. Plus to minus. In to out. So if homo is not hetero, it must be what hetero supposedly is not. Plus to plus. Out to out.

I will admit that when I was younger, this is what I thought I wanted. My ideal lover would be some replica of myself with a body so similar that if seen from behind we might be mistaken for one another. One of the last men I kissed, when I was twenty, was as lean-legged as I was then. His hair was just a little longer than mine and pulled back in a ponytail, and for a little while, I imagined the two of us might fall in love and take long walks together, arms encircling each other's waists, fingers tucked into the back pockets of each other's jeans. The first woman I kissed was put together like me, too, dark blond, part Polish, born in the urban Midwest. We shared all of our rebellions and beliefs, or at least if we disagreed, we never admitted it, and we were the same height, had the same sturdy cut of thigh. But all in all we didn't hold each other's attention for long.

Even lesbians and gays seem to take this ache for sameness for granted, at least if you go by the club and cruise ads in the back of the queer papers where the boys are mirrors of rippled chest, the girls an echo of each other's curved shoulders and moussed hair. The real people who pose for those ads probably clash and grind in more ways than I can imagine, but the image they portray is an erotics of reflection. Most lesbians I know, however, are at least a little bit wary of the identical-lover syndrome: female couples with the same haircuts wearing matching shorts and deck shoes. These matched sets seem to be lost in each other, and that is a state I have always feared, the erasure of what is me and me alone. If I notice that by accident Linnea and I are both wearing jeans and the same color T-shirt I'm embarrassed, and once we get out in public I'm unwilling to take off my coat to reveal our mistake. I am no longer attracted to the dream of falling in love with my twin, and, as another kind of folklore tells it, I am not wrong to fear it. Meet your doppelganger and you are soon to meet death. To me, it seems a kind of death to float in a merged suspension, sharing all your clothes, all your music, all your books and favorite foods, everything that shows the tones and shades of the particular chemistry that sparks within your one and only skin and bones.

I wonder if this mirrored-lover longing is a throwback to the preteen who stirs with girl-to-girl longings and can't quite admit that what she really wants is to kiss her best friend on the mouth, but can't risk it, so instead suggests they swap sweaters or wear each other's earrings. It's the fantasy of the girlfriend-sister-lovers, stretched out on the bed, propped up with all of their parents' pillows, who knock heads and knees and stocking feet while watching television and eating popcorn from the same bowl.

In real life, too much sameness seems to me to deaden the charge, at least once coming-of-age hormones or the thrill of doing what you are not supposed to or simple unfamiliarity wears away. When I look at the basic pull that has held my longtime lover Linnea and me together all of these years the easiest thing to notice is what lesbians have begun to speak of as gender differences among women—the reason Linnea prefers to wear men's boxers to bed and why I like painting my toenails. But this is just the stuff you can see. The longer I live with Linnea, the more I wonder what it is that keeps us together beyond the things we both love—fat-noodled Japanese soup or instrumental jazz recorded the year I was born or clocks made out of Las Vegas casino dice or the weight of a cloth-bound book in our hands. Maybe it's also the things that annoy us about each other that keep us interested. Such as the way Linnea tears paper matches out in exact order, front to back, a habit she picked up from her Swedish father, or the way she drives like her Italian mother, whipping around corners, waving her arms and flicking her fingers like a pissed-off fan at a soccer match. Such as my tendency to daydream as I drive, the rolling wheels beneath my feet massaging me, lulling me out of the moment, or the way I have been known to scrape the edging off the garage or lock bumpers with the car ahead of me at the autobank. Tension keeps us separate, and so still other, still a little unknown and beguiling.

Our daily differences are the outlines around each of our bodies, the sheath that keeps us from spilling out into each other. Then, when we rub our hard edges together we still get friction, still feel heat. For our most solidly coupled friends it's the same. They don't have opposite genitals, may not have different limb shapes or skin tones. Still, they all have significant disharmonies, alternate brain-wave patterns, some kind of genre shift between them even if what they have to say is similar.

For Linnea and me our differences come down to the ways we do or don't pay attention to things like birds. Linnea will stand on and on under that feather-filled tree without shifting her eyes. Her breath barely whistles in and out of her chest, her face placid as a saint's. Finally she will point up into the green rustling nothing. "Ruby-crowned Kinglet," she will whisper. "Do you see it?" I'll peer and squint and try to pay attention, but my mind will wander to the houses we just walked past and how I tried to stare into their windows, or to the tired sag of the woman's face who just hurried past us on her way to the bus stop, or to the dream I had the night before full of billowing scarves and waves of supple bodies. I know Linnea is anxious to get home to look up the bird in her glossy-paged guide. "Was it a Yellow-bellied Flycatcher?" she will mutter. "They both have a light ring around their eyes . . ." It was definitely a Ruby-crowned Kinglet she will decide, later, sitting in the rocker in her room recording what she saw in her bird notebook. I'll sit in another chair and watch her so deeply engaged in a thing I would never do. It is not just our bodies that pull us to each other, not just the passions that would match up on a compatibility chart. It's also the way we interest each other, the things we have to describe out loud if we want our lover to understand. This is what makes it possible to keep imagining the continually aging portrait of our two bodies. A knee grazes a waist. A hand on the ass. So known, so strange.

YEAR FIVE

Viscosity

Linnea stood on the hard-crusted snow of our yard with a garden spade and a big plastic bag, as I left the house to walk the dog. She would rather have been filling her bird feeder, or inside watching the news, but instead she was cleaning up dog shit. So much of our life together has been made up of this. We get up out of bed so the dog can shit. We stand in cold doorways waiting for the dog to shit. We save plastic bags to take on walks so we can clean up dog shit. We ask each other, "Did that dog shit yet today?" I waved at her from the porch and she waved back with the hand that held the spade, her breath a white rose of frost.

The traffic was heavy on Portland Avenue, the evening rush home from work. It was late February, the evening temperature was just starting to drop, and the hour held the last red-orange strands of sunlight. It was a good time to walk the dog, before it got too late, too dark, too cold. If I waited even a half hour longer the sidewalks, now wet where the sharp afternoon sun melted the edge of snowdrifts away, would glaze over, leaving thin, treacherous coats of ice. I slipped hard on that ice once, a fall that left my lower right hip aching for a year. So walking on wet sidewalks after the sun goes down became one more item on the mental list I keep—things I am careful about.

Patsy pulled on the leash and I yanked back, as the neighborhood lights began to flicker on. According to demographics, our block was a mixed-up collection of races—African American, Southeast Asian, a few Native Americans and Latinos, and about half Caucasian. And then there was what the demographics don't show. This was a part of town that for years lesbians have called Dyke Heights, because so many of us live over here. But all these numbers don't really mix; there are separate worlds circling in the same city space, twenty blocks from downtown. The houses are grand and crumbling on Portland Avenue. They are huge and excessive, with Queen Anne towers and Gothic edges. Linnea and I liked to fantasize about buying one of those old houses, painting it purple, dark rose, turquoise, and gold leaf, like the painted ladies gay men own in San Francisco. I looked at the fabulous, rickety turrets and the shabby, luxurious porches and wondered where it came from, this desire to live with my lover in a giant house with romantic curlicues and startling colors. I used to think I'd always live alone.

Years ago, I sat on the bank of the Mississippi River on the east side of the city with a woman named Angela and said, "My dream is to live by myself in a little wood house on stilts, on an isolated beach somewhere." We sat on a fallen tree trunk, on a riverbank littered with beer cans and cigarette butts, and we smoked, too. It was one of our sneak-away dates, and it was unusual that we were spending it outside talking, and not in my bed, or making love furiously in her other lover's red Mustang. It was one of those times when it was possible to recall that we started out as friends.

"What about lovers?" she asked. She was the one who was married at the time. Her lover was a domestic sort of woman who wore handwoven shawls and fringed skirts and knew about natural foods. They lived in a first-floor duplex with homemade curtains and a yard and two dogs and so much food in the cabinets they could make anything they wanted to eat, at any time. My refrigerator was usually empty except for cheap beer, crusted old bottles of condiments, and brownies leftover from the last time I had the munchies. Angela told me everything about her life with her other lover, and I never told her to stop. It fascinated me, even though with each new detail—how they planned to buy black-and-white café tiles for their kitchen floor, how the dog chewed through the dildo harness, how they always fell asleep holding each other—I wanted to cry, hit her, scream *stop it, why are you telling me these things?* I made mean jokes about it whenever I could, calling them Rob and Laura Petrie, telling her to go home to her goddamn picket fence.

"I'll have lovers," I told her, taking a long drag of my cigarette. "They can come by, as long as they leave before dawn."

"You are really a bitch, you know?" she said. I didn't understand her reaction, but then I saw things too simply then. She was the one who cut me. I was the one who stung. That was all. How could I hurt her when she was the one who left me, again and again, limp from her lovemaking, cradling myself to sleep, listening to the shrill shouts and dull yells of the married man and woman downstairs, fighting again. Still, what I loved about being with her was just this, the forbidden afternoon sex, the kind of high you can only reach with someone who refuses to stay for dinner.

Years later, I walked Patsy and stared at the ragged Victorians. Gay men with some money lived in the neighborhood now, too. Some of the restored houses had rainbow flags in the windows and I knew the owners were men, not lesbians, because I had seen them in the warmer months tending their intricate landscaping or hosing down the sidewalks. It was still too soon to tell if we should call this gentrification or neighborhood revitalization. I imagined living in one of these grand, polished homes with Linnea, preparing whatever we wanted for dinner on a butcher-block counter in the center of a roomy kitchen, planting lilac and rose bushes in the yard, holding each other until we fell asleep in an enormous cherry-frame bed.

Patsy and I paused in front of a big battered Victorian a block from where we lived. Chipped yellow paint, overgrown bushes, and spiky cast-iron fencing around the second-story porch gave it a haunted look. I had met someone who lived in this house, a musician with long black hair, Mediterranean coloring, and crazy circling eyes, who always wore a battered cowboy hat. I had seen him playing the violin in local cafés alongside a balding, sweet-looking man with sandy Norwegian features who always wore sandals and played the thumb piano. I wondered if I should try to know my neighbors better, start a block club or something. Patsy sniffed, looking for the perfect spot, as a small rusted pickup backed up too fast out of the driveway. A different balding white guy, with a straggly beard, I had never seen before rolled down the window frantically and stuck out his head. "Hey, hey, do I shit on your lawn?" My whole body bristled against this guy. I held up one of the plastic bags I always carry on our walks. "I'm cleaning it up," I called back, my voice a little too high and shrill to be mistaken for friendly. He glared at me, roared back up into his driveway. Patsy shit under a sloppy rhododendron, and I considered leaving it, but finally I thought of that block club, and I picked it up.

One of the reasons Angela always left me alone in bed was to run home to let her dog out. I never understood it then. I thought it was an excuse. "Poor Fally," she would say, standing next to my bed, pulling on her jeans. She named her dog after Falstaff, the drunk in Shakespeare's *Henry V*—homage to her equal love of beer and English literature. "Poor Fally. I left the house at 5:30 A.M., and now look, the sun is setting."

"You'd better wash your hands," I'd say. "The wife will smell me on you."

"She's working late. I'll take a shower when I get home."

"If she's working late," I'd whisper, "then don't leave."

She would pause for a moment and look down at me. The tangerine-colored sunset washed over her skin, already half-gone, a hologram of herself.

"Man," she would say, and shake her head. I could see her chest rise and fall a few times as she considered. "No. Poor Fally." Then she would kiss me on the forehead and be gone before I could take a breath.

Poor Fally. Years after, I finally saw a production of *Henry V*, and I couldn't help but notice how much that dog, with his raggedy beige fur and froth of hair under the muzzle, looked just like old Falstaff. And now, whenever I find myself rushing home to put Patsy out, I think of that dog, waiting, holding it, while Angela stopped by, for a minute, on her way home from work and ended up making love to me until we heard the fizz and pop of the streetlights coming on.

It was getting colder, so Patsy and I kept it short, only four long and four short blocks. Approaching Portland across from our house I saw Linnea bathed in yellow light. She was bent over her desk in her study at the front of the house, probably grading student papers, and I worried she was ruining her posture. The duplex we rented might have once had a great Victorian exterior, too. We were never able to tell for sure because of the pea soup green asbestos siding. The lights inside were too bright. She couldn't see me looking at her. I stopped at the red light, made Patsy sit at the corner even though there was a break in the traffic. Cars are another thing I am careful about now ever since I got hit, while jaywalking, by a university kid who whipped around the corner in her father's Mazda truck. I saw Linnea there, across the avenue, the details of her face obscured through the frost on the window. She was sitting in her room, so she probably hadn't started dinner, I thought, feeling pissy for a second. Then I remembered that she was the one who cleaned up all that dog shit, probably several weeks' worth. I was suddenly tired by all the work there was to do in a day. I missed the time when I didn't worry about my health and would be happy with an ice-cream sandwich and a cigarette for dinner. Somewhere since then I had became changed, older of course, but something else too, someone I once couldn't imagine being. Yet who I used to be was still there, hovering, a shadowy hologram I could see sometimes, peering down at me from just over my head and I wondered if that could really be *my* life waiting for me in that warm house, burning too many lights. I wondered if that was even the life I wanted. I imagined myself alone, without her, lovers standing over my bed in the tangerine sunset, leaving me to fall asleep, alone in what was once my dream house, four thin walls on stilts, on an empty beach, without a dog and without a neighborhood, as the last lights of the day faded without a sound. But maybe it wouldn't be that way. Maybe I would be able to handle the hazy life I once imagined, unbound, glancing fast over other people's lives like a particle of unattached copper-colored light.

But I had to laugh at myself. I knew too many people who used to want what I had wanted, another moment in that place where the body and all that surrounds it dissolve into one, pulsing, pastel wash. You can drink your way to it, smoke your way to it, fuck your way to it. Some people (not me) can even pray their way to it. As I remembered my own good old, bad old days, my chest unfurled with want, my hips started to sway with craving.

But I had come to know enough about what things can't last. Who would want to end up as some anonymous old lady with a stinking apartment and wine bottles hidden behind her shoes? But that was not the reason why I lived differently than I had before. The surprise has been the discovery of something better, the knowledge that two people can find a focus between four shared walls, can find purpose in the viscosity of undiluted colors that don't fall away at the end of the day.

The stoplight on my corner changed to green, but I kept standing there. Patsy looked up expectantly, waiting for me to come back to this day, this corner, this walk, and finally I did and smiled down at her sweet blond face. When we were halfway across the street, the light turned yellow, and so we ran the rest of the way home.

Leaving Bohemia

I used to dream I was running. For months I dreamt the dream repeatedly, even though I was safe at home, asleep with Linnea on our king-
sized bed, in the old apartment on Portland where we lived for a decade.
I dreamt of running, or trying to run, every muscle straining. My heart
was slamming, my arms were grabbing at the air before me as if to pull
my body forward faster, but my legs couldn't move. I was trapped in slow
motion, my feet dissolving under me like a lamp-scorched movie strip. I
moved, but just barely. The place I was running from and my destination
were each just a blink on shrinking horizons.

My dream did not specify where I was trying to get to, which blue
basin of water, which translucent city. I was caught between my first
home and another place. Bohemia? But not the mountain-rimmed
province in Eastern Europe where some of my family began. Not the industrial Midwestern city where I grew up with its littered streets named
for immigrant politicians and soldiers such as Cermak or Pulaski. Not
even the scattered regions of artists, thinkers, and other weird sorts,
named for bands of vagabond gypsies wandering Central Europe in the
fifteenth century, whom the French mistook for lost Slavs.

～

I do think I would have liked living in expatriate Paris, or in Greenwich
Village before Stonewall, the place New York City's tabloid reporters
called the Citadel of Slime, swarming, they said, with mannish woman
barkeeps and lisping boys in heels. But perhaps all landscapes look better from a distance and even my own geographies will read differently

fifty years from now. When Linnea and I rented our sloping apartment on Portland Avenue, a straight shot from downtown, our Bohemia was mundane and not always easy living. When we first set up house together, Linnea was in graduate school. I was a poet and a part-time arts administrator. It was a cheap apartment with nineteenth-century woodwork and stained glass, which allowed us our three cats and a dog, and it was big enough, one room for poetry, one room for Linnea's dissertation research, and still another left for the two of us to start the evening kissing, and end it with streaks of streetlight slipping in through the lace curtains, illuminating our bodies, unclothed, joined.

But our apartment was crumbling. The electricity was substandard; we couldn't blow dry our hair and make toast at the same time or the circuits would blow, which meant a steep hike up to the attic to push the button on the old screw-in fuse. We could take showers, but not baths because the crummy tub that must have replaced some grand old clawfoot was only a half foot deep and crookedly plastered into a spongy corner under a window so badly insulated that we found ice around the drain on cold winter mornings. For years we ate or whispered or made love in front of the hot face of the fireplace with its mottled green-and-black ceramic tiles and engraved mantel, only to finally discover that the reason we found loose bricks in the cinders was that it had no fireproof liner. Hundreds of nights we must have come close to setting the old place ablaze. All the walls leaked, rusty stinking drips, and when it was humid, mushrooms grew under the kitchen sink. There were only three electrical outlets in the whole place, so under our rugs and furniture lay a web of extension cords that were singed and useless once we finally moved.

∿

Linnea and I, queer daughters who still remember relatives who never forgot the Old Country, have inherited bits of all our Bohemias. The reasons our grandparents and great-grandparents wandered away from Croatia, Bohemia, Poland, Prussia, Italy, and Sweden must have been the same reasons we left our first beds with that ache for a happier life than the one we might have had if we stayed home. But the new homes we find sometimes resemble the places our parents and their parents worked so hard to leave, the neighborhoods other people stay on the freeway to avoid. We wear clothes other people discard, do work that offers up our skin, our throats, sometimes even the wet places between our thighs for the world's perusal, while the people we come from would pay anything for a little more privacy.

We latter-day bohemians demand the right to live outside family jurisdiction, the first generation of our relations to feel so free. And so Linnea and I, collegial lovers who study the body as if it were a city we need to remember, as if our flesh were a lost alphabet, choose to shack up. We have no wedding purse, no trousseau or trunks of family pewter and crystal. We carry nothing but our books and notebooks, old record albums and what's left of our precious childhood impressions, to the streets of New Bohemia where the population lives in gusty, sloping apartments, gets by without health insurance or new cars or good dress coats. It's not ancestry that defines us here, not patterns of speech, not bone structure, but our thrift-shop wardrobes, the loose way we spend our days, the lovers we never marry.

Linnea and I didn't mind our precarious apartment most of the time. It was so cheap, just $250 a month, and in the spring there was a blooming lilac bush just out our back door. While my cousins in Chicago, descendants of Italy and Slavic Bohemia, just one generation from *wap* and *bohunk*, were furiously adding moonlight shifts, making money, amassing property and while my brother Paulie, fresh from law school, moved into a lakeside Chicago apartment with a doorman, Linnea and I stayed on Portland Avenue. We were happy in our boho castle, especially in the years when I went back to school, when Linnea was reading for her exams and working summers teaching composition in a maximum-security prison. Yet we both grew up with modest comforts we missed. There were afternoons when the dream of a real home hung green-lit in our imaginations. We drove around the city imagining ourselves in that house, across from the park, the one with the little Queen Anne tower, or another house, just three blocks from Portland, painted deep turquoise, with a skylight and a pink-lit address plate made of real neon.

It was in my dreams that I was most dissatisfied. Awake, I loved every dusty corner of the place where I had set up house with Linnea, but in sleep I was filled with craving. I wanted something so badly that my upper body trembled, my mouth guppied and gasped. It was some solid place I was trying to get to, a spot where I could pull Linnea to my chest in the full light of day, a home where a chorus of dead voices with my name echoed through me. But where was it? Which Bohemia?

~

There have always been expatriates who choose exile, the bohos and homos, sometimes one and the same, some temporary residents, some lifers, some who drank themselves to death, some who stayed on, out-living all their old friends and then writing about it. Toulouse-Lautrec stayed up late sketching the seedy scenes of Montmartre cabarets. Gladys Bentley left Pennsylvania to dress in men's suits, marry a woman, and sing dirty songs at her after-hours piano in the Harlem Renaissance clubs. The walls of Gertrude and Alice's Paris flat were a tumult of their painter friends' radical brush strokes and shattered portraits, and millionaire Natalie Barney's home was a Sapphic salon of witty female literati in feathered hats and cross-dressing dames smoking cigars. Janet Flanner renamed herself Genêt, lived out of a suitcase in a Paris hotel room, wrote literary letters home chronicling Josephine Baker's bare-assed debut and the way Marlene Dietrich walked in trousers. Later came Ginsberg's hybrid Buddhism, Kerouac's boozy prose, Jimmy Baldwin's long prophetic breaths, Joni Mitchell's jilted love trills, Ru Paul's blond wig and push-up bust. Bohemia used to be the cheap cafés of Left Bank Paris, the speakeasies of prohibition Harlem, the bookstores of San Fran's North Beach, the disheveled rowhouses of the Village, the heroin alleys of the East Village's alphabet soup. Like Linnea and me, Bohemia's residents (the famous ones and the ones we never heard of) craved something. A new way to hear the notes. Another way to arrange the brain. A gangster suit or a sequined sheath from the other side of the rest-room wall. Then the big magnet that holds us all in place shifts on its center again, and all the cheap foundations topple. There are lesbians on the radio, a drag queen on TV, a marble and plate-glass chain store on our old corner that sells distressed jeans and faux bowling shirts that look just like the ones we used to fish out of a bin for a quarter, and Bohemia wanders on again.

Does anyone really stay in Bohemia if they don't have to anymore? Or is Bohemia blood culture after all, with us wherever we set up our beds? When I talk to my younger brothers about their big weddings, their steady jobs, they seem to know things I can't grasp—what to wear, who to invite, what songs to teach their children. For me, life is a long gasp of questions, and so I look for boho wherever I go, the unassimilated spots, the shadowy cafés. In Madison, Wisconsin, there's a coffee shop I adore, owned by lesbians. The walls are lavished with plaster- and glass-assemblage sculpture, a mosaic of mirror shards and broken tea cups my mother would find ugly, but to me is dead-on how life really feels. There's a little restaurant I love in Chicago, neon-lit with fifties' kitsch and waitresses in vintage dresses from the White Elephant Store. I am restless whenever I visit the south-side settlements of the second and third generations of Eastern Europe, where the lawns are neatly shorn, where there will be meat for dinner and the paneled ranch-house basements have fully stocked bars. So I sneak away north, to the messy city at Thirty-fifth and Halsted, gay Bohemia, where I order a cup of the Japanese tea they brew there by the pot, and eat carrot loaf with a side of vinegary greens and a slice of macrobiotic cheesecake. If I'm lucky, a young waitress with a buzz cut and Doc Martens boots will flirt me up, and although I'm not interested, I'll smile back and leave a big tip because of how she pulls me out of the old Bohemian fields of my family where I am the curious cousin, back to the boho lesbo republic where at least I look like a sister. In New York City I pour through the gay press for all the funny listings—a drag queen named Hedda Lettuce with her own cable TV talk show, heartthrob ads for lesbian dance clubs with babe shots of twenty-something DJs who show cleavage by day and by night spin vinyl in mustachioed drag. And in Minneapolis, exactly ten blocks up from our old Portland Avenue pad, a gay dancer tall as a pro basketball player with an exquisitely shaped German American face and a voice low as the bottom notes of a pedal organ is impresario to the storefront cabaret of my people. His shows feature abstract jazz and lesbian poetry, improvisational monologue and art against AIDS, tap dancers and performance painters, and once even twelve Super 8 projections of twelve months of the sun, setting and rising again over the west side of the city.

~

There are so many reasons that we left Portland Avenue, but the easiest truth is we have more money than we did before and when we moved it was to a place where our lives might be better. These days I can blow dry my hair and make toast and even iron my department-store clothes, all at once, although I have yet to take advantage of such luxury. Our new house with a little turret (that's really just a closet) is on a block named after a lesser poet, just fifteen blocks east of where we lived before. We have a bathtub, skylights, a washer and a dryer, just an alley away from where the neighborhood starts to slope downward toward the freeway, just 350 miles from the post-immigrant streets where I grew up. From my back deck I can see the alleys and yards of Powderhorn Park where long-nailed black trannies work the counter at the video store and white ex-hippies still dress their kids in tie-dye. Where young black men in fat-legged pants slam basketballs and Native American girl-gangs jump rope in the alley. Where teenage boys born in Cambodia bump what look to be volleyballs off their heads and blond boys with droopy pants chase loose dogs through the baseball diamonds and where lesbians going gray at the temples and wearing purple Birkenstocks walk their dogs on leashes around the murky park lagoon. Gay men in this neighborhood have excessive gardens, dread-headed white adolescents stalk down the center of streets showing off their camouflage pants and tattooed scalps, tense guys with rock faces pace by the phones at the corner food stores. This part of town has mural painters and puppet makers, Harley guys and drugged-out mothers, lesbians who might get married, straight couples who won't get married, and just off the park a coffee shop that hangs local art on the wall, and sells a damned good, cheap burrito plate.

From my front porch it's quieter, just one family per home, a messier, mixed-race version of the neighborhood of steelworkers and school-teachers where I lived as a kid. When girls in sagging pants and over-combed hair pass by sharing cigs I flash back to myself in junior high when I wore bell bottoms and jean jackets and ducked the doper guys in jacked-up Chevys. What is different are all the homosexuals who live here now. A permanent parade of rainbow flags flap over our fences. We live in a dry spot with all the lights on, old cars in the garage, and whatever still fits from our old thrift-shop wardrobes folded in our drawers. We live with the sound of laundry tumbling, the stereo humming with 1950s bebop, walls lavished with Elvis art, and rooms upholstered in enough faux leopard to make a drag queen cry. We have Mary Queen of Heaven icons from Italy and Poland, weeping Mary candles from Our Lady of Cicero in Chicago, and blond-haired Barbies dolled up like Marilyn Monroe. Our garden is sloppy, our roof doesn't leak, the vacuum cleaner has real good suck. We have built-in bookcases and at least 1,000 books, we have ten teapots, we have four framed valentines that match our cow-colored kitchen, and when the windows are open we can hear the echoing pongs of three different sets of wind chimes.

Today, in the second place I've lived with my lover whom I am still not allowed to marry, I dream of watery coastlines and finding tall, terraced rooms in our house that I didn't know were there. The running dreams are gone, maybe because life is happy enough, here on this street between Bohemias. At night we lie on our king-sized mattress beneath the moony light streaming in through skylights and listen to kids setting off firecrackers in the alley or to someone who needs money rummaging through the recycling in search of aluminum. The dim light colors our skin blue while we read from the alphabets of our bodies and when we sleep, I dream of swimming through unrippled pools toward a room I recognize as home.

Soulmates

Sometimes on my way home from work or the grocery store, I drive around the block just to get another glimpse of the house where I live. I sit out in the car with the motor running and stare, trying to recognize the contours and colors of my own life. Other times I look at my own palm and wonder if I've ever seen that hand before. I even have moments where I look at Linnea, my soulmate of so many years, and ask myself, who is that? Is she real, or just a flickering apparition? If I pinch her will she yelp?

I don't suffer from amnesia or some other malady of memory. It's just that I trip into these dazed moments where the world I know best becomes illuminated and unknown, a slowly spinning globe of light and movement, and I have trouble finding my way back home. This is why, many years ago, the spring I turned twenty-eight, just six months into my life with Linnea, I took the advice of a friend and went to see a tarot-card reader who met clients in her home. She lived in a bungalow on the southeast side of Minneapolis, probably not too far from where I live today. I don't remember much about her except the impression she made. It seems to me now that her hair was unkempt and thin, reaching unevenly to her shoulders, but maybe it was just that she held her head cocked and leaned too close when she spoke to me, and so I remember her as messy and haphazard, wearing a loose shirt, shapeless skirt, and Birkenstock sandals, her exposed toes a little bit dirty. My friend assured me the woman was a psychic and would tell me what I needed to know. What I ended up with troubled me so much that I never paid to talk to anyone like her again.

~

I have never been sure of what to make of tarot cards and psychics, dreams and ghosts, UFO sightings and astrology, power crystals and healing gems, all those faceted pathways into what glistens underneath the surface of our lives. Linnea approaches these things with a simple logic. She believes what seems believable and enjoys the rest. I tire myself out trying to discern between the real and not real, falling face first into belief, then pulling back so hard that nothing is any fun. I want to believe what the cards say to me; nothing in my experience tells me I should.

The first time I saw a tarot deck up close I was twenty-three years old and in love with a woman who had lived as a lesbian much longer than I. Elena had just moved to Minnesota from a small college town on the East Coast that was famous for the number of lesbians who owned their own restaurants, bookstores, coffee shops, and therapy practices. It was as if Elena emigrated here from another country where lesbians had their own language, cuisine, national religion. Her tarot deck was a souvenir of that place, and was wrapped in a satin handkerchief that had been soaked in patchouli. Today when I walk past the fragrance counter at the bath and body store where I buy my cosmetics a distinct fragrance I don't recognize at first awakens me to the presence of the boy with orange and canary yellow hair wearing an army fatigue jacket, or the girl in fat-legged jeans and a pricey fur-fringed jacket just like one Janis Joplin might have found in a Goodwill bin thirty years ago. As they diligently sniff up the new shipment of patchouli, and dig around in their pockets for enough change to take some home, I am transported back. It was a fragrance so common to radical lesbians in the late seventies and early eighties that when I first started sleeping with women, I thought that must be how all women smelled, under their clothes.

The cards of my lover's tarot deck were round. The figures had been recast in the forms of women of all hues cavorting around a campfire and singing to the moon. She laid them out on the floor next to her futon, gently as if they were old photographs or precious paintings in miniature. She arranged them in shapes, a series of pyramids, some upright, some overturned. Elena knew the patterns by heart, and the meaning of each card, too. She touched the face of each card lightly with a movement I recalled from Catholic churches of my childhood, the slight graze of fingertips over the still water of the holy water fonts. But Elena was not silent, not praying. She chuckled as she set each new piece down, and told me all the things anyone would want to hear from a new lover. You are so smart. You hear things that others will never understand. You will be amazing by the time you are thirty. She promised me. I was skeptical that these thin wafers of paper and printer's ink held the magic my lover promised, but I liked the feeling of watching the cards set down before me in an ancient, received pattern, from which arose an idea, a picture, a possibility of who I might be. Maybe there was divination here, just as my lover claimed. There surely was magic between us in that rumpled, candle-lit room that smelled of patchouli and bath salts and rose oil and our bodies moist from touching. Maybe I could believe.

~

Soon after the night my new lover spread my future across her dusty bedroom floor, my parents drove up from Chicago to see me in Minneapolis. We spent a Saturday doing the usual things young adult women who have left home to live alone do with their visiting parents. We ate in a nice fish restaurant, wandered through a mall full of tiny storefronts that sold nothing but lovely, useless gifts. Then we turned into a little bookstore with a focus on spiritual concerns. The shelves were full of books on matriarchal deity worship, Gnosticism, Buddhist meditation, Native American Shamanism, along with calendars featuring the Hindu god of the month, and candles of every diameter and color. There on a busy glass shelf, amidst a potpourri of appropriated faiths, I found a box of tarot cards, the old kind, with medieval-style line drawings colored in with what seemed to me to be illuminated inks. I didn't think about why I wanted to buy them. I just picked them up and started toward the register, when I noticed my father's big thoughtful face, watching me.

My parents had been watching me this way for some time now, trying to figure out my sloppy thrift-shop clothes, my one pierced ear that caused my mother to ask if I had joined a cult, my gang of similarly dressed friends, one of which was my favorite this time, another last time. I had told my mother I was a lesbian, confirming her fears, I suppose, that I had been captured by a band of doomed disciples. We hadn't spoken of it since. The fact hung there among us, a muggy drape, as I ignored their gaze.

My father, the first in his family to go to college, believes the world is a quandary to be approached with the intellect. He seemed then to think I was a problem he could figure out, if he just observed long enough. I had always thought of myself as very much like him. Certainly his approach—measured, introspective, verbally spare—had always seemed preferable to my mother's propensity to let out a howl of alarm every time one of her children tipped back too far in a kitchen chair. Yet once I had begun to have intimate relationships with women, a whole new world of physical pull and sensory intellect opened up in me. Mystery, magic, the texture of air between two longing bodies startled me alive and I wanted more.

Did I believe I'd find the way to what I craved in the tarot cards? I only know that the images, so iconographic, were a picture of something that felt true. I wanted to own them. My father must have been able to tell by my apartment with the rusted shower stall and the flat futon on the floor that my job writing press releases for a women's theater company didn't pay enough to allow me many frills. As I moved toward the cashier, my father kept watching me, and when I finally met his gaze he spoke.

"What are those for?"

"They're tarot cards," I said, holding them up for him to peruse at a distance.

"And what are they good for?" he asked again, the sound of his voice rising. What are they good for? I glanced down at the firm pack in my hand and wondered the same.

~

I met my first psychic in a supper-club bar. His name was Jason, and he looked like a Shriner, the kind you see in a holiday parade—retired white guy, tasseled hat, big goofy smile, speeding by in a tiny motorized clown car. Jason worked most nights in a downtown Minneapolis steak house that has been long since torn down. I might be remembering any number of vanished supper-club bars that I knew in my years of waiting tables, but what comes to mind when I think of Jason is textured red wallpaper, the dense smoke of Camel unfiltered cigarettes, a round, dim-lit booth near the bar, and the man himself. He had a gold-and-red-gemmed band on the ring finger of his drinking hand, and was sipping a sweet Manhattan with two red cherries floating over the ice cubes. The liquid in his drink glowed gold as an alchemist's potion in the flocked lounge candlelight.

I went to see Jason at the insistence of another friend. "He's amazing, really psychic," she promised, the morning after she sat down on his black vinyl cushions as a joke, but ended up leaving the bar crying.

"He knew I was pregnant, before I said a word," she told me. "But I haven't told anyone."

But how hard could it have been for Jason to guess? My friend was a slight blond woman who had just recently moved to Minneapolis from a smaller city three hours north, cheerleader pretty, dressed in a tight mini skirt and a thrift-shop jacket with abstract ceramic pins made by local sculpture artists pinned to her lapel. Her boyfriends were charming artist guys, soulmates, more than one had promised her. She was the perfect image of the girl who leaves an average lower-middle-class home to resettle in Bohemia. At first glance she was the type other women of this milieu envy because of the way she was always put together, but closer observation revealed that just the opposite was true. If I were a Shriner guy sipping a cocktail in a supper-club lounge, if I met this young woman with the funny clothes and the faint shadow of freckles under her makeup, if I looked into her fidgety blue eyes and held her unringed fingers in my open palm, my first guess would have to be boyfriend trouble, something gone wrong, what I might fear for my own daughters and nieces. She is pregnant and she doesn't want to be.

But all this happened before I knew my friend well. Later on I could see it too, how it was all coming apart for her, as it was for me, as it was for most of the women I knew in my early twenties who drank too much and got too high and wandered toward whatever our bodies called out to, the ones whose families watched us, wondering what they could do if we spun out completely, over the edge, out of anyone's reach.

On the muggy summer night that I drove my Vespa scooter with the sticky ignition switch downtown to meet Jason I was having troubles of my own. One lover, the one with the patchouli-scented handkerchiefs, was threatening to leave, unwilling to wait out the seven years it would take for me to become remarkable, if I wouldn't stop sleeping with my other lover, the one who wouldn't stop dropping by in her other lover's red Mustang just to go for a drive, just friends, she swore, all the while charming the buttons off my shirt. There was no way I was going to tell Jason, or anyone else in that supper club, any of this. Still, I was hoping my ten dollars would buy me something I could use.

Jason greeted me as if I were his favorite niece he hadn't seen since Christmas. He cracked a few jokes and puffed on his cigarette, as I offered him my long narrow fingers and barely open palm. He cupped it in his hand, heavy and cool. The fat band of his gold ring sent a shiver up my arm, until I relaxed and let my fingers fall open. He peered into the furrows engraved into my palm's flat plain. With my free hand, I smoked a Salem Menthol Light, and swallowed too fast from a glass of Chablis. He was quiet for what seemed to be a long time.

"Your life line is strong, robust," he told me first, something I had heard before. He paused again, looked up at me and back down at my hand. "I see you in a helping profession. A therapist maybe?"

I stared back at him. He squinted in the cigarette smoke and took another sip from his Manhattan. "Well, what I see is that you feel you don't belong here, is that right?"

My eyelids must have fluttered in surprise. Did he mean here, in this supper-club bar, in my baggy green fatigue pants, beaded thrift-shop top, one pierced ear? Or was he talking about something bigger?

"Some people," he went on, "are not from here. We call them star people. You're born here like everyone else, but you start in another place. You have a purpose, if you can find it."

"It sounds crazy, I know," Jason went on, taking another sip of his drink. "Little green people from Mars, right?"

Star people? I didn't say a word, just stared at my open palm, unrecognizably nested in his dry white fingers. But I must admit now that some part of me clamored, still clamors, to believe. I am not from here. I have a purpose, a mission. I have always felt underfed. I felt it most acutely when I was alone, late at night, the stereo up too loud, candles blazing, something inside craving what couldn't be satisfied with a tray of fresh brownies or a whole bottle of wine or playing the same scratchy Joni Mitchell track over and over again. Did everyone feel this way?

Now I wonder if this is why some young women do join cults. The craggy voice of a man who could be your father suddenly turning silken. The red-flocked room tilting a bit on its axis. A promise—you are fated, chosen. You are not from here. You belong with us, where we know you are remarkable.

But that night in the dim cocktail lounge I wasn't giving anything but the obvious away, and so Jason shrugged and laughed again. "Well, you don't have to believe me. Get the book. *Star People*, it's called. Read it and see if it fits."

I still wasn't talking. Jason sighed, held onto my hand, peered again. "And I see money," he continued. "$5,000, headed your way." With that he let go, smiled at me again, and sat back against the seat cushions. My ten minutes were up. I slid a ten-dollar bill across the tabletop, downed my drink, and left. Outside the lights of the summer skyscrapers throbbed as blue as the seas of a distant planet.

∼

I can't say for certain that I don't believe. There are some people in the world, smart people, who are born to faith. I don't mean a holy-roller devotion, although perhaps, if I could see past my prejudice of anything Protestant and churchy, I might be convinced that there are devout believers in the Christian God who have better things to do than pray for the mass conversion of the queers. But religion aside, there are some people who have no trouble believing in a happy universe full of necessary currents and the dead watching over us. Linnea has been one of those people. You can see it when she laughs, or when she dances.

I watched her once, the first year we were together, jitterbugging with an old friend. Linnea was a sturdy five-foot-eight in her cowboy boots. Her curly hair was longer and looser than she ever lets it get these days. Her worn jeans were hugging her butt. Her friend was tiny and short-limbed with permed hair falling past her shoulders. She was a veteran of a little theater company known for its tumbling choreography. Linnea took the lead, dipping and spinning, holding on by the wrist as her pal somersaulted and slid between Linnea's thighs. It struck me that I should be jealous. I knew it was too late to train my awkward five-foot-nine frame to move like a trapeze artist. I would never be able to dance that way with Linnea. But that thought flickered away when I saw Linnea's face. She was not wearing the look of a woman in love, a woman who loved another woman's body, another woman's heart. I had seen that look, up close, every night for weeks now. But this moment was different. Her look expressed something godlier than sex. Her face was filled with the sort of holy awe a person feels when they look out on a city from a high perch. She *is* from here, and she loves it.

∾

So what do I believe? That is the problem. I'm not always sure. Linnea dances. I wander off into a daydream. Linnea follows a dim beam in the distance, beckoning her forward. I stumble around in a fog of my own making. Why can't I just breathe, in and out? Why can't I just go out dancing and then come home again, just once, without watching myself do it?

∾

"This relationship you are in now will not last," that sloppy South Minneapolis psychic told me.

Almost a dozen years have passed since I sat at a card table in the psychic's living room. Her dogs were barking and howling in the backyard. Linnea was waiting for me out front, smoking cigarettes in the cab of her pickup truck. If I didn't have a tape recording of this meeting, I might convince myself that I have it wrong, that the psychic never said what I remember her saying. But the tape has preserved her precise words, her news that I was movie-star beautiful in one past life, that I lived in Persia in another, that I was prone to neurotic worry in this life, that I had executive potential in the business world, that I had issues with my mother, and that I would soon be taking a trip. Her voice was throaty and she rasped when she talked. I remember she was a chain smoker as I listen to her recorded voice for the first time since that afternoon when I careened out of her yard and slid into the truck next to Linnea. Her name was Shirley I see now from the business card tucked into the tape case. Shirley called herself a Counselor, with experience in

Tarot, Astrology, Numerology, and "other services." How could some-one with so much expertise be so wrong?

If there was one thing I knew the spring I turned twenty-eight-years old, it was that I had already met a soulmate. Linnea. I knew it at once, from the first time she kissed me. I had kissed plenty of lovers before Linnea, but the first time Linnea kissed me I heard a whoosh of spark and wind, and I fired up like an oven with the gas left on too long.

So when this rasping psychic snapped the cards on the rickety leather surface of the table, I interrupted. "This relationship now, it's a long-term commitment."

"Pick three cards," she said and when I handed them to her she slapped them down on the table. "They say you are not telling the truth. In your subconscious mind you feel this relationship is already over."

"No," I said. "I don't feel that way."

When she laughed I could hear the cigarette-phlegm rattle in her throat. "That's not what your subconscious says."

Could I really be so wrong about this? I hadn't asked her about my love life. Why did she bring this up? Shirley's face turned stony as she cocked her head to one side and leaned toward me across the table. "I'm sorry, but it's so strong. You think the relationship you are in now is it be-cause it's the most you have ever felt. But the next one will be huge. Your soulmate. In the next year you will meet the one you will stay with for the rest of your life. Except for maybe, later on, a little affair on the side."

I must have been staring, or not staring, or tearing up, or biting my lip, or something because she said, "I can see you don't trust the cards like I do." She gathered them up in her cigarette-stained fingers, shuffled them again, and told me, "Pick three more." As she slapped them out be-fore me again, she shook her head and muttered, "The cards don't lie."

I suppose I could have refused to believe her. Linnea did. And mostly I didn't believe her. They were just cards, after all. Just pictures. Yet Shirley's predictions created a little rip in our lives together that hadn't been there before. What if she was right?

The few months that followed this encounter were such a short period in the breadth of Linnea's and my long relationship that I barely remember them now. Yet at the time they seemed significant because they interrupted that long-held breath of falling in love. Up until that day we were at the stage where sleep didn't matter, money didn't matter. We were elevated and prancing over the heads of the people around us, living on touch and taste. I suppose something had to snatch us back down. I just wished it hadn't been the idea that there might be someone better for me out there. I wish I hadn't spent even a moment of our first summer together asking questions, looking around the way I did, my chest muscles thumping at the sight of any handsome woman I hadn't seen around town before. Was that her, my promised one?

But despite my new doubts, Linnea and I moved on, moved in together, moved ahead to the part of our love where we couldn't stop stumbling into the same fight, the one where I gushed with words that were supposed to be my feelings, where Linnea said nothing, shocked silent by my effusiveness. Something would have moved us onto the next stage, and then on again to the next. Something always does. But I'd like to know how long it's possible to hold the altitude of love's first fire, how long a pure and simple belief has the power to hold two full-grown people afloat in an image of themselves, two burning pieces of star, two shocks of an unearthly shimmer.

∾

I did buy that book Jason recommended. I found it in a rack at the back of the biggest spirituality bookstore in town. I knew plenty of people who shopped at this New Age supermarket but I had never walked through its doors before, scared away by too-cute unicorns in the window and a catalogue of eerily titled seminars as long as my leg posted in the entryway. I wish I had kept that book, so I could look at it again now to see if I remember it correctly. I recall a dark blue cover, and whirlpool-shaped swirls of starlight. The back-cover blurb read, RECOMMENDED BY THE NATIONAL ENQUIRER. Inside the type was large and the text consisted mainly of lists. How do you know if you are a star person? The list was extensive, and only a few of the items remain in my memory, standard alien-abduction fare with a few variations. *You feel you don't belong here. You dream of visitors to your room at night. You have chronic sinusitis. You sense there is a role for you in this life, but you don't know what it is yet.*

I thought of Jason and his star people again that Easter weekend when a California cult of computer programmers who called themselves

Heaven's Gate committed mass ritual suicide. I don't know if they believed themselves to be the same star people Jason spoke of, but their credo sounded similar. Heaven's Gate believed Comet Hale-Bopp marked the arrival of a long-awaited spaceship that would take them back to their home planet. They were certain it was time for them to disrobe from their clumsy human bodies. Like a ripped party dress, faded jeans, an old leather belt, they had worn this skin-and-liquid wardrobe for far too long. I had thrown my copy of *Star People* away years before, too embarrassed to keep it among my poetry anthologies and literary magazines. Now, with each news bulletin I was more relieved I hadn't taken Jason too literally.

"You will find true life with us—potentially forever." This is what the Heaven's Gate web-page manifestos promised any who would join them among the stars from which they believed they had originally come. "If you cling to this life, will you not lose it?" I do cling to this life, and will keep clinging until it dissolves away in my grasp. I cling to Linnea, hang on her arm as we stand in our backyard, gazing up at Hale-Bopp's burning yellow tail, twenty-five-miles wide, the newspapers say, but to our eyes smaller than a dime. I don't want to waste time on hazy beliefs I can't see or taste or touch. I want to live in this world, here in the nebulous swirl of what I am told and what I can see for myself.

~

If my encounters with psychics have taught me anything, it is that life is a jumble of what we hear and what we know. To my ear the words of palm readers and crystal-ball gazers are not the truth so much as they are figurative hardware designed to help me sort things through.

This is basically what I told my father in that spiritual apothecary before Shirley, before Jason, before I had even imagined Linnea. What are tarot cards good for?

"They're a tool," I told him, guessing, reaching for something that felt true enough to say out loud and would make sense to him as well. "For introspection."

I think the same today, when I pull them out of a box at the back of my closet where I had packed them away with my high-school diploma and grade-school report cards. When I pour them out of the brown-and-gold-tapestry bag I bought at a women's crafts fair I'm surprised at the pale colors. I remembered them more boldly, the pinks as red as Saturday-night lipstick, the transparent yellows as glittering gold leaf. In reality, they are the shades of watercolors. But the images still stir me. The woman sitting up in bed, her face in her hands, with nine unsheathed swords floating over her head, looks to me like the weight I carry those mornings when I awaken from a bereft, unfounded dream that Linnea is leaving me. When I look it up in my candle-wax-stained tarot book I see this card means loss, doubt, illness, death of a loved one. On another card, I see the back sides of two figures dressed in the garb of a man and a woman with two children dancing at their feet, ten golden cups hovering overhead in the pattern of a rainbow and I think of how it feels when I finally do stop staring at the outside of my house. I park the car, come inside where the lights are on and jazz singers croon from the stereo and Linnea is waiting for me. When I look up the Ten of Cups I see it means contentment, lasting happiness from above. What do I believe? The ambiguous truth of the image, of course. I believe in contour and color and what I see when I stare. I look at the drawing of the Nine of Swords and I feel cut with everything I miss in the world, every lost friend, every abandoned home. I look at the shimmering, hovering cups and I see what I have each night as I stroke Linnea's head before we fall asleep. The magic of the world comes to me in its pictures.

≈

Did I mention that Jason was wrong about my pregnant friend, who wasn't pregnant at all, just thought she was? Did I mention I was indeed remarkable when I turned thirty, a remarkable mess, in treatment for alcohol relapse, my stars temporarily burned down to a dull charcoal glow? Did I mention that it's been eleven years and counting, and Shirley is still wrong about Linnea and me? But I do have one good psychic story to tell.

Guinevere, my best friend from childhood, went to see a psychic once when we were both in high school. I wasn't there, so I can't describe the place, except to tell what she told me. The psychic lived in an old house in Harvey, Illinois, a gritty suburb just south of the Chicago city line, one neighborhood over from where we both grew up. The old woman's receiving room was hung with golden crucifixes and ceramic statues of hands folded in Christian prayer, and the incense she burned smelled like the stuff Catholic priests carried in smoking tin baskets and sprinkled over the congregation at the start of Sunday Mass. Back then we were wild teenagers who drank and smoked dope. The sitting room of Catholic lady mystics was not the usual sort of place to find us. But Guinevere was interested in pyramid power and meditation, mystical rock music and new weird ways to be religious, which is probably why she ended up in that churchy parlor.

The old woman held Guinevere's hand and said, "You have a friend," and it was me who immediately came to my friend's mind. The way I imagine it, the crucifixes glimmered in the candlelight as the psychic squeezed Guinevere's pale fingers and mumbled something unintelligible about best friends and poetry and what was to be done. But in the end, Guinevere told me, the lady spoke distinctly. This woman who had never met me knew a little about why I would become a person so compelled to stare at my own house, my own hand, my own lover. "Tell her not to stop," she told Guinevere.

Don't stop what? I've never known precisely what she meant, but her words come back to me often, a riddle I will never solve, a koan I can't answer. I thought of it again recently, on an average Sunday, when I had no particular plans. Linnea loves motorcycles, and on this icy February afternoon she talked me into going with her to the motorcycle show. This annual cornucopia of leather and chrome is held at the downtown Minneapolis convention center, and designed for bereaved bikers like Linnea, grounded for the season, waiting for the thaw that comes so late up here, pining for the gravely throat-clearing of the engines, the nasty cough of stagnant pipes heating up for their first spring ride. We looked at home there among the bikers and their babes: she with her steel-toed boots and long gait, me with my eyeliner, leopard scarf, and little leopard gloves. I walked with her through booth after booth, fingering leather vests embroidered with red roses and heavy black jackets with long streaks of fringe. I watched as she held a different heavy-soled motorcycle boot in each hand, comparing their weights, or tried on a pair of wind-resistant gloves. We looked at custom-painted helmets, packable toolboxes, emergency tire-repair kits, spanking new Yamahas,

Hondas, Kawasakis, and Harleys, sleek low-cut models, or the big touring hogs with built-in luggage racks. We chatted with a couple of wide-armed biker women with long shag haircuts and chesty laughs who were passing out brochures for the annual summer biker gathering in Sturgis, South Dakota. And then it was show time, today's feature an indoor performance by the Victor McLaglen Motor Corps.

The Motor Corps are a precision motorcycle stunt and drill team from California, a bunch of white guys who could have been my uncles, Knights of Columbus members from the south side of somewhere. They were dressed up in cop costumes, rode slick police Harleys with whitewall fenders that matched their helmets, and performed tricks with names such as "the peacock" and "the pyramid," ten guys standing on each other's shoulders, fanning their arms through the air like waterskiers in an Esther Williams movie. Their bikes balanced upright, the men smiled in unison, waved their hands down at us like beauty queens from a parade float. The crowd gasped and shouted for more. I stood there with Linnea, staring with my hands clasped over my heart. The exhaust from their tail pipes was stinking up the place and generally it doesn't take much to get me coughing, but at this moment I could have easily breathed in a furnace fire. We were witness to the best mystery. The Ten of Harleys. The holy pyramid of the paunchy patriarchs. A silly constellation of things done just for the fun of it.

"Tell her not to stop." I could have seen something else, a gang of white guys who might hate us and all of our friends if they knew who we were, a pack of stick-wielding cop lovers, a bunch of pricey bikes stinking up my breathing space. There have been times when that is all I've seen. But this is not what I saw on that day. "Think how long they must have practiced," I whispered to Linnea, as we stood in line to ask Dick, Mickey, Woody, Rex, Sam, and the others to sign our official Victor McLaglen Motor Corps poster. "Every Saturday. Every night after work," I said. If I stare long enough I see more than sputtering pipes and police clubs. If I could look up this picture in my smudged tarot book, I might see words such as devotion, or whimsy, or joy. Is this what Guinevere's psychic was trying to tell me? I like it that I don't know for sure.

The poet William Carlos Williams said there are no ideas but in things. A pyramid of precious metal goblets, illuminated and over-flowing. A pyramid of weekend acrobats in knee-high boots and brown cotton trousers with gold cord trim. The pyramid of Linnea's and my gaze as we stand in the cold spring yard staring out through the city haze for a glimpse of Hale-Bopp's tail. All of this I can scavenge for clues, but not answers. I don't know if it's possible to divine what will come to pass. What I do believe is that I can look out from my terrestrial body to Linnea at my side or toward the minuscule showers of comets and see either distance or proximity. I doubt our lives or loves are predeter-mined, at least not completely. Much of the time I get to choose, and I don't need a psychic to tell me which is the happier destiny. Today I choose to cling to this world, to Linnea's arm, as the planet where we live inches around its axis again and we breathe in and out, wondering what will happen tomorrow.

One Woman at a Time

Some people, not just lesbians, ache for a new kind of romance, a foggy bohemian vision, ghostly households of love's possibilities. I used to be one of those dreamers. I would close my eyes and picture everything changed, a new social order of amour. All of my lovers would be a pyramid of variety-show acrobats wobbling on one another's shoulders, ankles shaking but holding steady, me at the top, juggling plates. I never expected to end up in any kind of marriage, never imagined the tightrope of interchangeable days such as the ones I have known since I started to love Linnea. In all of my imagined constellations of love the exclusive couple was passé.

Things hardly ever turn out the way we imagine they will, at least not at age twenty or twenty-three. In my case I never did succeed in climbing up, holding on. My early adulthood was more of a sprint through a corridor of mirrors, a hall of opposites. I banged and shattered between the place I escaped and the place I escaped to. And I am not the only one. Look at the extremes of lesbian culture in the past twenty years. First there was woman as blunt object—bristle-cut hair and separatist collectives. Then there was woman as exhibition of unconventional lust—scalp bared, nose pierced, breast and hipbone tattooed. Each new group wanted to tear down the tent and trundle off to another town, to start over where it would be so much better this time. I understand that urge, and have found myself making and remaking the presentation of my home, my affections, my body, along with the rest, until finally I'm not so sure anymore that we have to keep starting again.

~

When I was in my early twenties, just coming out as a lesbian, there was an article circulating among my new radical feminist friends. I can't find the author's name, don't remember who gave it to me or where it was published. I only recall the title, "The Couple as Dysfunctional Social Unit." This was the time soon after I had dropped out of college, when I spent mornings and weekends stretched out reading on the thrift-store mattress I had stuffed into the hatchback of my old rattling Pinto and then dragged, with no help from anyone, down the stairs into my college-town basement apartment. The walls there smelled moist and rooty, and I smoked menthol cigarettes and drank black-and-yellow-brand coffee by the pot, with pillows piled up behind my back so I could balance a book in my lap. Artemis, my scrawny copper- and auburn-haired cat who would live on with me well into my years with Linnea, was still an adolescent then, curled up in a skinny ring against my thigh. I am not of the generation of women who wrote the radical feminist manifestos. I am from the first new generation to read them, and I did, unceasingly, barely taking a breath between each heady essay. Such twists and spins, these words, these startling ideas that caused the world that circled my bed to shift color and contour. I read of women who killed in self-defense. I read about when, how, and why to enhance offensive billboards. I read that feminism was the theory, lesbianism the practice.

It was the article that explained the political error in the concept of the couple that stirred me like no other. For years I kept five or six copies of these words safe in my files along with love letters and a few favorite poems, and it is only since my last big move that I seemed to have lost the article for good. I'm sorry to find it missing. I'd like to read it again, to see if it has any bearing on my years with Linnea.

In the late seventies, I was bored with some of what was presented as "true" lesbian culture. Goddess chants. Collective living on organic vegetable farms. Exhibitions of menstrual art—a sort of organic action painting created when the artist stood over a blank canvas at a time of heavy flow. It appealed to some, but not to me. What I loved was the hard backbeat of gay bars. Rally speeches that pulled waves of shouting from a fist-waving crowd. Record albums by feminist singers who belted from the belly up about ways to make love without losing pieces of ourselves. I was titillated by transformational politics. Take everything we had ever learned and all of our brain cells, too, and spin them in a centrifuge. The world, love, every detail of our little lives could be completely reformed.

But it wasn't just the ideas. The ideas were made up of words. Of images. Take my beloved article. It could have been something so simple as the sound, the slant rhyme of the title words, *couple* and *dysfunctional*, that first shook my senses. Or maybe it was the graphics, classical statues of the female form in hazy outline. Some were whole anatomies, both breasts, a pair of hands, two thighs. The rest were joined and half-vanished, merged bodies missing half an arm, part of a blank stone face.

∿

I worry sometimes that Linnea and I have become one of those merged bodies. If our love is not as layered and treacherous as the acrobatics of non-monogamy, then how do I describe the joining of Linnea's and my life? Have we become earthy and root-bound, a doubled corm, one flurry of blossoms, distinct plants only if split in two and planted again? Or is our attachment of muscle and mind even more symbiotic? A double-decker bus, two levels, one engine. A duplexed house, two complete and separate homes that share one attic, one furnace. For as opposite as we may be, Linnea's wing tips to my suede mules, her blistering motorcycle trips to my dreamy dog walks, we often think and act inside the same breath.

Our friends laugh when I start a sentence and am unable to finish, snapping my fingers because I can't think of how to say it. But Linnea knows what I mean, and so enters into the sentence with me. The missing word is always precise and polysyllabic. *Plethoric*, she will offer, or *proclivity*, and I'll say *yes, yes, that's it*, as I wave my arms around in the air and go on with my story. It has become nearly impossible for us to see each other as completely separate, a state of partial dissolve I had always vowed to avoid.

All the women I knew in my early twenties, even the ones, as it turned out, who would not live the lesbian life for long, yearned to find ways to keep from losing any of their parts. The ache to hold onto all of ourselves was physical, a chest-clenching, stomach-tumbling need to burst out of the gravitational field and spin free. Sex was part of it, the body-to-body thing, skin grazing skin, the temperature rising. But we were after more than that. It was an inexpressible something that we craved from life, for which orgasm was just a metaphor.

These were the cusp years between the seventies and eighties and revolutions of the body were supposed to have already happened. Yet I am certain that lots of women felt the same ache in the thighs, the throat, the nipples that I did. We may have passed beyond the influence of TV wives in ruffled aprons and heels married to good men who looked most handsome in their old army uniforms. But the squealing blond ditzes in the hot pants and halter tops of 1970s television weren't much better. I wonder if it's different for young women now. Then I still felt so vulnerable to a definition of the word *woman* that I could not accept. The one who disappears under a man's thrusting hips. The one who vanishes into the strange country of a man's name.

These were the days when lesbians of all persuasions tried to cut themselves away from the rest by chopping off all of their hair, wearing baggy corduroys, learning how to build things. And not just lesbians— straight women learned how to use a hammer and a hacksaw, let their hair wind into messy braids or a wild vine and sprawl, refused to marry their live-in boyfriends, even wondered if they might be lesbians, too. And some of the messy-haired straight women turned out to be the real lesbians, and some of the crop-topped lesbians turned out to be good Republican wives. In amongst the flurry, we all took some half-formed idea of alternative love for granted. We all read about it, if not in my favorite article then in another. Any kind of marriage was a trap.

And so non-monogamy was the way to go, but as soon as we tried to express it in words—we progressive college-town residents just relocated from the big city or its freeway-bound suburbs—our imagery was of a pastoral world that most of us had never known. Our bodies were currents. Our lovers were shores. Shores who became the current to other bodies, other shores. We talked big. Our words spun and caught, and in their wake left a map of a world we were so sure could exist. But lesbian feminists, like all lefty politicos, do a good job of creating these alternative geographies yet so often make poor work of walking the ground.

But maybe it was different in other crowds. Maybe they didn't drink so much beer, smoke so much pot. Maybe they really did break through to whole new countries of love. I admit, my own story is clouded with all that is lost to inebriation. My young friends and I drank and we toked and we rambled about how we imagined it would look, these new republics of love, thin blue lines along a road we had never driven. Our words gave us something we craved. We were hungry. We were throbbing. We wanted new brains and new bodies, too.

The bare-scalped and labia-pierced sex radical lesbians of the nineties charge the women's culture left over from the seventies with sexlessness, but that is not how it was. There was plenty of sex, and lots of words, too. The trouble was that all that flowing and correctly fertilized language had a way of obscuring the lure of what was really going on, in at least a good many of our beds. I knew women who sat up all night smoking cigarettes when their lovers were out with somebody else. I knew women who had sworn they would never pair off, yet hollered, threw things, got drunk, and called their wandering lovers unrepeatable names. And yet they continued on with nonmonogamy, and not only, I think now, because of how the words convinced them. The women I knew then, myself included, and the ones whose manifestos I read, all had trouble admitting to the parts some harder-sexed lesbians might be a little too obsessed with now, the erotics of naughtiness, the aphrodisiacs of pain, the turn-on of stinging our actual or metaphorical skins. And it did sting to have more than one woman at a time, no matter how hard we tried to feel otherwise. Every now and then, no one was mad and the sex was good as free fall. But it never lasted long. If our multiple liaisons were a forbidden trapeze act, then our moments of flight were augmented by how far we might tumble.

~

The faded photocopy of the dysfunctional-couple article passed from hand to hand like the final few pulls of the joints we smoked so frequently then. For years, its sentences were my personal mantra. I would not mimic the capitalistic tradition of wife as property. I would not possess or be possessed, own or be owned. I would not try to stuff another, or myself, into a box of wrongheaded promises, just to stay safe.

The years had inched ahead into the 1980s. There was rock and roll television. Mainstream pop stars with orange hair and studded leather neckwear were wearing lacy underwire bras on the outside of their clothes. I had moved from a cornfield college town to a big Midwestern city, and was still calling myself militantly non-monogamous. It had such a nice ring to it, such a rolling, repeating rhythm.

But I can tell you now, it was no cushioned roll along a riverbank. My lovers and I were still stoned much of the time, and there were sobbing scenes in idling cars as the light at a downtown intersection turned red, then green, then red again. There were drunken phone calls, pebbles tossed against windows in the middle of the night, diagrams I drew on bar napkins illustrating how it really could work. The endless juggling. All the plates in the air at once. Gorgeous orbits, a geometry I knew no more about than I did river valleys and mountain streams but that really did take my breath away each time I tried to describe it.

Then one evening the fighting got so bad I couldn't stand it anymore. I grasped for any gesture that could get me out of trouble, so I reached for the obvious antithesis. I cringe to think of it now, how Elena's face crumpled with sobs, how I slipped the paper ring from a restaurant bread stick over her finger, how she smiled and stopped crying and wanted to believe me when I promised to stay faithful. It lasted a day or two, until I ran into Angela at the co-op restaurant where all the boho lesbos ate lunch. Her eyes, I noticed, were the color of high-grade maple syrup. She whispered what she had just then noticed, how she adored the shape of my toes, the arch of my foot just visible under the straps of my sandals. Within the week we all swung back to where we had been before. Angela was peeling off first my shoes, then my shirt while her other lover at home was pacing and muttering and working up to a good yell. Elena was getting ready to leave me.

What this sounds like, of course, is not some ideological system of open love but just bad behavior, druggy drama, cheating, sneaking around. Which is exactly what it turned out to be, even though in the beginning we had more graceful names for it. At the start, our lovers knew about each other and even agreed to the complications, until we all discovered that some feelings couldn't be thought away, no matter how hard we believed in their shadow. Not the chest clutch and heave. Not the stone-knuckle punch to the gut that sent us reeling each time one of our beloveds opened her thighs to another woman's fingers or tongue. Pretty soon there were only a few nice words left. Mostly there was sex. Clever sex. Dexterous sex. Unforgettable sex. Make-up sex. Fights about sex. Or pining for sex we promised to forgo, which only made the sex better once we succumbed again.

It was during this time that Angela, the one who had become my sneak-around lover, began teaching college. One afternoon in the dusty Women's Studies teaching assistant's office, an undergraduate aide eavesdropped as Angela made a couple of calls. She promised her live-in lover that she would be home for dinner, promised me she would stop by on her way home from school. They were whispery conversations, the kind you only have with a person you have recently kissed. When she set down the receiver the second time, she saw the student was watching, smiling, almost stuttering in awe. She said, "You are my role model." She must have been reading the lesbian theories.

When Angela stopped by that afternoon for what had become our usual fast fuck before she went home for dinner she told me this story. Instead of making love, we fell back onto the bed laughing, and kept laughing until it was time for her to leave. Never again after that moment did I call our liaison anything other that what it had become, even though we kept it up for at least another year. It was not a political statement. It was not a body poem, not words into action. It was just an affair.

∾

Which is not to say that the women I know now who are still trying to live this way aren't onto something I have forgotten how to understand, a magic trick once explained to me but gone mysterious again. I can squint and stare for hours, but I just can't remember how it's done. These days lesbians younger than me call it by different names. Polyfidelity. Polyamory. More long chains of syllables to describe an old bohemian experiment. Lesbian feminists didn't invent it.

They say there are ways to make the experiment succeed. There is, apparently, a sort of religion to doing it ethically. I must seem such a crank when I admit how tired it makes me now to think about all that running around, all that deciding how much this one or that one really wants to know, all those unfamiliar futons and other people's pillows, all that time spent away from home. Yet part of me wishes I did still believe it was the only way. I clench a little when I hear the stories about women I am acquainted with who seem, from a distance at least, to be pulling it off. I see them in the park, walking their dogs with one lover or another, or at a party, exchanging glances, negotiating how they will handle it, all these lovers of lovers together between the same four walls. What I mutter to myself is, "It will never work," but what I mean is I'm a little homesick for the days when I was so sure it could.

Yet I surprise myself when I finally observe that without the booze and drugs and the buzz of what seemed then to be endless youth, these balancing-act notions of love are no longer my sexual preference. I pick up some of the current books on the subject, stare at cover art depicting rings of licking, stroking, nibbling women with thighs and breasts askew and the first thing I notice is how this does not turn me on anymore. I don't want to share, don't want to overcome the way my heart races and neck muscles brace when I imagine Linnea with someone who is not me. I don't want Linnea to fail to stiffen when she sees a pair of eyes following me from across the room. It's not that we imagine we own each other, like a house or a car, but there is an edge between us and all the others who might be our lovers, a sharp explosive wire that keeps us just alert enough to stay sexy to one another. It's basic, physical, common, human, which is what I love about Linnea and me. We are two bodies all bound up with each other, with better things to do than learn to love in some different way. Is it so bad to reach for one of those old, imperfect models for living, instead of always trying to build something better?

And yet I'm still so troubled by some of what those old models insist on, those images of losing oneself to union. And so I keep looking for new language, another tumbling run of metaphor, wondering if Linnea and I might be described as compound words, a different meaning alone than we have together. *Backdrop. Limelight. Ropedancer.* But that is not enough. *Dancer, drop, light, lime.* It's too easy to break apart any of these words into their loosely joined pieces. So perhaps, instead, we can see ourselves as a sonnet, a trapeze act of all the precise words we love and hate. We don't lose the singular meanings of each little utterance, but together they make a noise we were unable to hear before. Our repeating sounds and the music of our sentences pitch us into the big din beyond our immediate bodies. Not the first poem. Not the last. Free fall achieved within a fixed form.

Some would say the old forms are dead. We should try to compose in another mold, something new, our own invention. I can only answer by trying to describe what Linnea and I want from our monogamy, and it is easier, first, to talk about what I don't want. So much has happened since I lay in the thin light of my basement bedroom smoking too many cigarettes and reading crookedly photocopied manifestos. I've been a messy-haired straight woman who learned how to change her own spark plugs. I was an anti-pretty lesbian in thrift-shop sweaters and hiking boots, with pages of opinions on all that sex I had yet to encounter. I was a queer girl in denim miniskirts and studded ankle boots who was one of my lover's other women. I had woman lovers whose touch I don't really remember and others whose pull made me willing to try things that at the time I was sure I'd never be able to tell anyone, secret trysts on dirty floors or games with bedposts and scarves. There is none of this that I regret. There is even less that I want to try again.

What I want now is harder still. I was incapable of imagining, when I was twenty-three, that years of one-on-one intimacy could be another kind of high-wire act. The work of two women who choose to stay together—with our lack of models, without fixed rules and roles, an empty auditorium of words for it—is surely as difficult as any Las Vegas circus act, as astonishing as any blue-green pattern of late summer stars.

One afternoon, in the polyamorous days of my youth, I sat by a muddy city river with one of the women to whom I was attached and swore to her I'd never want just what I have with Linnea now, falling into sleep together, waking up together, this wordless map of minutes. I shuddered at the thought, and ran my hands up and down my own arms, as if to brush such a tiny, crawling, earthbound mortality away from my exposed skin.

And yet now I do exist in just this way. At the start monogamy was Linnea's credo. She was a swan, she told me, the type to mate for life. I went along because I was in love, but now the credo is mine as well as hers, not a philosophy so much as just our day-to-day. There is so little reason to try to defend it. Surely I've lost that old dysfunctional-couple article because I don't need it anymore, and as it turns out its warning did not come true. I have gone ahead and merged my life with another's. Yet I have achieved what I wanted anyway, an existence that resembles that classic marble figure, the first full-bodied ideal illustrating those earnest manifesto sentences, that whole self I craved with every electric nerve ending.

But I still need the words to explain the obvious to myself. Our skin-to-skin is important, sure. Linnea and I are not planning to give it up, but neither will we stop making dinner, or gazing out our front porch screen with cups of black or green tea set flat on saucers and balanced on our thighs, or working, or reaching for the fathoms of sleep or listening for the chimes we still discern in each other's voices. I got what I wanted. There is still more here than I'm likely to find if I look further, so I don't stray.

But I might not see this if I didn't have Linnea, if she didn't have me, to keep putting it to words. What good is a balancing act with no one there to witness? Our fidelity affords us an unobstructed view. We are each other's audience, madly applauding each somersault of breath, each dangerous sway, each firm step back onto steady ground.

Bad Thighs and Easter Turkey

"I knew she was bad news when I saw her thighs," Grandma Rose said, sitting as she always has, her smooth knees pressed together. She was talking about Janey, my cousin Antony's last wife, the one I never met, who according to my mom had a good job working for Jenny Craig Weight Loss Centres. It was cocktail hour in Grandma's gold-toned living room, a few minutes before Easter dinner, a few hours before we all said good-bye to my brother Paulie who had just finished his air-force training and was about to be shipped off to Japan. The early evening Florida sun was just starting to stretch into long-lit strands that cut across our laps, making the glass of sherry Grandma held in one hand appear to be on fire.

The living room looked exactly like Grandma's old living room in Chicago—fancy, shimmery, gold- and silver-threaded furniture and polished brass candy dishes that had once decorated the home she kept with her second husband. He'd been dead for years, that jokey, grizzle-voiced, cigar-smoking guy who hunted deer and was the only person we knew who worked a desk job in a corporation. With the money he left her, Grandma Rose built a three-bedroom ranch house on a golf-course development in Panama City Beach, the Florida white-sand panhandle, what the guidebooks call the Emerald Coast and Southerners call the Redneck Riviera.

Just a scattered collection of family gathered at Gram's house that Easter—my parents and the newly engaged Paulie and Mitsuko, along with Uncle Tony and Aunt Cecilia, and me, waiting for the Easter turkey Grandma won in a raffle at the hospital where she volunteers. I had a map of Japan next to me on the polished table. I wanted Paulie to point to the spot outside of Tokyo where he would be living. I wanted Mitsuko to point out Kobe where she grew up. That was not the way the discussion was going. The cocktail hour was a little staged; my father knew how Grandma loved this performance, as if we were a family that lived within the frame of an old black-and-white film, Grandma played by a white-haired Elizabeth Taylor. But she never sat still for long. In a bit she would pop out of her chair, stride fast to the kitchen with her satin hose flashing in the deepening sunlight. She would wipe down the immaculate counters again before she pulled the gift turkey out of the oven; the bird none of us were especially anxious to eat on this warm evening.

Earlier that same afternoon, his face just starting to flush red from the sun as we stared out together at the big tumbling ocean, Paulie said, "How often are we in Florida? Why aren't we having fresh fish for dinner?" I shrugged at that. Gram had it in her head we were having turkey. My dad had already tried to talk her out of it, but she wouldn't budge. Then Dad had planned to roast it on the grill to give it a summery, barbecued flavor, but Gram crept out of bed, while the rest of us were sleeping, to get to it first. She had it stuffed and into the oven before anyone was dressed for Easter Mass.

I had already complained about the turkey dinner on the phone back home to Linnea in Minneapolis. I called her once a day, with updates. "No one but Grandma wants turkey and stuffing," I told her, at least twice. "It's too hot for turkey. But you can't argue with Gram. She's the queen."

The turkey was just part of the strangeness. Holidays with my family had always been winter occasions. Gray Chicago snow and ice frozen so deeply into the pavement you couldn't see it until the rear wheels of the car slipped out from under you, while bare-armed trees cast shadows under seedy yellow streetlamps that popped on at 4:30 on Christmas Eve. By Good Friday we were lucky if the trees had budded, the sun was shining, and the wind didn't have too icy a center. On Easter Sunday we always wore coats to Mass. But in Panama City it was eighty-two degrees, and the trees and bushes were aching with color. Birds with bright crimson, blue, deep orange tail feathers, so bright I had to squint, fluttered in the palm trees and low green bushes. The flowers were red as valentine hearts, yellow as egg yolks, purple as a bad bruise. For three days I had been walking around this place with my eyes half-closed, resisting the urge to dissolve into the sun and colors that were still too much. My body was still too rigid with the crinkled brown, gray, and pale blue palette I had left in Minnesota.

Grandma Rose, my father's mother, had lived in Panama City Beach for over ten years now. My parents, schoolteachers, had been coming down at Easter break since I was in high school. I made the annual trip with them in the beginning, eighteen hours in a truck camper from Chicago, almost twenty years ago. We stayed in a trailer park called Venture Out, across the road from the wild white dunes scattered with clumps of blond sea oats and the roaring gulf that never stopped slapping itself against the flat sand. This was before Panama City Beach became a college spring-break destination, before the beach was crowded with high-rise hotels, drunken volleyball games, and little metal huts that rent sailboards and Jet Skis and fat-tire water bikes to ride over the rollicking surface of the big purple water. Gram's been in Florida so long she's always telling us she can't bear icy Chicago winters anymore, that forty degrees feels like below zero to her. When I got there, she wiped a puff of her bone white hair out of her face and said, "We've got a *half a million* kids here this season." She tucked the loose strand into the knot she has worn at the top of her head for as long as I can remember and her voice rose on "half a million," as if they were all coming over to her house, and she would never get the kitchen clean.

Wind chimes made out of a thousand tiny seashells tinkled on Gram's screened-in back patio. The sandy clatter sounded odd against Gram's shiny upholstered chairs and couches that belonged up north, not in this beach town where it seemed wrong to sit on anything but rattan or brightly flowered cushions. My Chicago relatives looked vaguely out of place too, skin brownish-red from the sun but still carrying that winter-upholstered look.

"Janey lifted her dress, at the wedding, so Antony could take off her garter," Gram continued, taking a tiny sip from her sherry. "I noticed it right away." This conversation made my heart beat too fast. Didn't they remember how they used to love Janey? I remembered those stories. The weekend Antony's mother Cecilia spent picking out that perfect kitchen wallpaper and hanging it with Janey. The long bike ride along the north suburban Chicago shore of Lake Michigan, how Janey and Cecilia pedaled the fastest. And they loved the one before her, too, the long-legged Catholic schoolgirl who looked like Bo Derek, whom Antony married when we were in our early twenties, the year I started telling people I was a lesbian. And the one before that whom Antony was with when we were both in high school. She had long caramel-colored hair, wispy at the ends, and always wore faded jeans with a perfectly matched faded-jean jacket. Once I helped them sneak into Grandma Rose's old house back home, when Gram was out of town. I was staying with Gram the summer after both Antony and I graduated from high school. He devised a scheme more complicated than it needed to be. I would slip him the spare garage-door opener, he would slip her in through the garage, I would spend the evening somewhere else. I came in just before dawn, and Antony and I nodded to each other over the liquor bottles Gram kept under her sink that I had left open and strewn across the kitchen floor. They exited out the garage door with their arms around each other, dressed in identical denim, center thighs pressed together. From the back they were mirror images. I figured they would get married, and Cecilia acted as if they would, by scooping the girl into her kitchen and chattering like best friends. But when it was over, all Cecilia could talk about was how unfriendly that girl was, how badly she dressed.

I looked around my grandmother's living room, hoping someone would admit with a look, at least, how nuts this conversation was. Although the family's feelings about Janey had changed, certainly the size Janey's thighs were at her wedding had not. Every woman I had ever seen Antony with had been *Sports Illustrated* swimsuit-model beautiful. For years I wondered what these knockout women saw in my cousin who had seemed to me mostly silent and sullen since sometime in mid-adolescence. Then I saw a music video, Bruce Springsteen in his clean-shaven, worn-out blue-jean years. Girls in rock and roll T-shirts were swooning and smiling, trying to catch his eye, and I started to understand that some women see poetry in such hard, sloping shoulders, in that heavy-lidded, hard-to-read gaze.

And who knows what makes the pretty sentences between any two people in love fall away? I doubt that anybody's thighs have much to do with it. I let my eyes flutter closed and imagined Linnea was sitting here with us in her long men's shorts and clean T-shirt, with a silly-looking sunburn line across the side of her face from her sunglasses. I wanted to catch and hold her gaze. I wanted her to give me that look she kept ready for me in these situations, the look that returned me to myself when she knew I was in danger of slipping away into a dull white fuzz where I wouldn't be able to do what I came there for, which was to talk to my brother about his enormous move to Japan when he had never lived anywhere but Chicago and a little college town in Indiana. Instead, we were all transfixed by the way our memories of Antony's former wives morphed like a video trick, one face shifting into another, the cover girl whose nose lengthens, whose thighs widen before us, as we begin to believe she always looked this way.

Tony Bennett's voice played softly on Grandma's scratchy old hi-fi, the same one she had when I was a kid. The sun coming in through long windows that ran along the front door stretched lower now, catching Gram at her knee's center point. My dad was sitting next to her, the ice and olive were spinning in the martini he held in his hand, his lips were slightly turned up at the edges. Cecilia and Tony, Antony's parents, sat across from Grandma, nodding, the sunburn line on Cecilia's thighs exposed where her long tan shorts slid up. Cecilia's thighs were wide across the top, like mine, like my mother's, like the thighs of most of the women from both sides of our family. Grandma Rose might be the exception, but it is hard to know, as she has always kept her thighs covered with neat creased polyester slacks, pastels now that she's in Florida, and slim skirts that don't expose her knees until she sits. Linnea tells me that none of our thighs are bad. She says they are long and luscious, just not skinny, not narrow and hard. Women's legs, not steel poles, not a drag queen's muscled gams.

Once, long ago, I showed a photograph of my mother to a friend. It had been taken when my mother was in her mid-thirties and she was wearing a short culotte dress. She was posed against a dark solid background with large wallpaper-sized flowers, and her thighs were exposed. These days I can look at that photo and see that, yes, my mother's legs do widen above the knee. They are probably wider than she would have liked them to be, but they are not ugly. But when I pulled out the photograph all those years ago the only thing I could see was how much her thighs looked like my thighs. So I was amazed when my friend, who was, like myself, a lesbian in her early twenties, said "I love your mother's legs."

"Really?" I said, glancing down at my own wide thighs that I always kept covered.

"They look so strong, so sturdy, like trees," she said, and I laughed. I'd always dreamt of having skinny sapling legs, like a Barbie doll.

The only woman at this family party with anything close to sapling legs was narrow-boned Mitsuko, who was sitting with her feet tucked up under her on the blue-silver corner sofa with my mother, looking at snapshots of the sand-colored pyramids from Mitsuko's trip to Egypt. She was moving back to Japan to be with Paulie, but not right away. She had a few more trips to take first—San Francisco, maybe China. They wouldn't see each other for a while, after this weekend. I probably wouldn't see either of them until the wedding, and that was a year away. Mitsuko's long black hair was hanging loose tonight, and the sun that afternoon had turned her skin copper. That morning, after Mass, Mitsuko and I snuck into the country-club whirlpool a block from Gram's house that no one much used because of how the water temperature fluctuated, one day lukewarm, the next almost boiling. The late-morning sky was hot blue, and the shrubs around the pool were so green they looked unnatural, and I wanted to turn the color dial down, mute them out. The sun was warm on my bare shoulders, but the whirlpool water was hot enough to steep tea. I was able to dangle my feet in, no more, but Mitsuko, who grew up in Japan taking scalding baths in houses without heat, was immersed to her chin. Her black swimsuit with its plunging neckline and cutouts across the stomach was shimmering under the swirling water.

"Your mom said ooo-la-la when she saw my suit," Mitsuko said, her eyes closed, her hair spreading out around her like sea vegetables, her face turned up to accept the sun. I was starting to be able to accept it, too, feeling really warm, even under my skin, in my bones, starting to feel my muscles unfurl as they hadn't for months, since before winter. Here alone with Mitsuko, soon to be my new sister, my feet sunk in the steaming hot pool, the breeze warm and whispering, my body was almost relaxed. "I told her I lived in Hawaii," Mitsuko said, "where everyone has suits like this, but she kept saying ooo-la-la."

My suit was not as daring, fluorescent pink with big flowers and a zipper between the breasts, two sizes up from what I wore in high school. "I don't like being around my mother in my swimsuit," I said, running some of the hot whirlpool water up over my thighs that were just a little rosy from the sun. "She wishes I was little like you."

"Japanese are littler," Mitsuko said.

"We have Slavic thighs, strong like peasant farmers. I wish we could just admit it."

"My mother had cancer," Mitsuko said, opening her eyes. "Before she died she got skinnier and skinnier. I don't think it is good to get too skinny." Just then a big yellow-feathered bird fluttered out of the bushes and shot away over our heads. Its feathers were so bright we both squinted as it flew away.

Now this Easter evening, Paulie's eyes were fixed on the TV playing without sound, baseball players in cool white uniforms tossing a white blur of a ball across a startling green field of AstroTurf. Paulie had just finished his air-force training a few hours north of Grandma's in Montgomery, Alabama, at a special camp for lawyers entering as officers. When Paulie told me he was joining the air force I was against it, though I knew he hadn't been able to find a job in Chicago, even with his law degree. He told me the air force had promised to send them to Japan. I told him not to believe it. They would lie just to nab him. I was speaking as the sister he had never really encountered, the one who had stood on cold Minneapolis street corners during the Gulf War, holding signs that read NO WAR FOR OIL, while ducking obscenities hurled by stubble-faced white men in passing pickups with flag decals on their bumpers. But this time I turned out to be wrong, at least about Japan.

Paulie didn't look any different to me now that he was a military man. Just a little more exhausted. I'm not sure what I expected, perhaps that he would have changed already into one of those military spokesmen I peered at on the TV during the bombings, the guys describing the damage done by the new computer-managed explosives that blipped across the screen like the Pac Man games I used to play in bars. The TV soldiers' stiff faces lit up as they pointed and narrated, just like my dad's used to when we were kids as he described why he loved his old bebop recordings.

Sitting on Grandma's Chicago couch in her Florida living room, Paulie's sunburned legs were sprawled in front of him, his long thighs hard and muscled. Earlier that afternoon we drove out to the beach, a couple miles from Gram's, where I had stretched out along one side of Paulie with a long, sheer, leopard-spotted scarf knotted around my waist, covering my legs and part of my pink swimsuit, while Mitsuko lay out flat on her back and fell asleep on his other side as the skin exposed by the cutouts in her bathing suit was already darkening. Now that it was Easter Day, the college kids were gone, the hilly, white-sand beach was nearly vacant. The wind was stiff, sending empty beer cans clattering past, blowing Paulie's and my hair straight back from our heads. The waves pounding against the hard wet sand sounded like kettledrums. The repeating beat got inside me, left me defenseless, impossibly content. The sun dissolved my flesh away into the fast-moving wind. I noticed Paulie's legs then too, his olive-toned thighs and calves covered with curling, dark brown hair, his feet long and pale, his big toes callused, an adult man's feet. I was startled, remembering him barefoot on this same beach as a boy, his skinny legs and doorknob knees, a square shock of blond hair falling into his eyes. I was a haughty teenager then in a yellow bikini, brushing him off, walking away, my thighs covered by the beach towel I had tied around my waist like a sarong.

Later this Easter afternoon, back at Gram's, my cheeks stinging slightly from sunburn and the wind, the mineral water I was drinking fizzing a little in my mouth, I nudged Paulie and whispered, "Mmmm, smell that turkey."

He turned his head slightly, met my eyes. "Where's the fish?" he whispered through closed teeth.

"That Janey," said Uncle Tony, shaking his head. "She thought she was beautiful, but she wasn't so hot." Grandma and Cecilia were nodding. They remembered the same Janey. Not so beautiful.

"Janey met some guy," Tony continued. "He told her she was beautiful and she should be a model, and she believed him I guess, so Antony came up with the dough to take all these photos of her. He spent all this dough making these photos, but she didn't turn into any model."

"She was not a beautiful girl," Grandma agreed.

The settling sunlight played over her smooth knees. They were shining, two flashlight beams. Gram was the only one who was dressed up. I glanced down at my hands and realized I was squeezing my own thighs through the thin denim of my blue-and-white-striped engineer overalls cut much too large, the urban hip-hop style that I hadn't seen anyone wearing in Florida. I could feel the slight sting of sunburn as I squeezed. I had been with Linnea now longer than Antony had been with any of his wives. When I first told my mother about Linnea, way back in our first year together, she sighed and said, "Why don't you lesbians ever stay with the same person the way regular people do?"

"You mean," I said, "like my cousin Antony?"

It's not as if anyone ever mentions Linnea in these moments, but I do wonder what they see when I remind them she's usually with me at family events. She wasn't at this party, but I could picture her as if she were, her wide fingers, her men's rings, the silky, almost blond, nearly invisible hair on her legs, her dark Italian eyes on the other side of her glasses, her flat feet. I pictured her thighs, long, squarish at the top, not skinny like a stick, no shapely showgirl curve, but not thick with muscle like a man's thighs either. What do they see? Does the video shift when their gaze falls on Linnea, her chest flattening, her upper lip sprouting hair so they can pretend she's a man, my boyfriend? Or do they focus on the quarter inch of cleavage revealed along the top seam of her sports bra, as the video shifts in the other direction, away from the hot current of marriage that is always there between us, allowing them to see her as just my friend, some old-maid roommate? These people were my family, and I did love it there with them, the swell and crash of such familiar voices, a bittersweet wallop I felt in my bones. But why wouldn't they ever see things as I did, one marriage of my generation reduced to broken feathers and gristle, too sad, but another one, mine, full-winged, still ascending. Both things were present at once there at our Easter table.

The light in the room was dissolving, sinking into the purple wash of early twilight. Through the open screen I heard those paintbox-colored birds embroiled in their end of day twittering. My skin was warm and tight from the sun and finally there was the slightest edge of chill in the air. It brushed against my bare arms like a dull knife, and my eyes teared up a little. I hadn't meant to let it in, this heat, this blooming. Once I was back home it would be a long six weeks before the ground burst open with these hard summer colors. Now I would be impatient for it.

The television had all of Paulie's attention. I hoped I could get him to look at the map with me after dinner. Mitsuko was fingering the gold base of the lamp next to the sofa where she was sitting, but she was not finding the on switch. My mother was frowning, holding the photo album out into what was left of the scattering light, and ignoring her mother-in-law's distant pronouncements. My mother had liked Janey, maybe now even more, on principle. I wondered if Mom worried what her mother-in-law might have to say about how she looked the day she married my father. My mother hated the photographs of her own wedding. "I've always regretted my gown," she told me, more times than I could count. "I should never have bought a three-quarter-length dress." Her memories of a wedding-wardrobe decision—how much of her legs she had left undraped—still left her misty after thirty-five years. She didn't join in the conversation about Janey's misbegotten day. "Is this the friend you traveled with?" my mother asked Mitsuko, nodding toward one of the photos. "Will she be in the wedding?"

In my family's old eight-millimeter home movies there is no evidence of big thighs. My mother looks trim and modern in her Capri pants. My eight-ten-twelve-year-old thighs are unremarkable below the hem of my red cotton shorts or yellow-flowered culottes. In the later scenes when I was a teenager my cutoffs are so short that my butt is barely covered and my legs are narrow. Now, as I approach middle age, there may be some truth to my ancient fears, but how could I have believed it then? As for Janey's legs, I admit, I've never seen them, but I'm willing to bet it's not her thighs that were expanding that Easter evening but rather what none of us, not even me, wanted to admit, which was that unhappiness tends to attack randomly, and no marriage is guaranteed to last.

Grandma Rose finished her sherry and stood. "They were big," she announced. "That girl had big thighs. Antony shouldn't have married her."

My father laughed, shook his head, and so did I. Cecilia and Tony were nodding, agreeing with Grandma. The green scent of spring dusk mingled oddly with the too-sweet smell of the roasting turkey. I opened my mouth, started to say something to Gram, but what? I wondered if, in her eyes, my thighs were the size they were when I was in high school, just as Antony looked to her to be an undivorceable husband. This is how she loved her grandchildren, by recasting them as sultry celluloid ideals who gathered, adoring, at her movie-queen feet. It was only our spouses who spoiled the picture.

Gram swept away into the kitchen, Cecilia close behind. "We'll need you to carve," Gram called over her shoulder to my dad. My mother looked after them but stayed seated with Mitsuko, who found the light switch and pointed to another photo. I heard the wind chimes clatter and a gust of cool air rolled into the room. I looked at my dad, who looked back at me, still laughing. I wondered what Linnea was up to at home as the day's late rays cut across our kitchen. Was she feeding the cats? Talking to the dog? "Time for that turkey and stuffing," I said to my dad, and he laughed again, nodding and shrugging as we waited in waning light for our Easter bird.

Falling Down

Patsy and I walked south down Portland Avenue that cloudless afternoon. The center-city skyline fell away behind us. The late March sun was a distant white throb. The sidewalks were wet with melted snow. The straw-colored grass was strewn with garbage that had been suspended in the winter drifts. My skin felt straw-colored, too, dry and drained, kept too long from the sun; my flesh felt too heavy, still half-suspended in winter.

It wasn't my usual dog-walk route. The rusting mufflers of big gas-guzzling sedans and the rumbling side panels of delivery trucks made Patsy shiver, drop her ears, rub up against my knee. Ahead I could see the crumbling old brownstones where friends of mine used to live, in the years when this was the nice neighborhood I envied from another crumbling street, ten blocks closer to downtown. Now I didn't feel completely safe walking in this direction. The condition of the neighborhood was on again, off again, and on this day, walking south on Portland Avenue, things got worse before they got better. Still, it was almost spring, and I needed to walk off all my closed-in thoughts accumulated over the long winter. I needed to walk south, where I hadn't walked since autumn, to see what was still standing and what was falling down.

Linnea, do you remember when I first moved onto this block? Lovers just two weeks then, we carried in the last of my boxes, found the lost cat who had been hiding under a pile of my clothes bags, closed the door on the man from my past who had come by to help me fix a hole in the bedroom wall. I knew him from the months surrounding my twentieth birthday. He was the last man I ever slept with. It was nice of him to lend a hand, so many years later. Still, there was a strange moment where my past and my future stood together in my kitchen. Then he left and you and I were alone again. The stereo wasn't hooked up yet. I didn't even have a dog. The only sounds were the heat bumping on, the rattling motor of the old refrigerator, the thumping of my two cats leaping in and out of empty cabinets. We had already wandered from room to room, stroking the sworled leaves and roses carved into the fireplace woodwork, already watched the light ripple in through the stained glass, already gasped and whispered, "All this space. It's so huge." Finally, we fell back onto the stiff springs of my old vinyl sofa, let our arms and hips and thighs fall against each other, let our heads loll back, let our eyes float up toward the ceiling. The plaster was textured, flecked with hundreds of silver specks. "Constellations, " you said.

⁓

On the corner, across from our house Patsy and I passed by Dorothy— thin-boned, white-haired, with skin the color of powdered sugar. She was chipping ice out of the gutters along the curb, as she did every day in early spring if the sun was shining, if there was not too much snow. In the summer, she swept the sidewalks with startling upper-arm power, or else she edged the lawn by shoving a serrated blade along the sidewalk with rapid jerks of her narrow wrists. All year long she picked up what other people tossed out on her grass—sticky paper cups, fast-food bags, a child's torn shoe, an empty fifth of vodka. She brought her radio out on an extension cord, and tuned it to a talk show. Her hearing was bad, so she had it turned up loud enough for us to feel the constant static thrum, waw waw waw, through our closed kitchen windows. From the street I could make out the grating, know-it-all voice of Rush Limbaugh, harping about the usual—lazy, unemployed, welfare-mother, lesbian Democrats. Dorothy hacked frantically at the ice, as if it were a cold fungus, a creeping mass that would swallow her white stucco house on the corner if she didn't keep chipping away.

A lot of people said our neighborhood was disintegrating. Was it? Even our landlord said so and his son, who lived next door to us, agreed.

That is one of the reasons they charged us 1950s rent. The last time I had worked a temp job in the suburbs I met some people who wouldn't even drive down that part of Portland Avenue because African Americans, Southeast Asians, and Mexicans lived where once there had been only Norwegians and Germans of the merchant class. I thought the neighborhood was going somewhere, too, sliding earthward, but I saw it as mostly a physical fall. The buildings, some of them owned by those same white people who used to live there, others owned by the sort who make a living off renting out houses unfit to live in, were crumbling away into the dirt. Even our house. When we pounded a nail into the wall we heard a current of plaster rushing into the basement. Talking to the assorted chorus of our friends, some who lived nearby, others who didn't and thought we shouldn't either, I took a hard line. "Landlords who abandon their property in the inner city should be put in jail." But then our rent wouldn't have been so cheap. I would have been forced to work more, would have had less time to walk the neighborhood in the middle of a weekday afternoon while mulling over how these vistas, shingles falling from roofs, dissolving steps and cockeyed railings, looked like still photographs of an earthquake's first moments.

∼

Darling, do you remember when you finished off the fence? It was a few months after we got Patsy. The dog needed a plot of her own. You wanted a safe place to park your motorcycle. The old fence horseshoed just half of the yard, and it was so dilapidated that it swayed up and back in every stiff wind. It was the summer of the Midwestern drought. We bought the posts and cement ourselves and, on the hottest weekend in July, you and one of your buddies propped up that old fence, marked off the open spaces where the new fence would go, set foundation posts in hollows of new concrete, nailed up the new cedar slats. The heat beat down on your sweating back. It seemed as if the sun was falling, hurtling itself down into our private patch of mud and green.

∼

I came to be afraid of all that crumbling. I was afraid of the faces of boarded-up houses, hands pressed over their eyes. I was afraid of anything that might have caused my home with Linnea to shake and slither into the ground. This is what I thought about on my early spring walk down Portland Avenue—that time in our third year together when we almost lost hold.

The time I am thinking of was four years before that melting afternoon. Then it had been autumn. I walked Patsy south down that same street. It was a gusty night; funnels of fallen leaves were swirling at every corner. After 11:00 P.M, dark for hours, it was late for a walk, but I was trying to shake a feeling from my body. I had just gotten out of a car with a woman I wanted to kiss so badly my chest ached from my neck to my navel and I was constantly clenching and re-clenching my hands. It was inexplicable, this desire for a woman who was nothing, dull compared to Linnea. She was not even comfortable saying she was a lesbian. My lips felt too warm whenever I saw Ricki and I was jumpy, abnormally alert. I knew this was a crazy craving better left unfed, but the ache would not stop, no matter how I tried to talk myself out of it.

The years that had passed since then had nearly erased that illicit flush from my body. When I returned to the present, to this day's walk, I was relieved to see how changed I was. Looking around on my bright March avenue I noticed there was still a little snow on the roof of the house two doors down from Dorothy. We liked the people who lived here. Laney and Jo's house was three-story and shaped like a barn, with a carriage house out the back. Laney was on the sidewalk in front of her house, picking up trash and tossing it into a big plastic sack, just as Jo pulled up in a little red car.

"I got a job!" Laney announced. I noticed she no longer wore a turquoise hair extension tied into her bright blond hair, and I wondered if she had just gotten tired of it or if this change marked the difference between graduate school and the academic job market.

"Did you hear about Laney's job?" Jo called from the street as the car door clunked closed. Jo came up from the street to the sidewalk and leaned over to pet Patsy who was smiling and wagging her curly tail. The copper glimmer of Jo's long hair complemented the fox blond of Patsy's fur. In full dog love, Patsy hurled herself higher, muddy paws grazing Jo's tight black jeans and high black boots. I yanked back on Patsy's leash. "Sorry," I said to Jo. "She doesn't understand about outfits."

Jo didn't seem disturbed, kept on petting her as Patsy's mouth hung open in a tonguey smile.

Linnea knew Laney from the university graduate program where they both did their Ph.D. work. Laney's specialization was avant-garde poetry, Linnea's the lesbian novel. I had met Laney years earlier in poetry circles. Then her husband Jo had struck me as a skinny guy with a Billy Idol tough-artist look—leather pants, rough-cut bleached hair. Now Jo's hair was waist length and dyed a deep shade of auburn that shifted color in the light. Along with black jeans tight as a plaster cast, Jo wore foundation makeup, powder, and deep brown eyeliner. The effect was punk-sultry femme fatale, Cyndi Lauper meets Veronica Lake, a look that drew whistles from passing cars.

Jo was one of the artists in our neighborhood, part of Portland Avenue's boho element that kept me here amidst the earthward ripple of brick and glass, rust and the rest of Rush Limbaugh's least favorite things. Jo made films, dim-lit meditations on AIDS, and Jo painted: lately, anatomical males laced up in mystic bondage and wearing lacy bras and fishnet hose, penises swinging out from under black garters. "It looks like a card from a transgender tarot deck," I said to Linnea the last time we got a postcard in the mail advertising one of Jo's openings. We wondered whether to refer to Jo as he or she or maybe even he/she. We supposed Laney was still a straight woman, but wondered if Jo's changes had altered her identity, too. Laney and Jo's parties had mysterious visual themes. Animal skulls. Squid. They were full of thin men in shiny black party jackets escorting feather-light, chain-smoking cross-dressers in skin-tight minis, along with graying English Literature graduate students wearing striped shirts and bad posture. They all mingled under Jo's Dantesque paintings, around an elaborate font of champagne and beer.

Both Laney and Linnea came out of graduate school into an impossible job market. Hundreds and hundreds were lined up for every opening. Their lifelong dreams of oak-lined offices and placid professorships fell away like an image in a crystal ball that faded and reformed into the shapes of other, less discernible, more temporary careers. Sometimes, back in our apartment, I watched Linnea with a black marker in her hand, filling in the rejections on the big job-search chart she had hung on one of the oak pocket doors. "Nope. No No No. Nah. No way." I watched her and felt a trickle descending through the center of my body. Would we ever get what we had pictured in our heads for so long, or were our dreams made of the same stuff as our old dissolving plaster ceilings, once sound but now hardly up to code? But the news that Laney got work, this was big. "What's the job?" I asked her.

"Comp, at a community college in Rochester."

"Rochester? What's that, two hours? Will you commute?"

"An hour and a half each way. But it's a good job." Laney's face was round and pale, china-doll pretty beneath her platinum bangs. She always waved wildly when we passed her on the street, rushed up to talk to us at art events, but we never got any closer than these chats on the street. That is why I've never asked her what she thought about Linnea and me, her queer girl neighbors who look more like husband and wife than she and her husband do. Never asked about whether she missed the time when her husband looked more like her brother. Never asked about how it was to watch a body change, one person falling away, a new one appearing like an image hiding under the top layers of an oil painting.

"I'm going to get her a cell phone," Jo said, looking at her sweetly, "for those long winter drives." As Jo set a gloved hand on Laney's shoulder, protective, husbandly, I remembered how Linnea worried about taking me to faculty parties as her spouse, but then thought of Laney and Jo and figured for us it would be easy.

"Congratulations. I'll tell Linnea," I said, yanking Patsy back from trying to jump up on Jo again.

As they started to move together toward their house, I began to walk away. "Isn't it amazing," I called back over my shoulder, "how much trash is uncovered when the snow melts?"

"It looks like the center of the city is unraveling," Jo said, looking desolately at the wadded paper and broken bottles on the boulevard in front of their house. Laney squatted to pick up a pile of broken glass, shard by shard.

"Our end of the block usually gets together to clean up," Laney said.

"God, not our block. I don't know anyone on our side of the street, except the landlord's son. They keep moving in and out."

"You two are the stable corner over there," Jo said, and I laughed.

We were stable by then, but once there had been tremors. That woman I had wanted to kiss a few year's back, her name was Ricki. And actually, I did kiss her. But just on the cheek. Still, it had been enough to shake the foundations, cause a few bricks to fall. She looked like Mariel Hemingway, only boyish, I thought then, although no one I pointed it out to could see it. I met her in alcoholism treatment. The first thing I noticed about her was that she reminded me of my old ex-lover Angela, the one I had ended up sleeping with on the sly in my anti-couple years, before Linnea. Ricki didn't look like Angela, except for something in the cut of her body, the jock-muscled shape of her legs and torso. She looked like someone who could play tackle football and not be afraid of getting hurt. But what really drew me to her was the way I was sure she was attracted to me without admitting it, maybe without even knowing it. If I wore bright mauve lipstick I'd watch her watching my lips when I talked. If I wore a lace bra, which I did, intentionally, I made sure to un-button my shirt so it would show. My chest would flutter hard as I felt her stare at my neckline from across the room.

But this wasn't the bar, not a dance nor a party. It was treatment. Four nights a week I sat across a circle from her and admitted, crying, to everything in my life since age fifteen that drinking and pot smoking had screwed up. And she did, too. We were there together, listening to and telling stories of banged-up cars, banged-up bodies. We loved each other for each word, for each newly exposed wound.

But if this was love it was dimly lit. The drunkest of our stories—barfing in the shower, punching a lover in the eye—shimmered and beckoned like a drive-in movie screen flickering at the edge of a long dusk. It was hard not to fall in cynical love with our worst selves. And I was falling for her, in an aching, shooting-pain-through-the-body sort of way. But only sometimes.

Other times I was still in love with Linnea, even though her face was so often too pale, too stiff with protection even when we kissed. She was furious with me, ever since she had witnessed my slip back into who I used to be. Linnea watched a woman that looked like me emerging from under a mottled corner of history she had noticed too late. The sober woman she fell in love with had thrown her over, started drinking again. Linnea had never considered how important it was that she had fallen in love with a woman who didn't drink anymore. It was the first time since her childhood with a boozing father that she could see how thin the window could be between one kind of life and another. Her lover drank again and was in treatment for it. What would I do next?

What I wanted to do next was keep on drinking. I wanted this so bad I'd sit up straight in bed at night and try to wipe the craving off my lips with the back of my hand. And I'd think about Ricki, how I wanted to stroke her head and hold her while she cried, how I wanted to kiss her mouth, and lie down with her naked, our skin aching and shivering together as we mourned the loss of the booze, our other lover.

∽

Linnea, do you remember the day we made love in the kitchen? You took me by surprise. The southern sun was beating in through the blinds, the kitchen carpet was scratchy and tufted where you had just vacuumed. Our kisses that first year left me bendable, boneless, willing to do anything. But it wasn't the kiss that got me that morning. It was the way you grabbed me by my waist. Your wide fingers, your arms were strong enough to lift me, hold me airborne. Even though I'm taller than you, when you pulled me toward you I felt I was rising to meet your kiss. For a moment I was quick-winged, a hummingbird. When my feet touched down on the carpet again you wound your heel around my ankles, tripped me. We fell, tumbling to the floor. When you opened my shirt, kissed me between my breasts, stroked my crotch with one hard hand, I laughed and whispered, "You want to do it here?" "Right here," you whispered back. "Right here."

∽

That sunlit afternoon of our seventh year I walked on past Laney and Jo, beyond five or six well-kept homes with trimmed shrubs, homes with polished stained glass above the doors and window frames. Then all of a sudden things fell apart. Three apartment buildings in a row had orange condemned stickers pinned to the front door. Patsy sniffed the bare dirt in front of the first, then crouched to pee. Usually I pulled her off people's front lawns, tried to redirect her to a less conspicuous spot, but there were no people living within these broken bricks. Chunks of cement, cracked off the front-door steps, were scattered along the walkway, and there was shattered glass everywhere. A skinny mother cat ran by with her feral kitten in her mouth and disappeared through a punched-out opening in the basement window glass. Most of the windows were boarded up with splintered plywood, but a few of them had been overlooked. The glass was punctured with holes the size of a big stone, or a fist.

A long time ago I ate Thanksgiving dinner in one of these buildings, years before they were condemned. I couldn't tell anymore which one because they all looked so different now. I had brought mashed potatoes in a big ceramic bowl that is gone now, too. A few weeks after Linnea moved in with me my youngest cat nudged it off the counter and it smashed into pieces on the floor. But before that it had been a splendid bowl, and the potatoes were rich and buttery, and our friends cooked a turkey with stuffing and other women came and brought sweet potatoes and bread and green salad with artichoke hearts and pumpkin pie that we ate with real whipped cream as we sipped fresh ground Nicaraguan coffee served in my friends' big cobalt blue mugs.

All these years later, Linnea and I watched out our front window when police cars swarmed to corners like this one. Their blue and red siren lights spun like roulette wheels. That afternoon, the sun still pulsing, the ice still melting, I tried to move by quickly, but Patsy had found something irresistible to sniff, so she locked her legs and hindquarters. I was stuck there for a minute, before all that falling brick and cracked cinder block.

That windy night four years earlier, before those apartments had been condemned, I fled down this same street with Patsy in tow, trying to walk my feelings for Ricki out of my body, trying to keep my life with Linnea from tumbling away. Earlier that evening Ricki and I had given each other letters. We exchanged them in the upstairs bathroom of the old house that had been converted into offices and treatment-center meeting rooms. I sat on the edge of an old porcelain tub and she leaned against a tiny porcelain sink, five minutes before our treatment group met. We hadn't planned it. We both just showed up with these crinkled gifts in plain white-paper wrapping. We read them together, in front of each other. My face and the smooth blond back of her head were reflected in the mirror just behind her. Our bodies echoed back and across

the tiny white room. My letter was verbose and complicated. I was trying to tell her how I felt without giving anything away. Her letter was
simple and too cute, like a letter a high-school kid would write. At the
end she wrote, "I care about you more than you know." That is the part
that stuck with me.

It was no accident that I needed a ride home that night. I had
stranded myself on purpose, so I'd have to ask her. I knew I wouldn't see
her for a while. She was about to go to jail for a week, the sentence for
her last drunk-driving ticket. It was on that ride home that she told me
she would not be back at all. When she was released from jail, they were
transferring her to inpatient treatment. All this time, these long fall
nights, as we scrupulously documented everything that had ever happened to make us want to be unconscious, want to be dead, Ricki had
been secretly drinking.

"So you've been lying to me," I said, as if she were my lover, as if she
had cheated on me.

"I'm sorry," she said.

"I'm so angry," I whispered. I feel like hitting you, is what I was
thinking.

"You look like you're ready to hit me," she said, crouching back, away
from me as she drove slowly down yellow-lit side streets.

I laughed at that. "*I've* never hit anyone," I said.

When she pulled up alongside my house I leaned in close. My kiss
landed hard against her cool, smooth cheek, leaving a lipstick flower. I
meant it to be a good-bye peck, but I knew it was more. I knew that I was
trying to get nearer to her lips that even then, so full in the glare of the
streetlamps, made my lips ache to look at them.

Walking that same street years later, in the bright afternoon light, I
could see that the sidewalk in front of these crumbling buildings was
jagged and rough-going. It hadn't been shoveled all winter. A narrow
path had developed after a while from people's footsteps, but it was
choppy and slick. Now the snow was half-melted but still treacherous,
especially with the broken glass uncovered in so many layers of melted
ice. I told Patsy to heel, jerked her collar to keep her next to me, tried to
maneuver her paws around the sharp edges. When I crossed over to the

next street I looked back, expecting to see my old friends stepping out, one tall and dark as coffee, dressed in bright pants and a loose shirt, carrying a big woven bag, the other one shorter, carrying a Y bag, on her way to her daily swim. Her round, always-smiling, cream-toned face was framed by black hair pulled back with a headband. But those friends were long gone; they had lived in Seattle for years. The only thing I could see from where I walked was all the time that had passed. I crossed over Portland Avenue, heading east toward another block.

That night all those years before, after I kissed Ricki, I did not keep walking away. I stopped myself suddenly and we turned dead around. I remember how Patsy looked up at me, her head cocked expectantly as we paused on the corner. The copper-colored leaves were gusting up around my knees and falling back again as I tried to decide whether to turn around and go home or to keep stumbling on. When we turned back, I walked more slowly, something in the musty night air snapping me back into focus. What had I been doing? When I had left Ricki's car a half hour earlier I thought I was waiting to make some choice, some clear-cut yes or no. To Ricki. To drinking. All along I knew that with Ricki would come drinking. It was chilly out there and my body ached. My feet were sore from my pointy-toed boots, horrible for walking. My arms were sore from the dampness of the night and from Patsy's constant tugging. Lights flicked on and off in windows above our heads. Other apartments were bathed in blue, the glow of televisions. But my danger-ous cravings began to fall away. I don't know why. Maybe the walking cured me. Maybe luck. Maybe good sense. Maybe a fleeting contact with belief in some force bigger than me. Or maybe it was just the bald fact that Ricki didn't kiss me back. Whatever restored me to my better self that night did its job well. That's the last time I've needed so much help getting home.

We walked the block back quickly that night, past Laney and Jo's where all the lamps were turned up high, past Dorothy's house where all the lights were out. Inside Linnea had been waiting for us. She wore the red kitchen apron her mother had given us, and the sleeves of her blue denim work shirt were rolled-up. She had been washing the dishes. The apron matched our red kitchen table. There they were, my lover, my kitchen, all color-coordinated, and despite everything, still waiting for me. Linnea's face was too pale, too creased with worry. "Did you see any stars tonight?" she asked me with the dish sponge still in her hand.

~

A paint-stained rag wadded up in the hand. The smell of turpentine at the back of the throat. Under the layers of old oils, my living self rises. The best we can hope for is that new life thrives beneath a ruined landscape. It did not happen in a day. Linnea, do you recognize me? It took seven years from the moment we met to recreate, cell by cell, this body I give you now. These days I still fall into your chest, but not boneless. Now I am full boned. I meet you, invite you, bone to bone. This winter, on a Sunday afternoon, I wrap my heel around your ankle, trip you so that we fall into the unmade bed. You come to me as you always have with tousled hair, eyeglasses set safely on the nightstand. Your wide fingers are holding my waist. Later, if I want it, you will reach into the basket under our bed, strap our pleasure-emporium phallus to your hips, come into me until I shudder, but for now we approach each other as we are. I rise up to meet you, my hips, my heart emerging out of all my other lives. We both fall down, fall back, lose ourselves in the old paint and debris of our histories. We both rise up again. Old surfaces vanishing. New light emanating.

~

Walking away the afternoon in the throbbing March sun as the downtown skyline fell back into a misty haze, Patsy and I headed away from Portland Avenue. I felt the blood start to move through my body, the exercise awakening me. I felt my cheeks flush, the muscles around my stomach loosen. When I looked back again, I could see Dorothy still frantically chipping. I could see Jo on a ladder high atop their house investigating the loose shingles, copper hair glimmering like pennies in a wishing well. When we got to Park Avenue we turned north again, passed a big old Victorian with scaffolding partly installed up one side. This house had been on the market the year before as a HUD property. It had been condemned, but now people lived there. The walks were clear, and there was not so much garbage on this corner.

"Look, they put up a fence," I said to Patsy. "I wonder if a dog lives here now?" Just then a big white Husky stretched in the corner and ambled over to us. She was the same color as the big patches of snow left on the grassy parts of the yard. Patsy and the Husky looked a lot alike, the same curly tail, the same upright ears. Only their coloring was different, this dog white and black, Patsy fox-colored. They stared for a moment as if they were confused by a skewed reflection, then they sniffed each other through the chain links. One of them started barking and the other one joined in, together a racket of yaps and snuffling along the muddy base of the fence. As I pulled her away, I looked up to see that the people there had removed some of the old siding. On the top story, just above the attic window, was a carving, barely visible under the old chipped paint. It was the same design I had seen on a lot of these old houses, a half circle of sun rays, narrow streaks bursting from the center, an arc of new light.

Reasons to Be Happy

Imagine a party, a bottle- and can-cluttered kitchen, a couple, two sunny women in their early thirties, who are standing just close enough for their bare arms to graze and set their translucent arm hairs on end. Imagine they are a pair everyone has met, one of them a muscle-bound heartthrob with spiky platinum hair, wind-burned skin, a knee blown out by rugby, history with half the women in the room. She was the one nobody expected would ever settle down. The other is newer on the scene, taller than her lover, with a face not so much pretty as interesting, creases starting to form at the outer edges of her eyes, long hair pulled back in that messy-on-purpose style you see in all the casual clothing catalogues. Her clothes are a little sloppier than she grew up able to afford. She is not as well known as her lover but just as impressive, the one who got the heartthrob to stay home. Imagine how they adore talking about their relationship, how they love to show off their engraved commitment-ceremony rings.

A muggy summer evening in an upper Midwestern city. A household of lesbian roommates. A birthday celebration. A vintage-eyeglass and cool-shoes sort of crowd, women in their thirties or younger, everyone holding a sweaty glass of bubbly water or a bottle of imported beer. If you are anything like my longtime lover Linnea and me, you are getting to be a little old for this crowd, and you just don't party the way you used to. So you watch.

You watch as women who used to be sober tip vodka into their mineral water. You watch the ones who used to be someone else's lover perusing the crowd in search of a current girlfriend, or maybe someone new. Dance music, female vocals, a hip-twitching beat, but no one is dancing. Women go outside to smoke and only a few are drinking hard. It's the sort of party where people can hear themselves talk, so they do. Their voices form a murmuring swell that builds up and falls away again as this summer evening drains into night. In the kitchen, leaning against a red kitchen table, the couple tells a nodding circle the story of their beloved domesticity. It's the taller, better-schooled of the two who does all the talking. How one of them is neat, the other one sloppy. How they buy one piece of used furniture each month, then work together to strip it down, polish and paint until it is ready to live with them. How they are always able to laugh while they work. How they are always able to make each other happy in bed.

A shared flush rises from their faces. Their bodies, just barely nudging each other at the elbow, are the apex of a hot triangle that beams out over the kitchen and out into all of the rooms of the throbbing wood house. Pretty soon the whole party stands around them, half-hypnotized, listening to the talky one talk, the hunky one shrug and hold out her gold-ringed finger for anyone who wants to see. "I knew it from the start," the talky one tells us. "We were meant to be together."

Then someone, maybe you, maybe me, asks, "How long has it been?"

"Two years," they say together, each word drawn out, hovering, as they hold each other's gaze.

Two years? This might seem a long time to most of the gaggle gathered around to listen. Linnea and I stand at the fringe of this party and wonder, with our eight, nine, ten years together and counting, if we're getting too old for parties. Two years is barely a beginning. We lock eyes too, and bite our bottom lips. Two whole years.

This is not really a portrait of any one particular couple, but a version of so many couples Linnea and I have come across, all of whom are broken up by now. It's not that I mean to laugh at them. Most of us have armloads of former true loves, and I have no way of knowing if Linnea and I will be together forever. But if I roll my eyes when lesbians hold out something like two whole years for us to pick through, as if it were two tons of precious gems they had so diligently collected, it's only because Linnea and I get tired of being the ones who have been together longer than anyone else in the room and because I've come to the point where I want to wait a little while, to see how it goes. I'm reluctant to get close to one more young couple only to live through another of their breakups.

I am still a little shaken when lesbians I know break up. I'm not talking about flings and sneaky affairs. Those always seem to be just what they are, a spike of black-light-poster glow, stoned and purple-blue, then pop, the color's gone. It's the way an affair thrives under the crust of the rest of life that makes it so captivating. But most us can't live forever in the basement. No, what I mean are the couples, the ones who share a groove, buy food together, have two cats and a dog, a mortgage, a shared car, photo albums, season basketball or theater tickets, the ones whose parents know about them, and visit, and know the birthday of their daughter's lover, and maybe even send a gift. I mean the ones who go to the gym together every Saturday, or to the same cluster of pine cabins up north every July, or hold a huge bonfire party for all their friends every autumn or an open house every Christmas Eve or who come to our house carrying yams or fruit juice or a salad every Thanksgiving. I mean the ones whose names roll from our tongues in one long breath, the ones who look good together, who complete each other, until all of a sudden one of them leaves.

Linnea and I have been together the longest of almost everyone we know, and each time another pair of longtime-lesbian companions tear in two we move up another notch. "How long have you been together?" single lesbians in their twenties will ask us as we stand in the kitchen of one more party where we are older than the hosts, and when we tell them, almost nine, ten, eleven years, their eyes widen and we can see their lips move as they silently count backward. "That was the year I graduated junior high," one of them will say, as Linnea and I exchange crooked smiles. How could anyone have been in junior high in 1986, we're thinking, but by then the young ones have moved on to get another drink, or stir to some rough-hewn song that has just spun onto the CD, and we wonder how to dance to a beat that sounds to us more like words than music. We start to notice the sticky smell of keg beer and the veil of cigarette smoke clinging to our hair and that is about the time we decide to go home.

Home is, after all, where we longtime lovers recognize each other best. The longer I live with Linnea the more important home becomes to me. Lesbians and gays still don't have enough big images of themselves. Not that things are what they used to be before we had bookstores and big-budget movies and openly lesbian rock and roll stars. These days there are photograph books of couples like us, pairs of women or men who may or may not still be together, posed on their sofas or in their front yards or up against a stark studio backdrop. There are volumes of interviews—about choosing family, surviving conflict, planning a gay wedding. There are film documentaries, gay histories, even library archives of lesbian cross-dressing wedding scandals dating back to the turn of the century. Evidence of our unions, a glimpse into the speck of what must have been billions of lives, exists for anyone with the time to study it. But it's still so little compared to the saturation of themselves that straight people have little cause to notice every time they channel surf or page through a magazine in the dentist's office or drive under billboards on the way to work. So I wonder if lesbians and gays might feel more bound than most to rely on the places we live to make our relationships look real. If we don't see enough of ourselves out in the realm, why not try to spot our reflections in what gleams in our day-to-day?

I have friends who don't like the idea of lesbians married by the power vested in them by their dwellings, a phenomenon prevalent in a city such as mine where it's often cheaper to buy a home than rent a decent apartment, which means that some get into it before they are ready to really commit. "That house fetish thing," one of my cohorts calls it, referring to weekends spent at estate sales, flea markets, or even Dumpster diving in the upscale alleys where people toss out perfectly good possessions. I would like to say I'm one of these domestic divas, a bohemian budget-hunting type, as it seems a serene way to spend our hours. And now and then this is just what we do. Linnea and I will use a Sunday afternoon to poke through antique malls or pick through what is left of the weekend's moving sales. We look for objects to add to my collection of teapots, to Linnea's assortment of antique barware, to both our array of Las Vegas kitsch and Madonna tchotchkes. But usually we don't have the time, or would rather read a novel or eat lunch or go to a matinee, or we simply can't see our way past the clutter we have already accumulated, stuff that seems to come to us without our bidding.

The lesbian couples we know who take their decorative quests more seriously live in houses that never appear to be a mess. Their homes are full of dried-flower petals. Century-old framed botanical prints of roses or violets or yellow irises. Gay nineties lady-head lamps with beaded lampshades. Maxfield Parrish prints of two barely dressed women on a swing that hovers over a blue-green mountain lake. Old metal bread boxes with hand-painted appliqué. Shabby Victorian dressers with the old paint purposely left to peel. Funny framed magazine ads from the fifties of coffee-crazed housewives with sparkling kitchens and Valium smiles. An ancient garden gate propped up like a trellis in the center of a well-tended perennial bed. Their rooms look the way I'd like to feel, possessed by the caress of a finger that transforms static air into an off-beat garden. "I would pay to come here," I've so often said, when visiting one of these homes. This sort of thing used to be gay men's territory, but based on what I've seen lately lesbians are doing it, too, and sometimes I envy them their Midas touch.

I understand my friends' arguments that women who spend all their time making a photographable home might be sublimating something important under all those Martha Stewart-meets-lesbian-kitsch surfaces — sex or a real conversation or their checkbook overdrafts or booze on the breath or the truth about what they do when they are apart — but I still see the possibility of another kind of story. Imagine a Sunday morning, a brunch held before the Gay Day Parade. Linnea and I are sitting on a swayback sofa with a hand-stitched slipcover, set against a hand-ragged wall hung with antique photographs of women in bustled skirts, next to a trunk, the type in which a Victorian lady might have once packed her trousseau, stripped to the grain and hand-decorated with gold swirls and a mosaic of vintage buttons. It was in a room something like this, on top of this trunk, perhaps, or on a slightly scratched mid-century tiled coffee table, or in an art deco rack full of glossy gay magazines, where the two women we were visiting kept one paperback volume, the only book we ever saw in their home. *14,000 Things to Be Happy About.*

"Look at this," I almost shouted to Linnea. I leafed through page after page of lists. *Leaded-glass doors. Prune kolache. Magic Lanterns.* It went on and on. This might help me find the image I had been searching for, my long pursuit after a picture of what it looks like to be lesbians in longtime love. Perhaps if we could embrace a simple meditation on living, fresh

paint on an old chair, the smell of chicken stewing in a pot. It's too simple, too saccharine, I know. I ought to have jumped all over these insipid
lists that sever objects of affection from the lives that love them. Linnea
laughed at the page I showed her. She is an English Ph.D., after all, accustomed to reading for subtext. Why would happy people need a
primer on happiness? And yet I am astonished to recall that I fell for that
catalogue of jelly jars and zipper teeth, high-heeled shoes and cobalt
blue bottles. I could even add a few bright items of my own. Our dog
Patsy stretched out in a patch of kitchen sun. The first time Linnea and I
saw Manhattan from an airplane. Our refrigerator full of sourdough
bread, free-range eggs, all-fruit jam.

But why should I always be so troubled with questions, with the bleari-
ness of the future? Why should I treat the world as I do, like a continuous
crossword puzzle full of witty clues and wrong answers? Maybe I was
wrong to wonder if women like the two who bought this book ought to
be better prepared for impending cloud cover. Maybe some people just
know how to keep the sun beaming in through their clean windows. I
ought to be more focused on the sound of sandpaper scraping away the
surface of old wood, I thought. I ought to spend more time feeding the
purple echinacea flowers I see out my kitchen window. Think less. Clean
the house more. That is what my mother always told me. Is this what she
meant?

But it's this sort of mirage that fools me, perhaps because I want it to.
After all these years with Linnea, I'm still not sure I know happiness
when I see it. Then I'm stunned when another of our friends calls with
the bad news, and I wonder again, what does a happy lesbian couple
look like? I realize, of course, that there are women who have been together much longer than Linnea and me. Some have been at it so long
that if we leaned against their kitchen counter, boasted of our long love,
held out my finger so they could admire the little ruby ring Linnea gave
me for our second anniversary, if I stroked Linnea's curly head with my
ringed hand, right there, in front of everyone, and tipped her face to one
side to show off the matching ruby earring I gave her the following
Valentine's Day, if we told them, eleven whole years this December, they
might exchange looks full of all we don't know yet. Remember what hit

us in year sixteen, my dear? Remember that peak we hit at our twenty-fifth, and how hard it was to know what to do after that?

I've read about women who have been together a quarter of a century or more, but I don't know how they have managed to stay happy. Would it help if I did? Imagine two white-haired women in matching slacks, women who love to smoke cigarettes together, and drink Diet Pepsi, and watch old World War II movies on cable TV. Maybe their thick beige draperies reek of old smoke. Maybe their back hallway is cluttered with empty Pepsi bottles that knock together when a truck pulls too fast down the alley. But when they step in through the back door from shopping or from visiting a friend who's been alone ever since her last companion passed away, just as twilight begins settling over their back stoop, they might hear those bottles ping, a familiar ringing, and they might not even notice the intimate smell of the upholstered room where they have sat together, so many evenings. It is in that moment that they might draw a long sigh. Homecoming. An easy falling breath that I could never know in that particular place, with a woman who is someone else's long love. Not mine.

Just last year another of my good friends left her lover of thirteen years. It was an inferno of a breakup I never thought would happen, a forest fire where I didn't even know there were trees. My friend stored all her stuff in cardboard boxes in my basement for eleven months—a cookie jar, her good dishes, photo albums, a weathered blue garden Madonna. And one Saturday night another of my friends tried to explain to me why she and her lover were splitting up. "But what happened to the way you used to play the electric piano together at midnight?" I asked. And the way you used to snap photos of yourselves, heads touching in the afternoon light, faces hot with laughter, I thought, but didn't say out loud.

"I'm going to give that piano away," she said.

I was standing in our kitchen when I heard about the rift between one of the young couples we met at a party, the ones who had hosted the Gay Pride brunch. Linnea hung up the phone and turned to tell me the news and my hands flew up to cover my heart. So it wasn't enough, the fragrance of drying rose petals, the reflection of light in the lampshade beads, a garden that keeps growing whether or not its gardeners do. "But they had 14,000 reasons to be happy."

"I guess they ran out, " Linnea said.

Maybe so. Yet while I can nod to Linnea's cynicism here, I still believe there is something genuine about the love any of us feel for what we imagine, collect, or make to bedeck our everyday. But I can see it's not reason enough to stay married. First comes love, then its adornments.

So who's there to show us how to do it? Our heterosexual aunts and uncles and parents? Some of them have been married more than forty years by now. They must know something about it. But we don't have what they have—names for their union in every language, the weddings of a square-chested prince and a big-busted, cinch-waisted princess at the end of every Disney movie, every Shakespeare comedy, not to mention Mary and Joseph, Hera and Zeus, and those little bride and groom figurines they have saved from their wedding cakes. And they don't have what we have, freedom from all those rules about how it's supposed to be done. But we also have years of TV evangelists sobbing over our poor lost homosexual souls and the majority of our elected congress pronouncing that our marriages have no right to exist.

So what's left? The idols among us? We have all heard the stories about finally getting to meet that famously monogamous lesbian couple. Then, when you shake the hand of the princely one on the right, you see she's staring at you as if she might want to slow dance. You feel her vapor gaze and in a woozy moment you imagine taking her up on it, until you remember why you were so anxious to meet her, this fleshy wedding-cake icon, and as fun as it is to have a little flirt, a stone or two slides away inside. Anyway, most of the time, it turns out that Linnea and I have been together longer.

It may be that we have one advantage over our heterosexual counter-parts. At least we don't have anyone insisting that there are maps, and the experiences we do have to draw on are our forebears' traditions of finding the way en route. But creation is hard, too hard sometimes. This should not be news to lesbians. So many have tried to invent and re-invent every kind and variety of relationship since the first among us stomped with boots and banners down the centers of big city streets, more than thirty years ago now, screaming the name of the love that for so long dared not speak. An army of lovers cannot fail, our slogans read. But what about an army of lovers who no longer speak to each other?

I suppose I should have long ago just relaxed and given up trying to find an image to contain what Linnea and I have created between us. Yet I crave that very thing I've hardly seen, some reflection, some echo to surround us, some dry wash of wind and morning color that tells us this is just too normal to spend another second thinking about. I'm still looking, in books, in films, in other people's stories. I even traveled to a lesbian archive in Brooklyn to see what I could dig up. What I found there, in that dusty house of haphazard shelves, crooked files, strangely labeled boxes, was a cabinet full of snapshots of lesbians in love.

There were photographs of "Sandy and Trudy," nuzzling in blue-plaid shirts on their brown-plaid living-room couch. There were photographs of a smirking couple, who seemed a little uncomfortable posing, one tall and long-limbed, the other short and droopy-eyed, and holding a newly golden loaf of bread atop their flattened palms. Behind them, beyond what must have been the buttery, grainy fragrance of their baking, out through the ruffled eyelet curtains that framed their faces I could see a clean blue car parked in the driveway. "Our house," the photo said on the back. And there was a photo of a plump woman lying on her back on rumpled white sheets and wearing nothing but a sleepy morning smile—a view only a lover could know, her nipples as dark as her molasses-colored eyes. The caption of this one read, "birthday girl."

Here it was, not a lesbian decorative-arts catalogue, not party chatter, just a raw vein of common happiness. Thousands of little windows into the way we love. But why, I wondered, would anyone give away their marriage photos, even to keep them safe for history? These photos weren't that old and I recognized a few of the faces of writers and artists known in lesbian circles. I knew at least some of these women were still alive so I couldn't assume these snapshots were all deathbed bequests. I thought of the boxes and drawers I kept of photographs of Linnea and me. Sitting in shorts with knees touching on a green wool blanket at Gay Pride. Scaling the water-sculpted rocks of the Lake Superior shore with our dog Patsy, still a dish-eared puppy. Me in a zebra-patterned hat and a mock-glamorous face in front of the Christmas tree. Linnea holding a string of newly snagged fish in a photo shot at an angle that showed off the purple and blue peacock tattoo on her left upper arm. Who would let such a precious hoard out of their sight?

That is when I realized the other possibility. I flipped over another shot of Sandy and Trudy, stretched full out on the couch, kissing hard on the lips. "Together five years," it said on the back. The time to give away such photos is when you no longer want to look at them. These were former lovers, couples that had been, but were not anymore. They were lesbians who had run out of reasons.

Linnea was with me at this archive, doing other work in another scattered and dusty room. We had spoken barely a word all day. At the end of the afternoon we had to take a subway from Brooklyn to Manhattan, where we had rented a room for a week. It was January, gusty and damp in New York City, and I was groggy and choked up from the archive dust. And still, those snapshots lit through me, a melancholy slide show. As we stood on the underground platform waiting for the train, one month after our tenth anniversary, I watched Linnea, standing apart from me. She was distracted by her day's work. Her heavy leather motorcycle jacket was zipped up to her chin; her neatly zipped black leather briefcase pulled one shoulder down lower than the other; her black fur hat, the exact color and texture of one of our cats back home in Minnesota, was perched on her head. I should have known her silence simply meant she was still working, her brain clattering on with whatever old magazine documents she had unearthed that afternoon for her research on dime-store lesbian novels. I should have remembered how often Linnea believes she is speaking to me when she's only thinking my name. But I hadn't told her how I had spent my day either, and didn't tell her then about how full up I was with the faces of those real women who had once awakened every morning with the scent of one particular lover on their skin. Did they have new lovers now, or did they live alone? Did they go back to the bottle, or to parties to peruse for someone new? Did they ever wonder what went wrong, why they stopped loving the birthday girl or the one who filled their kitchen with the smell of baking bread?

I didn't tell Linnea about the gray maw collapsing there between us, deeper and wider than the space between subway platforms. So far from home I forgot how to see that we were still wired together, even without talk. I have trouble now, looking back, believing I took my bad mood so seriously. Yet there I was, stunned by gloom. It had to be happening to us, too, didn't it? That had to be why we weren't sitting beside each other on the hard wooden bench, why we had barely uttered a sound on the windy walk out of the archive, around the traffic circle, down the narrow cement steps to the subway station.

There had been an afternoon, six months earlier, that could have been a snapshot. It was the day we moved into our new domicile, once a garbage house renovated by previous owners, now our happy home. Linnea's truck was parked on the garage pad in the back. My rusted junker was parked out front, and the dog lounged with her tongue hanging out on the sunny back steps. On the shady front porch our new swing whined and creaked in the hot breeze. Right there, four reasons to be happy. The first ones to stop by to see our new house were those women with 14,000 reasons. They were unexpected guests, as we never did know them well. They brought us some black-eyed Susans from their perennial garden, to plant in ours. A blessing from them to us. A fifth thing to be happy about. But maybe they should have saved that last reason for themselves. Or maybe we needed it more than we knew. On that subway platform, so far from home, I thought I saw all the photographable light draining out of Linnea and me, and without knowing I was going to I said, "I don't feel you anymore."

She turned to me open-mouthed as the train shuddered into the station. We got on the train. I was crying. "What are you talking about?" she said sitting there next to me, hunched and deflated as we hurtled through the mottled underground. I was feverish with words. *You don't talk to me. You don't look at me. I don't feel you in my heart.*

What I should have told her then, instead of later, was the story of all those smiling women's faces, the photographs taken before they knew it would all come apart. When I tell friends who aren't paired-off about this moment they narrow their eyes at me. "Why would you think these women aren't fine? Lots of people are better off away from each other." And of course, I know this, that the couple is not automatically sacred. That is a right-wing zealot's view of marriage. Not mine. And yet I grasp at whatever I can see in order to find ways to honor what Linnea and I have made. I went to that archive to find pictures of it. I wasn't prepared to encounter the opposite. Were these photographs documents or were they premonitions?

And so I fell into a spiral of questions. Why should all those women break up while we stayed together? Who are we to think we could do any better? Why not admit the inevitable? It seems idiotic now, to have been so overcome, but my skin was crawling, my breath wet and sludged. In the car around us, the local people were reading newspapers or dozing as their necks rubbered from one side to the other. The only thing to look at outside the windows were the billboards hung at the incline into the next station. Ads displaying happy heterosexuals running in the grass, laughing and smoking cigarettes. I couldn't think of anything more to say except what I had been saying. "What do you mean?" Linnea kept sputtering. "I'm working, that's all. Just thinking about work. You think this means we're ending?"

Lucky for us the Brooklyn subway line doesn't stay underground and it was not yet night. When we rose out of the depths, I could see the smoke-draped sky and everything I was feeling reversed again. 14,000 reasons to be happy. 14,000 reasons not to be. It's not that we ever run out of either. We decide, everyday, whether or not to wait it out, to see how long it takes for our part of the world to cycle back toward the sun. Finally, this is what any marriage looks like, a journey over and under the dirt, moving too fast to be contained in a snapshot. In that ember of a moment, too tired, too hungry, both our eyes stinging and wet, we rose up from the underground into the day's last rays and Linnea pointed it out to me. A simple out-of-towner's awe was all it took. "Honey. Over there. The Statue of Liberty."

Madam Liberty glistened green-gray over the dirty Brooklyn rooftops. Her torch was set afire in the ebbing sun. I wish I could tell you she spoke to us. "Give us your tired, your huddled, your illicitly coupled . . ." But it was nothing so dramatic. We just saw her there for a minute, and Linnea lay her gloved hand on my thigh. I felt her, that most familiar touch. I felt her still, as the light blinked out, as the train plunged us all back under.

Will You?

"Will you marry me?" Linnea asked, cradling a black felt box in her palm. The little ruby and diamond-chip engagement ring she bought for me at Montgomery Ward captured the yellow light of dinner candles flickering in honor of two happy years since the first time we touched in love. I looked down at her grinning face gazing up from where she knelt on the dusty dining-room floor. I answered her with the only words that tolled through me then, a cathedral bell peeling yes, I will, I do, oh yes. The bells kept sounding for as long as I understood that the words *will you marry me* meant no more or less than I knew she meant them to. Did I love her, did I take her, was I hers to hold in her arms for as far ahead as we could think? Yes.

But a breath or two later I had more to say. "But what does it mean?" I whispered, as she moved in closer and wrapped her arms around my waist, rested her curly head against my stomach.

It is in moments such as these that I have stopped to wonder. I am unable to look the words straight in the face without seeing the history of the wedded world piled up behind them. It is not that Linnea's and my love feels suspect, but rather the language we consider using to describe us. Married. What did it mean when a woman asked a woman to marry her on an evening eleven years shy of the millennium? Such a story was still well outside the major motion-picture frame. What did it mean when Linnea got down on her knee to offer me these rubies, this circle of gold, and even diamonds, the biggest a graduate student could afford, which was not too big, two spots of glitter no wider than the point of a pencil lead?

I see all you easy romantics shaking your heads, rolling your eyes at my annoying uncertainty. Why has Linnea put up with this? How could I fail to know what this means? We all know what it means. It's that teary scene in the back of the cab at the end of *Breakfast at Tiffany's* when it's raining and George Peppard tells Audrey Hepburn that they belong to each other as "Moon River" swells from just beyond the frame. The watchers, you and I, we swell too. This is a happy ending. But the lines the actor speaks are more than just the words of the script. Can you hear how it resounds through the dark like the thunder we wait for after the crack of light that breaks the night sky into pieces? When you promise to cherish in sickness and health you become each other's plot of land. Marriage is the borderline between this moment and all you had imagined of yourself, before love. We belong to each other. A flag tied to a barbed fence, a brand on the soft part of the thigh.

I don't believe the love-as-ownership version of the story. Linnea doesn't believe it. Most of our chorus of friends don't believe it. We were not the ones to put words between George Peppard's lips, and yet those words echo in ways so bright and beckoning that it is nearly impossible not to cry when the movie is finished. Even if we have seen it before. Even if we know this is just another Hollywood rewrite of a novel about a beautiful doomed girl who could never have ended so happily.

When I asked Linnea what does it mean to wear a ring of promise, I did not fail to see her bright and beckoning face, did not fail to know that I was more than a boozy blaze of a girl imagined by a famous alcoholic homosexual who died too young, did not miss the fact that Linnea was no stock-studio savior positioned in the back of a cutaway cab. She was real husband material, reaching for ways greater than words to say she loved me. It is just that I wanted to know who would write the story of this tempered metal I should wear so close to the skin. The ring was not an idea that Linnea and I imagined between us. Whether leather, stone, bone, woven reeds, copper, sterling silver, or gold, the never-ending roll of the ring's circle has forever been an image of on and on, a precious-metal wish for the circle of love to remain unbroken. But it has also come to mean other things, a woman taken by a man, a geography possessed, a glittering stamp on the appropriated body.

I know this is not what Linnea was after when she fell to one knee.

And yet there is something of what I wish to avoid inside the thing I cherish most in Linnea's courtly proposal. The dilemma is not so much how to ignore the teary taxi-cab scene, but how to reclaim it. Ever since the radical feminist rampages of the 1970s, lesbians have specialized in tearing down the picture shows in our minds. I worked toward that end for a while when I was barely twenty, circling the sidewalks in front of the campus movie theater in an Illinois college town, distributing lavender leaflets that listed all the fates worse than romance that befell women on the big screen. I look back sweetly on my former self, that girl who was just getting up the nerve to grow out the hair on her legs, who snuck looks into the faces of the other new lesbians she was too frightened to kiss, lesbians so beautiful she thought (but would never have said) even without makeup and cute haircuts, in the way, I know now, only twenty-year-olds can be pretty. That girl who was me chanted under the cinema marquee, *hey, ho, pornography has got to go.* She was determined to purge all of the world she had learned so far from under her skin. But this day in front of the movie marquee was no more than a year after a night in 1977 when all the air in her lungs swelled like a full mast on Moon River. A man she met in a photography class, senior to her freshman, took her out for a beer and then pulled her to him by the empty loop of her painter's pants, as if she were as otherworldly and weightless as Holly Golightly and destined to belong to him. Even today, almost twenty years later it is not the man I want to revive, but that swept-up feeling, that full-sailed swoop.

I was wrong when I said I needed to know who wrote the story. I used to think that was important, but now there is something I want instead. To be all those people I have been. To find a way to be both the girl who would tear down the world and the girl who would float on its rushes. A woman smart enough to discern the patterns of meaning under the image while she is the image herself. She swells with yesses. She arches her back for the last kiss before the credits. She is free to collapse into bliss, but is still present, in mind and flesh, the morning after.

I did accept Linnea's ruby and diamond circle of protection to wear on my right hand, the queer ring finger. I still want it to mean that I belong to her, that she belongs to me, as the music rises and we embrace. Yes, I will come home to you each night, and I won't sleep with anyone else, and the nights we don't make love we will read in bed before we douse the lights and fall away into our private wishes. Linnea says the ring means she wants to be with me. She promises I don't annoy her with my questions. She tells me I am the moony sky reflected in her river, that I open her to what is beyond her reach. She says the ring is a circle because that is the shape of a finger. The night she slipped it on I was distracted. I swelled in love, yet worried the words would hurt me. Now I have worn her ring for a dozen years. No harm has come to me.

What Kind of King

We are standing in JCPenney men's department when I realize what sort of king I've promised to marry. The woman who gave me my little ruby ring is holding up ties, one with fluorescent triangles and intersecting lines, a pop-art geometry assignment, the other a delicate Victorian print with inlaid roses that shimmer under the too-white department-store lights.

"I'm leaning toward this one," Linnea says, lifting up the geometry lesson. The harsh lights above her head highlight the gray in her hair. We are surrounded here by the base elements needed to conjure up what is commonly called a man—hangers hung with navy blue, forest green, and magnet gray suits and the caramel brown and unadorned black leather of men's accessories under glass. Paracelsus, who inspired those Renaissance alchemists who wanted to cure the world with the medicine of transformation, declared that to conjure meant, "to observe anything rightly, to learn and understand what it is." Linnea conjures herself between the neat department-store racks, and I'm suddenly aware that for some time now she has been buying all of her clothes in the men's department, even her classic black wing tips. Even her white tube socks with the red or green stripe along the top. Even the silk boxers she sleeps in, or wears under her clothes on special occasions. Even her everyday underwear, the bright red, green, and blue bikini briefs that come in a clear plastic tube, tagged with a color photograph of a hard-jawed man of northern European descent with blond hair on his chest and a long-muscled swimmer's body.

I wonder what I am to understand about our bodies when I observe the two of us. I look at myself, my heavy eyeliner and mauve lipstick, the silk scarf tied around my throat that matches the leopard print of my gloves. Under my shirt I wear a satin underwire bra. I look at Linnea, noticing that the only items she buys outside of the men's department are her plain cotton and Lycra sports bras, the kind designed to hold the breasts still and out of the way. They are more comfortable than the Ace bandages women passing as men once used to bind their breasts, but have a similar effect, the aim to draw attention away from the possibility of a bust line, never to lift and separate. In the days before gay liberation, women could be arrested, charged with transvestitism, for wearing fewer than three articles of women's clothing. On any day of the week, Linnea does not pass that test. Friends ask me why it matters what any of us wear. Our clothes, they say, are just the facile presentation of our surfaces. The real person is within, contained in the intangible soul. I want to agree, and then I find myself daydreaming about a leopard-print dress of silk georgette I saw in a mail-order catalogue, or I watch Linnea, a woman with a doctorate in literature, and see her face pursed in concentration as she tries to choose between the two silk neckties she holds in outstretched palms. I feel certain there is something more than a surface at stake.

Here at JCPenney among the racks and cabinets of what is called men's clothing, I can imagine Linnea in another time and place. She has an unremarkable singing voice, but is a fine dancer. She has been known to pull off a terrific lip-synch, and unlike me, Linnea is a model social drinker and can strike up a conversation with almost anybody. She would be great working in any kind of watering hole. If this were the 1940s, New York, the Village, she could have easily been one of the butches who worked as drag-king impresarios in the mob-run show bars. She would be elegant onstage in a fine tailored tux with her hair cut short just as it is now, but slicked back smooth with Brylcream or Rose's Butch Wax. She would change her name for the stage to Lenny, or maybe Johnny, after her Italian grandfather from Hell's Kitchen, a gentle man whose skin had been inked with tattoos from head to ankle. In the Village drag shows Johnny/Linnea would be the king with the approachable face, handsome in her command of the gentlemanly arts, the mystery date all the ladies dream of, their faces lit amber in the boozy candlelight.

Johnny/Linnea would waltz out before the bare-bulbed footlights, just as airborne as Kelly or Astaire, escorting Dietrich in a sea blue sheath, dipping a reluctant Bette Davis, or twirling a taffeta-clad Ginger Rogers under her arm.

But what is it I see when I conjure up the image of Linnea on a drag-king stage? The old European fairy tales say the kings are the ones above all the rest, the rulers of countries and people, but there are kings of property and also those who possess a kingdom of self-knowledge, the low-rent regents of self-rule who have always known who they are. A drag king is no one's boss, but an illusionary monarch, a magician with the alchemist's amber light in her eyes. Some kinds of kings are easy to see—military leaders, oil barons, presidents, prime ministers, and prom kings. There is the King of Pop, the King of Rock, the Elvis impersonators swinging their hips in their beaded white jumpsuits. There are drug kingpins and kings of the road, the King of Kings, the King's English. There's Linnea's and my king-sized King Koil mattress. I wonder what, if anything, this catalogue of kings has in common with Linnea in her two-toned wing tips and creased trousers. Does she share some qualities with the kingly crested birds, the kingfisher, the Ruby-crowned Kinglet? Is she the chessboard king? The laminated-paper King of Hearts, ruler of the subconscious? The King of Pentacles, protector against evil spirits, a reliable husband but also a patriarch? What I see is the everyday checkerboard king, the player who has made it, panting, all the way to the other side of the board and can now move in whatever direction she chooses. So she does. She's a woman who wears men's clothes, except they aren't men's clothes to her, just her clothes, the clothes she likes.

At JCPenney, she hands me the geometry-lesson tie. I move in, squint to focus, then hold it back at arm's length again. "No," I tell her. "It's too awful. It hurts my eyes."

I hand it back to Linnea, who falls away from me in a long sigh. "So you really hate it?"

Behind the glass counter a thin-boned female clerk watches our exchange with a steady smile on her orangy lips. This Penney's is in a suburban shopping mall. I can't tell if she knows what kind of king her customer is. I won't know unless she says the words, *thank you, sir* or *thank you, ma'am*. I've yet to meet a lesbian who doesn't recognize Linnea as one of her own kind, but straight people often address her as a man. When we walk through the gay cruising zones of Minneapolis, Chicago, San Francisco, I watch the eyes of gay men fall from her face to her crotch and back up to her eyes, with just a fast glance toward me to wonder, I can only suppose, if I am his sister, his fag hag, or his wife of convenience. What people see depends on the context, on what they want to see, on what they are afraid to see.

I think of an old friend of mine, a woman proud to show off her unshaved legs, "untraditional beauty," she called it as she strutted in short, striped skirts with big Doc Martens boots. She put up with every kind of heckling for years, but it was a department-store clerk who finally did her in. One day, walking through a downtown Minneapolis store my friend passed by a young woman working behind the polished-glass cosmetic case. The woman had thin tweaked eyebrows, pores smothered under foundation cream, and a twitch, some violent itch to spit at a queer. She leaned over the glistening glass and actually shouted, "Look. A transvestite!"

My friend's breasts were not bound. She was a woman wearing many more than three pieces of women's clothing despite her unisex boots and the long gait she learned in the military. She wore Hanes Her Way panties, a crop-top bra, a black-and-white flared miniskirt, a black scoop-necked top from the junior women's department, slouch socks from women's hosiery, red sunglasses from the women's wall of the optical shop. Her furry legs, her soldier stride, her British-made punk-boy boots—do three male props make her a masquerading woman? Would she be arrested? My friend stopped dead and said simply, "I'm a lesbian," then continued on her way. When she got home she called the store to complain. The skin around her eyes was too pale when she told me the story. She believed in being visible, in being out of the closet even under the bleach-bright department-store lights, but this had been too much exposure, like a bad sunburn. Sometimes you have to cover up. The next day she shaved.

In fairy tales, it is common for a king to come upon his bride in disguise, masquerading as a beggar, a frog, a swan. The night I started falling for Linnea our clothes were costumes for a big night masquerade, but also harbingers of what we would come to wear on any Monday morning or Thursday afternoon. I was the house manager for a lesbian theater and she was a volunteer usher. We were still in our mid-twenties, and it was Saturday night. She was wearing a gray tuxedo with full tails and black velvet trim. I was wearing a little Jackie O suit—narrow skirt, bolero-length jacket—made from a black knit fabric with a sunspot design sewn in with glittering amber thread. We had run into each other before at parties, at the grocery store. We had never been unattached at the same time until now, but I had been watching her. I'd had fleeting daydreams of leaning into her embrace. I warned friends not to date her first. When we talked I felt jolted into a full habitation of my body, surrounded by a bell of amber sunset. My skin glowed the color of that resin gem said to cure all ailments of the flesh.

That night in the theater, there was an elemental pull between us. I couldn't keep myself from touching her elbow, her shoulder, her collar. When she offered to help me set up the box office I accepted, but it was slow going. We kept stopping and staring, watching each other's faces. The flimsy aluminum card table and battered-steel cash box floated like a Ouija board between us until we both just laughed. I laughed because it was ridiculous. We had work to do. I had to find something to cover the table, had to sell tickets, had to ignore her. She laughed, she told me later, because she thought I was so pretty in my Jackie O suit.

This night was the last in a series of shows I had been working on for over two years with all of my closest friends, a group of lesbian actors, writers, and techies who had stumbled together through so much bad gossip, so many misbegotten love affairs that we needed to hire a professional mediator before we could finish what we had begun. My plan was to creep up to the front to watch this last show up close, but when we stood at the back of the auditorium the houselights dimmed and Linnea stretched one arm around my shoulders and whispered, "This is it." She meant the show, the end of something, but I heard more. *This* is it. The next part of my life was beginning. In that moment of total darkness before the stage lights came up, I leaned back into her. That golden brown bell descended again, my muscles fell limp as she held me up. If she'd had the nerve to keep her arm flung across my shoulders I would have stayed by her side with my eyes closed, magnetized, and ignored the show until the houselights came back up again. But she pulled her arm away and I was muscle and bone again. I was still hovering near but too shy to touch, and wondering when we would really get together.

The next time I saw her she *was* masquerading. Linnea was Patsy Cline, the crowd favorite of the women's lip-synch show at Sappho's Lounge, Tuesday nights when a downtown gay drag stage was transformed into a lesbian dance bar. That night's performance featured a Janis Joplin in a floppy felt hat, with limp blond hair, patched jeans, and a tie-dyed T-shirt, who dropped hard to her knees at the final shout of "Piece of My Heart." There was a short, square, fair-skinned woman in a plain black tux and sand-colored crew cut, Whitney Houston's polar opposite, who leaned into the words of "The Greatest Love of All" so earnestly she nearly knocked the unattached mike off the four-foot-tall stage. There were two women in vintage black dresses with bright bleached hair, one a big girl, over six feet, the other short and thin-waisted. They did a number in which Doris Day sings a duet with herself. Another woman who squinted without her glasses wore a flouncy white Ginger Rogers gown and spun around the stage like a folk dancer to the tune of "Hernando's Hideaway." The sheer hem of her dress fluttered like a flock of magician's doves.

I didn't see Linnea until she stepped between the glittering tinsel curtain strings. She wore a ruffled red dress that cinched tight around the waist then belled out to her knees, a plain brown wig that had been set in curlers and ratted, three-inch heels, and lipstick a brighter red than the dress. She was perfect, a Patsy Cline concentrate, a refracted and amplified twin, in the same way any gender illusionist is so much more than the real Judy Garland or Diana Ross or Barbra Streisand could ever be. I had never seen anything like it before, a woman impersonating a drag queen. When Patsy Cline mouthed "I Fall to Pieces," twisting her hips to an unwired mike, the girls in the audience screamed. I fell a little too, into fascination, witness to the best magician's trick as Linnea vanished into another skin.

But when I approached her after the show I was confused to find nothing between us but dead air. It wasn't until later that I understood. She didn't recognize me from inside her disguise. "I *was* Patsy Cline," she told me. "Linnea couldn't be there, inside those clothes." But that night, surrounded by red-bar fog and the hot thump from the DJ's speakers, she smiled at me politely, with red lips that seemed to throb, too, in the pulsing light. A backstage star nodding generously to a subject fan. I was dizzy with deprivation. All my body's elements pulled, scattered, spun, but still I was left unacknowledged, uncaught.

In the old European stories the king rescues the soiled queen-to-be curled up like a feral cat in front of a cold hearth, or redeems the selfish princess who only reluctantly shares her dinner with the croaking frog, her unrecognized lover. But I couldn't wait for Linnea to recognize me. I needed to make a move; I had to conjure my king.

I knew I'd see Linnea next at a party, so I planned my wardrobe carefully. I chose an old pair of jeans, dyed green with knees worn through, my sex-catching clothes, ass-snug and knee-revealing. The pants had once belonged to a woman I went out with only a few times. I'd borrowed them one night the summer before, after she and I were soaked in a thunderstorm during a long walk around a dark city lake. She was pretty enough to have been a high-school prom queen. I had never been involved with such a girlie-girl; all my women lovers had lived a few degrees closer to the guy side of the scale. I wondered if this was how it felt to be my stoop-shouldered boy cousin from Chicago, born just a month after me, with his souped-up cars and back pockets full of date cash. His girlfriend was always the prettiest one in the graduating class of the neighborhood Catholic girls' school. But I didn't feel like a boy. Instead I was experimenting with stepping through the mirror, expansion through reflection, the double Doris at Sappho's lip-synch.

Not that this woman and I looked much alike. She was shorter, had smoother features, fuller breasts, no ethnic nose, no South Chicago accent. The similarity was from a deeper place, as if we were broadcasting from the same pole. This woman and I went for lots of long walks and I began to feel like an image from those soft-focus greeting cards you see in the drug store, two women in Victorian sheaths and heavy streams of hair, riding a bicycle together through the too-green countryside, bare skin touching, one nipple almost showing, one woman's hair falling over the other's shoulder as she leans forward to whisper. I was attracted to the sameness, the echo, and she seemed to like me too, so for a little while I thought we might be able to tune each other in. But then she stopped returning my calls. I was not heartbroken, but a little miffed, so I kept her pants.

These were the jeans I wore to the party, along with the sunspot jacket of my Jackie O suit. Linnea wore tight jeans, cowboy boots, a wide belt. All night we circled each other in our friend's kitchen. My body was shifting inside my clothes like the shapes we used to make in grade-school science class with metal filings and a little red magnet. Later, we heard friends had laid bets. Would I take her to my two-room apartment with the whistling radiators? Would we do it right in front of the house on the hard bench seat of Linnea's pickup? But she was too much the gentleman for that. She promised to call. We each left alone.

During the week before our first date I was a planet without an orbit. I wandered through shopping malls looking for a costume to impress her, but found nothing. The week dripped by. I sweated when others shivered, bundled up in wool shawls and fake-fur coats while others complained the heat was turned up too high.

Years later, Linnea took me to see the famous magician Harry Blackstone Jr. He stood on an empty stage in a white tie and black tails and levitated a lit lightbulb over the astonished, upturned faces of the crowd. Audience volunteers ran their hands over, under, alongside it to prove there were no wires, while Blackstone kept the bulb circling over our heads, an incandescent vision. Anyone watching Linnea's and my first kiss would have seen something similar, a suspended moment, amber and hovering. I wore black Capri pants and a little cashmere sweater from the 1950s. Linnea wore jeans and cowboy boots and a man's dress shirt, just pressed. We stood close next to a steaming radiator on the bright white stage of my bare-walled apartment. My body floated before her, quivering in its own glow. The slightest furl of her fingers hurled me closer.

A decade has passed since that first kiss, and last week a woman we both know said to me, "I've noticed over all this time that you and Linnea have shifted the way you look, to opposite poles." Have we? I wear lipstick more often these days. I used to think it was too much trouble. The sunspot skirt doesn't fit, but I still wear the jacket. Linnea owns more suits, more ties, but she's older, too. She takes dressing up more seriously.

She doesn't do lip-synch shows anymore, although we did name our amber-haired dog Patsy Cline. Linnea used to wear women's underpants (she refuses to call them panties) but switched because she likes how men's underwear feels against her skin. It's the same with men's shirts, men's pants. Linnea also abandoned her thin-ribbed white cotton men's undershirts for sport bras because of gravity's demands on her upper body, and I recently bought a Wonderbra, the movie-star-cleavage-push-up kind to wear with a velveteen dress I rented for a gay wedding. We have both put on some weight, so our undergarment needs have shifted, that's the main change.

When Linnea first started dating me some women warned her not to. "She seems strange," they told her. "Look how she dresses." I did always wear more than three items of women's clothing in the years most lesbians honored androgyny. Were they referring to my denim miniskirt? My black eyeliner? My Jackie O suit? Linnea just smiled. She knew her chemistry, which base elements yearn for each other. These days lesbians speak with another kind of certainty, separating our genders from our genitals, lining up beneath myriad headings, *butch* or *femme, femmy butch* or *butchy femme, femme top* or *butch bottom, femme-to-femme* or *butch-on-butch, transgender,* or even still, plain old *lesbian feminist.* And there are scientists now that tell us the old simple division of the world into easy categories, man or woman, boy or girl, is not precise enough to describe what may be five or more discernible sexes. But I don't trust science to be expressive enough to catalogue the variations in a magnetic field that pull some to their opposite, others to their mirror, others to a mosaic of variations between the two. The clothes available for us to wear may be to some a utilitarian surface, something to cover and protect the skin, to others another industry designed to profit from our confusion about our bodies. But to me, to Linnea, they are the choices we feel compelled to choose, our connection to some hum in the distance of existence to which we feel drawn as strongly as we are pulled to each other.

But on this day, at JCPenney, we masquerade as regular shoppers. What I haven't told her yet is that I love her men's clothes because of how they make me feel, Queen Moon to her Sun King. I don't think it's commonly known that you don't have to be heterosexual to conjure such a feeling. "Buy the rose tie," I tell her. "You'll see."

"So you really hate the other one?" she asks, glancing back at it over her shoulder.

"This one is so nice," I say. I hold it against her chest; my knuckles graze her breasts, and I feel that old amber levitation, the pull of positive and negative poles, even on this cluttered stage, beneath this too bright and unfocused light. Over Linnea's shoulder I see the clerk watching us, biting her orange lips. Her head is cocked the way our dog Patsy's head tilts when she doesn't understand what we're trying to tell her. I'm not sure what she observes in us. I would kiss Linnea right here, but getting kicked out of Penney's might ruin the feeling.

In Sanskrit the word for magnetized rock, the lodestone, is *chumbaka*, "the kisser." In Chinese it is *t' su shi*, "loving stone." The central image of the alchemists was marriage, the union of opposites. They weren't talking about women who broadcast from different poles, but then they were men among men and not talking about women at all. The lodestone is also a conjuring rock. We see ourselves rightly. We learn and understand what we are, king and queen of our own desire. At JCPenney, Linnea turns from me, but the kissing current keeps on flowing. She steps away for a moment, but only to buy the rose-stitched tie.

The Last Three Seasons

Rain drumming on a streaked windshield. A bleary face in gold-wire eyeglasses moving toward my face. A circle of sunburned knees and the hard sparks of a burning driftwood log, splitting in two. A long gauzy scarf of a horizon, hazy and water-colored. I remember so much and so little of the last three Aprils of my adolescence. Which moments really matter, the ones we have forgotten or the ones we mull over ten, thirteen, eighteen years after the fact?

Twenty years later I surf the cable TV offerings. It's a few weeks before Easter and I pause at the spring-break specials on music television. Ensconced as I am in an upper Midwestern city, where it is still winter, I turn the red-gemmed ring Linnea gave me a decade ago around and around on my finger as I stare at the television screen. How far away it all seems—hot sun, party-populated sands, the ideas I once had of how to spend a free week in March and of who I might turn out to be. The spring-break beaches are crowded with bikini-and boxer-clad college kids chugging beers and dancing in the sand. I recognize the beach, and not just metaphorically. Panama City, Florida, now my parents' retirement home, was not well-known among Northerners when my public-school-teacher parents drove the family down from Chicago during school breaks. I partied on that very sand, but not out in the open like these kids, polished sorority and fraternity types who seem barely aware of the television lens zooming in on their pierced navels.

~

My best friend Guinevere and I were still in high school the spring break she rode south with my family and me. Most nights we crept out of the trailer park and down onto that white-sand beach to drink cheap wine in the hollows between dunes around a bonfire with a pack of wild local kids led by a guy a few years older than us whose name was Moses. Our Moses wore his hair tied back in a ponytail, and his fingers were as long and finely formed as Charlton Heston's fingers were when he played Moses in the movie. The robes of the movie Moses swooshed as the windy Red Sea parted its lips. *Let there be light,* our Moses uttered into the windy dunes over the big roar of spring surf, as his buddies, stringy-haired guys, always stoned, always smiling, soaked the driftwood stack with kerosene and scraped the match along the sandpaper spine of the matchbox. The flame billowed into the starless darkness while we all swallowed another throatful of red wine, sweet and heavy on our tongues, and the joint was an orange blossom riding a wet trail, mouth to mouth. Guinevere laughed when she was stoned. The higher I got, the more I sunk inside my skin, but Guinevere pulled her heavy hair off her narrow face and talked. Her pronunciation was slow, each word a new discovery she stopped to taste before letting it slip out of her mouth. Guys who love to party loved Guinevere. They shut up and listened to every slow word she spoke, at least at the start. I had seen it happen before. What was new this time was Guinevere. I watched her fall in love on that beach, and even I had to admit that the bonfire made Moses' face look blessed, beautiful enough to cause anyone to swoon.

But the ones at the bonfire I adored were the Southern party girls, the way words poured out of their mouths so curvy and honey slow. I loved the way those girls always seemed to be almost dancing to some tune that moved them from the inside out, something slow and hard and guitar twangy like Lynyrd Skynyrd's anthems to white-trash pride. I loved the way they ran around in bikinis as if they were regular clothes, wearing them so easy, the way girls at home wore jeans. It seemed as if their skin must be thicker than mine, more able to repel whatever they did not want to touch them.

But I was far from falling in love the way Guinevere did that April, unless you count the way I came to love the feeling of my drunk head lifting up off my shoulders and the sound of pounding waves that rose up from the sand and into my bones.

Guinevere and I had talked so often about running away together. We would save all the money we made at our after-school jobs and buy an old VW van. We would graduate from high school then party awhile before going to college. We would drive around the country, get high, meet cool people, listen to music, and live on a beach somewhere. Watching her with Moses I knew for the first time that it wasn't going to happen. I came to a new understanding of myself that spring. I didn't want what Guinevere wanted, although I couldn't have said at the time just what I did want. That is what I thought about while Moses and Guinevere smiled at each other in the flickering dark, as they tunneled a passage under the beach surface with their fingers until they touched and held hands under the sand.

～

All of this seems nothing like what young college students have told me happens on spring break these days. I hear about beachfront dance bars flooded with some kind of industrial foam, a mass wet T-shirt and boxer-short party. I wonder, do these kids lay their heads back and laugh at the fun of it, the suburban-high-school-car-wash joy, the bare thrill of getting sprayed with the hose as hair falls wet around their sunburned faces? Or is it more of a group grope that the drunkest of the girls will only remember slightly, the touch of an unknown hand on her ass, the disembodied pinch of her sudsy nipple?

When I was their age I decided to take one last spring-break vacation with my parents, but once we got to Panama City I ditched the family whenever I could. I had been studying photography with an abstract photo artist visiting my university for a semester and had become fascinated by images of things burning. Every night I crept down with my camera past the deserted spots where Moses and his friends had held their beach parties, and I photographed crumpled balls of paper that I lit with a match in my open palm and then tossed into the wake of the waves. I don't remember if I really saw something in those vanishing balls of fire and soot, or if I was just behaving in the way I thought an artist should. Perhaps that was all it was, an affectation, but it might have been more, a picture of something I wanted, or felt, or dreamt of possessing. That is how I spent my time until I actually ran into Guinevere's old flame, our Moses.

After months of frantic correspondence and botched promises to visit Chicago, Moses had dropped out of college and taken a job as a trailer-park security guard. By then Guinevere had long abandoned her plans to run south to marry him, had already fallen in and out of love with someone else. Moses was still only a few years older than me, but he looked like a guy over thirty—wide-bodied, big-belted. His ponytail had been cut away and there was no more holy bonfire in his face. Without his beach flock, without fire rising under his outstretched fingers, he seemed regular. He was a nice guy in a tan uniform. He spent his days riding a slow security route past mobile retirement homes stacked up on cinder blocks and little patches of plug-in patios reserved for the temporary residents in truck campers or motor homes or long silver Airstreams that mirrored the white sands and big Southern sky in their polished hides.

This was before Panama City Beach was lined with thousand-room party hotels with massive parking lots, and Las Vegas–style marquees promising Joan Jett or the Chippendales. This was the spring I got my first perm, a long mess of curly ringlets, a style that today might be called mall hair but then was the latest fashion-magazine thing. On my nightly photo treks to the beach I had taken to wearing thrift-shop dresses from the 1940s that my mother hated because they reminded her of the clothes her mother used to wear when they lived in the projects. And I tied bright scarves over my ears so that the curls sprung like sea foam around my face. This is how I looked with a camera slung over one shoulder and my face burnished red by the afternoon sun, when I spotted Moses waving in cars from the glass security booth at the park entrance.

I used to say back then, that I didn't believe in romance, that girls could want sex the same easy way boys did, just for the rush of it. I'd like to believe this still, except I see now that for me it was a lie. I didn't start talking this way until Guinevere starting meeting the men who loved to get tangled in that hair of hers, always so long, heavy as pails of water. She had a way of talking to guys, shy, almost angelic, but still letting them know she wasn't a good girl. I think they saw her as a still pool of warm water that could embrace a man, surround him, take on his shape as her own. I had been her best friend since kindergarten. I understood she had depths those guys couldn't see. Still, she wanted to draw them to her, needed to try on what they imagined her to be. Moses was the first. Perhaps this is some of what heterosexuality is, or at least the way it is commonly played. Both the man's body and the woman's body shift in tune to some shared soundtrack, a sound that becomes the touch, the smell, the taste they crave in each other. Perhaps this is the dance step I was never able to master in those last three heterosexual Aprils.

Later, after Guinevere had already fallen out of love with Moses and was regularly sneaking out to sleep with her new boyfriend at the Starlight, a grimy suburban strip motel that rented by the hour, I began to try to lose my virginity, too, but each time something went wrong, the cock did not rise to the occasion, the boy turned away, too ashamed to call me again. I was never mistaken for a reflective pool, like Guinevere. I was a surf, pounding and pummeling, or a hard fist smacking against an open palm, pissed-off, ungentle, wanting. Looking back I can see that this wasn't a turn on for most guys my age.

My body banged against its own boundaries. My hands set fires. My eyes were watching, recording. Then I ran into this new version of Moses. *Let there be light,* I remember him saying. He looked so different, but once he started talking I saw it was only his body that had changed. His eyes still cracked and shone. He could still lead his shivering people across the dry bed of a parted sea. He told me he knew all the local hangouts, the best places. Would I let him lead me on an evening through the Southern bars? Yes. Whatever he said that night I had the same answer. Should we go to the red-flocked hotel lounge to listen to the Fleetwood Mac cover band? Yes. How about the heavy-metal bar where the biker babes wear snakeskin halters and their boyfriends barf in the parking lot, or the forties piano bar where the gentleman sitting before the ivories can make a sound like a champagne cork popping. Yes. But as the sun rose purple and pink over a wave-scarred fishing pier, and the beer buzz started to dissipate, I turned down Moses' offer to lead me to one more spot, a cheap motel bed somewhere along the Gulf Shore. I don't know why. I liked him. We'd laughed. Perhaps it was because I felt no feeling for him stronger than curiosity. He was, after all, the first one Guinevere left me for. Perhaps it was because I knew my parents were waiting for me to return to the camper. Or perhaps, standing there shoulder-to-shoulder over the billowing, crashing sea, I was bored by the prospect of a groggy grapple with a romantic fellow who had once planned to marry the girl I knew so much better than he did.

~

It's around this time that everything gets so foggy. Was I eighteen or nineteen the spring I re-met Moses? One of these springs I was still what my party friends in high school called a technical virgin, finger-fucked but waiting for the rest. By the next spring the technicalities had fallen away and I was drinking all the time. I loved how drinking made me feel, liquid from the outside in. Guys were no longer afraid of me, or if they were, they had stronger words for it, language that described only by taking some piece of me away. There had been at least a half dozen men, maybe more. I don't remember any of their names. The names that have stayed with me are the names of the ones who did not get what they asked for.

After Moses, or before, I am no longer sure, there was another invitation I turned down, the spring break of my sophomore year of college when most of the students at my Midwestern university had fled south to crowd the beachfront bars or gone home to punch the channel changer in their parents' TV rooms. I had stayed at school, alone in my dorm apartment that usually slept four, and was getting in trouble with building management for playing the stereo too loud. Supposedly I was studying but really I was just passing time in between work and partying with whomever was around—customers from the Holiday Inn where I waited tables, a bearded graduate student who fixed the dishwasher at a bar where I washed dishes, and an older journalism student, Hank, whom I had met while writing news stories for the campus paper.

Hank had a special significance for me because he used to be a student of my father's. He had been, in fact, my dad's favorite student. He was an editor of the newspaper produced in my father's high-school journalism class. Hank would probably hate to hear me say it, but I always saw him as a satellite from the home planet, the sort of guy my father would have loved for me to marry. That must be why I was always so cranky around Hank. It seemed to me then that the world was booby trapped with pockets of suction. If I didn't watch out I could sink into a life without choices, where I would just be a woman men liked, nothing more. Not a person with work and experience and sensation. Just a girl, the one who makes the babies and the Jell-O molds, the one who sweeps up. I don't know what it was about Hank, the way he looked at me or the way he held his body or the things he said, but I sensed he was one of those sinkholes. Then again, there was something about him I liked. I wouldn't have admitted it then, but now I can see that I flirted with the feeling of being dragged to my own demolition.

I went out with Hank and a gang of journalism students at loose ends over the break. We went to a bar where we sat on pillows on the floor and drank cheap brew by the pitcher. I was drunk, as usual, and outside it was drizzling, as it seemed to be always drizzling that spring. Hank drove me home and idled the car in front of my building. I don't remember just how drunk I was. I remember only that the rain peppered the windows and I didn't pull away when he leaned forward to kiss me, the wire rims of his glasses picking up the lights of the streetlamps. I've often wondered why I did some of the things I did back then. Why kiss a man whose body felt like a storm warning, a man who caused a hurricane of NO to pummel from my bones to my pores? Was it just the drink? Was it just that I wanted to see what would happen next? Was it what a therapist once suggested, that I wanted a story to tell later, something to impress my woman friends? I wish I could say it was a simple ache from my lips toward the lips of another, a nipple-tightening, the inside wash that threatened to let all barriers of skin fall away. I'd like to remember myself as a woman who just wanted sex, but the truth is I hadn't experienced that washed-away feeling yet, and wouldn't for a few more years. I have no distinct memory of that kiss, only that it happened, and that afterward Hank said to me, "I've been wanting to do that for months."

⁓

Today, when I watch TV footage of the spring-break kids, I recall the smell of beer from a keg served in a plastic glass, and other fragments of colored moments when I was surely too drunk to know what I was doing.

On one of the TV programs a video jockey interviews a circle of young women in a hot tub. They all wear bikinis, and none appears older than twenty-one. I notice one in particular, a voluptuous girl in a red bikini who smiles and sways when the VJ asks her which of the current video stars she thinks is the most sexy. "LL Cool J," she sighs and the other women sigh along with her, but she takes it further. "I'd lie down with him any time, here, right now," she says, and the way her body almost imperceptibly undulates, the way she wets her lips and smiles into the camera, she seems to know what she's talking about. Maybe she imagines herself a video diva. Maybe she pays for school with what she makes dancing in strip clubs. Or maybe she's a big-mouthed sorority sister partying hard for a week before the last tough month of studying. Maybe she's all talk, or maybe she really knows the way to feed the ache in her nipples, the pull between her legs. What strikes me is how easily she can say, I want this kind of touch from this kind of guy, as if her body really does want just what she says it does. As if she knows.

I didn't know what my body wanted in those last three seasons. I said, *men, men, men,* back then, and I have to laugh thinking about it now since it is so obvious to me that it was the girls who were really on my mind. My beautiful college roommate who slept some nights without pajamas, the Southern girls in faded bikinis at the beach bonfire, Guinevere who called to tell me she had another new boyfriend.

Now I wonder if I should worry about those girls I watch on TV. And the boys, too, I suppose. I heard a story on the radio about a boy on spring break in Panama City who fell to his death from a hotel balcony. "There's at least one of those every season," my dad tells me. The young man must have been drunk, of course, but was it just the full charge of chemicals coursing through his body that caused his recklessness, or was there something else he wanted, a choice waiting to be made that would allow him to unfurl into the world as he felt unfurled once he let the drink take charge. It could have been me twenty years before, blasted on the cheap wine it was so easy for a teenager to buy with a fake ID at the Florida roadside liquor stores. It could have been me who never returned from a night out with the party hardy security guard—my father's indescribable fear rising as he sat up, waiting for me on a lawn chair, on that tiny trailer-park patch of patio. "They had been drinking," the paper would have said the next morning.

But this isn't a story about accidental death by drinking or fast driving or thoughtless sex or the toke that leads to the hard stuff, or any of those things they warned us about when we were kids, those things teenagers aching to feel more alive will always do anyway. It's too easy to tell a cautionary tale, harder to just wonder what might have been.

~

I watched an interview with a famous pop star on the same channel that airs the spring-break specials. She told the story of being discovered on the stoop of her East Village apartment. "What if you had been inside, rehearsing?" the interviewer asked. "There are no accidents, I really believe that," she said, which seems to be what incredibly lucky people like her almost always say. "Things happen for a reason."

I don't know about that. What I think about are all the ways any of our stories might have been different. Is there a reason that boy fell off the hotel balcony while I got to grow up, stop drinking, fall in love, live a long life with the woman of my dreams?

After Hank kissed me, the car engine was still idling and he asked if we could go upstairs to my bed. I said no, but what if I hadn't? Or what if I had said yes to Moses that morning on the pier? What then? Maybe nothing but another forgettable encounter. I might have moved on as I moved on anyway, leaving Moses to his sweet Southern surf, Hank to the shrubbed suburban streets he would soon return to. But what if one of them were seduced by the burnt sunrise or the shapely fog of a central Illinois morning or the challenge of my unreachable core, the one they might have tried to thrust and shiver their way into but would never have reached? What if they decided they were in love with me, and told me so? What if I were half-seduced as I still am by almost anyone who tells me they crave the shape of my lips in their mouth? Would I have tried to love them back? Donned the white veil and knelt with them before the altar? Had their babies? I like to think of my life today, my cluttered domicile, my sunny room overlooking the local beer-and-hamburger joint, "home to the Juicy Lucy," my beloved companion downstairs in the kitchen grading her student papers. I like to imagine this is the life that has always been waiting for me, an orange ember glowing in the distance of those long ago springs. Linnea and I met at just the right moment and when we did the sparks flew but that might have been just another lucky accident.

At another drunken journalism student party, a week or so after Hank dropped me off unfucked at the door to my dorm, he said the sort of thing he was always saying to me. "You think you are so different, but all you really want is to get married and move to the suburbs." That same week he proposed to the redheaded Breck girl he'd been dating. They moved back to the Chicago suburbs and Hank became a high-school English teacher in the same school district where my father taught for thirty years. I might have never thought about him again, except that ten years later I ran into him. We stood in the corner of a red-flocked suburban banquet hall, minutes before my father's retirement roast. My mother watched from across the room, excited to see me talking so intimately with a man. When I mentioned to Hank that I was in love with a woman, the same woman I am in love with still, he told me that the Breck girl had cheated on him, divorced him, and was now dating a married man. Hank's face was more narrow than I remembered, his eyes a paler shade of blue. He laughed and shrugged when he told me the story and I noticed that his voice no longer caused my skin to bristle. "I remember, you were a great kisser," he said and I laughed and shrugged. It was more than I remembered, and I didn't know, as I hadn't known years before, how he wanted me to respond.

How thin was the window between what we did or didn't do those drizzling nights? Was there anyone whom I'd have allowed to carry me away on their backs? I've already admitted I had yet to feel what that MTV girl in the red swimsuit seemed to savor as she swayed and hummed with all that her body wanted. The strongest physical calling I had ever felt the year I turned nineteen was that sandstorm of NO Hank brought forth from me, and I can see how I might have mistaken that for love. Isn't that what Scarlett O'Hara felt for Rhett Butler? What Katharine Hepburn felt in every film where Spencer Tracy carried her off on his shoulder as she kicked, screamed, bit, and finally fell in love. Feisty was what Hank called me back then, and even then I knew what the word meant, the long growl before she falls.

～

The last three seasons of my heterosexuality wash together, an abstraction of men I don't remember, or men I do recall but I don't think I wanted. Perhaps it's true that there are no accidents. Maybe I said no because I feared those guys would have staked some claim on me had I said yes, and the one thing I knew then was that I never wanted to get married. Sometimes I'm certain I can track the chain of events that led me to where I sit today. Other times I get confused; my memories don't make any sense. I see myself writing Moses a letter on a ripped sofa on the sloping porch of a campus house I couldn't have lived in yet the summer after I met him. I might have it all wrong. He might have been the last one I turned down, not the first. Maybe I was not the one who wanted to catch up with Guinevere but the one who was already way ahead, recoiling from all the bad times I never said yes or no and sex happened anyway.

If there are no accidents, then Moses must have married one of those honey-mouthed Southern girls, and Hank would have married the Breck girl no matter what. She had such a placid model's face and that long red hair, so plush, so electric with that just-brushed look. I was strung tight, a kid with a crazy perm. I was wasted and falling out of my favorite red clogs. I was a funny drunk, everyone said, stuck on some notion of being free. I must have been the kind of girl a guy like Hank would have loved to mess around with, for a minute, before he got married. When he told me ten years later that he still remembered my kiss it was probably not because he might have made another choice, but because with every choice we make comes a fantasy of its opposite.

What I chose was not even one night with Hank, but instead a few years of nights with one more man who asked me out for a beer that inclement spring-break week. He was the bearded bisexual guy whom I met in the dish room of the bar where I worked. He introduced me to his lesbian friends, let me read lesbian manifestos in his bed on Sunday mornings, and loved me enough to be the last man of my heterosexuality. Still I wonder about the shadow print of my life, carried away to a suburban tract home with those wadded paper clumps burning away in my belly, kicking and screaming and finally, what? My shoulders falling back, my just-fucked face golden with that promised satisfaction I had always heard I was supposed to crave? Scarlet O'Hara wears that look when she steps out of the bedroom, finally in love with Rhett, pregnant with his child, and we are to believe that the greatest sadness of the feisty woman is that she doesn't realize she loves him in time. I can't follow this fantasy too far without laughing, as I laughed at Hank the night he told me all I wanted was to be married. Then I remember that the first woman I entered in love was confused with Guinevere in my dreams, her face and Guinevere's face lifting off each other's like kids' Halloween masks. But Hank was right about some things. I haven't moved to the suburbs, but I did, after all, end up married to an English teacher.

I don't think anyone can say for sure how our bodies come into their own, and clearly some know what they need by age five, others not until sixty-five. I suspect the truth is a stew of events and feelings that no one will be able to sort out. Meanwhile there are a million daily choices to be made, good or bad. We don't know which is a seed that will grow into the life that ends up as my life, or your life, and which is just a bit of dust, soot from a beach fire, a burning crumple of paper that floats before us for a moment then vanishes into a purple sea.

Looking Forward, Looking Back

A live vine is crawling up my shin, tripping me, pulling me slowly into the leafy brush. A snare is tossed from horseback, cinching my ankles and dragging me through a tornado of dust. The creature's hands are around my throat, squeezing until my body drops like a silk scarf to the floor.

This was not exactly what I was afraid would happen if I did what I was told and became what a woman is supposed to be. Married to a conventional man with steady work and suburban aspirations. The mother of three. These were the pictures of how I imagined I'd feel if I acquiesced, became that sort of man's girlfriend, any man's wife.

And yet today I have pictures of the kind of woman I decided not to be, the *Photoplay* sirens adorning the walls of the same room where I keep my books. Marilyn in little red shorts cringing as the froth of waves creeps up between her thighs. Betty Page in a leopard-print sarong, lounging against the furry torso of a live leopard. It's not that I can picture myself so fantastically sexual—that flawless skin, those red pouting lips, those full and perfectly erect breasts—or that I don't know that there were real, less perfect women behind those Maybelline masks. I can't forget that I'm too tall, too long-nosed, too bespectacled to fit in that frame. I look at their eyes, sometimes staring down the camera lens, other times looking away as in Richard Avedon's portrait of Marilyn, her eyes tired, or sorry, or lost. It's not that I see my own dropped gaze. Yet there is something in those photographs that belongs to me, not the women themselves but rather what they seem to possess.

I feel guilty saying it because I know these are not paintings of

Athena or Venus, not statues of Mary with a serpent squirming under her bare toes and a constellation hovering over her head, but real women, posed to look the way they do, or caught just falling out of that pose in a moment where the woman and the story of the woman accidentally mingle. I understand the argument, that these photographs, these Hollywood posters, these calendar pinups are just depictions of a fantasy put upon us by men. A version of our lives that allows us to be the ones dragged into the forest or squeezed until we exhale our last perfumed breath.

Once this was the only thing I could see, but now there is more. This multiplied femaleness might be a religion, like the Catholicism in which I no longer believe but by which I am formed. I mouth the words of the Hail Mary when I'm frightened, my chest shivers when I hear one of the old songs about the body and blood. That kind of femininity is a homeland, the country an emigrant must leave but still longs for, a city where I once lived and still live in any daydream I have of myself as finally grown, but that has not been my home since adolescence.

This is one of the differences between my long-time beloved Linnea and me. Although there is only a year and a half difference in our ages and we grew up no more than fifty miles apart on different ends of metropolitan sprawl, we do not share identical coming-of-age stories. When we watched old Saturday afternoon movies on black-and-white sets in our mothers' kitchens we were not the same. Imagine two little girls in yellow shorts slumped forward on kitchen chairs, the ridged vinyl leaving tracks on the back of their bare thighs. One of them is me with long, blond locks pulled back with rubber bands and barrettes into a tight ponytail and the other one, Linnea with curly, caramel-colored hair chopped off in a pixie. The TV flickers before both our faces. *Too close, you'll injure your eyes,* our mothers would say if they caught us staring into that little square of a story.

I was Lauren Bacall with hair falling over one eye, slinking into Bogie's room in a skin-tight suit, and, despite biology, Linnea was Bogie, wordless and wooden the first time Bacall kissed him, but alive with wanting the second time. I was Cyd Charisse with high heels, high kicks, and bored bedroom gaze and she was Gene Kelly, muscled and moving, like a ballet dancer who also played baseball, always ready to catch her in his liquid embrace. Nobody knows whether or not we are born with it in our cells, the simple identification with one or the other of opposite choices, Lauren or Gene, Bogie or Cyd, or if we learn it somewhere along the way and store it always within our reach, along with the alphabet and the way to ride a bicycle. But even if it's just a lesson kept in two or three spots of the brain, the brain is the body, too, connected to the toes and elbows and clitoris with veins and capillaries and lymphatic rivers and, if the acupuncturists are right, invisible currents of energy. Some things won't ever be walked or even wished away.

And some things will. Some people leave their homes and tell us they never look back. Some people let the songs of a new religion sink into their corpuscles and, if you ask them, they will swear that the old music is gone. Some people never did watch much TV. Others did, but in spite of it, wear androgyny as mindlessly as a birthday suit. That is not my story. The past and present are alive in me at once and so the dance steps are trickier. To at once comply and resist, these are the footprints I lay on the floor before me. I am a woman who casts off the waltz of heterosexual womanhood yet still wears the markings of the female on her back and face. I am in love with another kind of woman who searches for a better word for her sort of womanhood. We love together in our world of distinct and opposite words for this and that, at once both deeply married and not married at all.

For they are in some ways the same, the institution of woman, the institution of marriage. I know the history, how women were either bought or stolen, how we have been since the start of time posed to fit the convenience of the ones with the money. I nod in assent when women I meet remind me of the feminist credo, that the history of marriage is not in our favor. And yet I can't look at my married heterosexual friends without noting the obvious, that these women are not just a lovely swirl of scarf on the floor, that these men do not have the acid-distorted face of the creature that squeezes the breath from her curvaceous frame. What marriage came from and what it is are not *always* the same. Lesbian friends have said to me that weddings are just another mindless obligation, another cultural lockstep where everyone says their part and weeps their choreographed tears and goes home believing they are fulfilled. Perhaps. Ritual can be the Sunday obligation you show up for because you are convinced that you must, or it can be the shrine you want and really need to kneel to, from the oldest part of yourself.

I know the history. I know what my body craves. A silk scarf around the throat and a bit of color on my lips. Music swelling up from under my beloved's and my feet. And so I hold onto Linnea's shoulders and we shuffle a few steps. When the music takes over I ride for a while, just a minute or two without thinking about it, to see what it feels to be who I have become inside a world that already is.

The Hard Hollow Heartbeat

When you are lucky enough to be in love and to live happily with your lover year after year, some days are a slow embrace and dip, a long sigh of private heartbeats. Other days are not so easy, but still, the tango can't help but captivate. Then you look up, as Linnea and I did, and can't help but notice what they're saying in the daily news.

What we saw was trouble in Bohemia. Finally, we had to admit it. On any blue afternoon, as daylight careened into evening, sliding without sound into what would soon be twilight, everything seemed fine. But it shouldn't have been so quiet.

These were the hot months of the middle 1990s, when the *New York Times* renamed our city Murderapolis and we came to refer to the steamy South Minneapolis summer as gunshot season. The guns got to be all I thought about those languid afternoons, every time I sat on the porch or stepped out of my car or got ready to take the dog for a walk. Every year, those last few mosquito-filled weeks seemed worse. By September things would start to settle down. By November the gunplay would stop, or at least move indoors. But in the middle of August, just a half block from the house where I had spent nearly a decade with my lover, two boys were shot.

You were kids, junior high age. The streets that night spun with red lights and siren wails. Our dog Patsy threw back her head and howled. I wanted to lay back my head and howl, too. This was too much, too close. Our neighbors' voices mingled with the echo of gunfire under our skin and the lights, the mumbled conversations, spun too wild, too hot purple crazy.

Just a day later it seemed as if the street had forgotten. The avenue was no longer spotty and tumbling, the high-pitched noise and police lights were gone. On this day it was the opposite, sheer blue and muffled as the wet sandy bottom of a big lake up north. Was it a mirage? A gaslight trick? I wondered if I had imagined the wild lights, the blotched pavement. Linnea has always told me that I tend to overdramatize, that if I weren't a writer I'd be, like my cousin Dino, an operatic anecdote teller, so naturally I wondered if I was making too much of all of this. I walked through the house gingerly as if I expected to misstep and trigger some hidden explosive. Summer on our block had become a constant wariness, every breath cloaked. I didn't fully realize then how much I had become accustomed to such frequent fear.

Take a simple dog walk. On that quiet weekday evening less than twenty-four hours after the shooting, Patsy was trotting back and forth across the apartment, begging to get out and sniff around in the big blue day. I knew I had to get going and walk her before it got too late. I even got so far as standing on the porch with Patsy's leash in hand, but I didn't step out onto the sidewalk right away. Patsy didn't share my hesitation. She was wearing her no-pull halter, her leash was clipped on, her whole body was quivering. The pockets of my leopard-patched dog-walking shorts were stuffed with plastic grocery bags for dog shit clean-up, my driver's license, some change for an emergency phone call. I had touched up my eyeliner, re-parted and sprayed my hair, put on snaky earrings and cats-eye sunglasses, while the dog did whirl-arounds, her body a spinning doughnut, *let's go, let's go*. But I paused to listen. Was the neighborhood beating steady today?

We waited on the side porch of our tottering duplex apartment, full of raggedy chairs and unsteady tables old tenants had left behind. During our first few years there a guy named Barney lived upstairs. He was a ponytailed jazz guitarist who, like me, spent some of his days working horrible temp secretarial jobs, others just hanging around at home. One unemployed afternoon while poking around in the attic treasure trove—a disheveled heap of Victorian headboards and dressers, old metal pots, fabric scraps and record albums, paperback books and newspapers from before World War II and metal-legged chairs that eventually ended up in our kitchen—we found some old spray-paint cans. So we painted all our porch furniture in spirals of red and green and blue. Neither of us were painters, but this was so easy. We grasped the can between our fingers and pressed down on the spray nozzle, slowly releasing the paint in concentric circles. A little bit of color got on our knees and fingers, but when we were done, both the upstairs and downstairs porches looked more like home.

But the day we painted the chairs was already more than five years in the past. Now Patsy was waiting for her walk. Barney was long gone to a quieter neighborhood in St. Paul. Our porch furniture paint was flaking away; the porch floor was splintered and flimsy but still marked with splotches of spray paint in the spots where we missed. There was a hole in the side porch above ours that one of Barney's friends put his foot through, years earlier. After that, the upstairs tenants kept their outside furniture on the wide front porch that looked over Portland Avenue and we wondered, as we had so many times, how long we could keep living in that place.

Lately the corner outside our house had become the place strangers most often chose to sit in their cars and wait, fingers drumming the dashboard, heads jerking along to the radio, while their pals jogged kitty-corner across Portland to buy drugs. But on this day there were only our cars, the rusted Escort I drove that we called the Pony, Linnea's wide rattling Blazer, and the spotless Acura that belonged to Elena. She was the latest friend we had talked into taking advantage of the cheap rent upstairs, before the landlord could rent the apartment over our thin ceiling to someone we might hate.

In our makeshift yard beyond the porch, below where I stood on that day with the dog, Linnea was working on her motorcycle, looking sexy. Her knees showed through ripped jeans, and she wore a cutoff shirt that bared her tattoos. Linnea is nothing like the fantasy woman I thought I'd fall in love with back in 1979 at my first women's music festival, when I was twenty and new to the bohemian world. My dream then of a woman lover was a mingling of some part of my inaccessible college roommates, some part of the lesbians I watched gather in their 1970s feminist garb on the grassy University of Illinois quad. She would, I thought, be prettier than me with long hair swept off the forehead with a purple bandanna, with eyes that looked made up even without makeup, with long feathery earrings.

Linnea is square-shouldered and masculine. That afternoon, standing on the porch looking down on her, I loved her beyond what my body could contain. It was as if my skin, bones, blood vessels expanded. In the old days I got stoned to feel this way, but that feeling was nothing compared to the wave of giddy dissolve that came over me in those surprising moments when I was suddenly aware of all that I loved.

In the slanting afternoon sun I could see how gray Linnea's hair was getting. When we met her hair was the color of cherry-wood stain, but now a thousand strands of silvery wire wound through the short clipped sides and the rumble of curls across the top. She stood with her legs apart, wide and rock solid, wearing thick-soled motorcycle boots that made her look taller than she really is. It's partly this stance that makes strangers mistake her for a man, even on the hot days when it's hard to miss the rise of her breasts beneath her thin cotton T-shirt. Although she was not looking back at me, I could feel my own body respond to hers, my hips loosening, my mouth softening. There were days in that old neighborhood when I couldn't stop thinking about the danger, about people who died or who might die, about the sudden blasts that could snatch away happiness. Those where the moments when I wondered if I should let Linnea out of my sight, even for a moment, even to walk the dog.

~

I couldn't entirely blame the neighborhood for those thoughts. My sense of danger is linked to other dangers in a connected rumble, as a snake of box cars trundling to a stop across an outer city intersection sends a shudder all the way down the line. Still, the city where I live now did not create me and my fears are nothing new. I've always expected the worst, that Linnea will crack up her truck, or her motorcycle will slide off the Lake Street Bridge, or she will spontaneously combust before my eyes. I've always had trouble trusting any kind of happiness, suspecting that bliss is a set-up, a trick to get me to relax just before the final big blast. Linnea has never obsessed about these things. Not that she didn't worry about the guns—she was the one who pulled me to the carpet whenever she heard them, the one to dive first for the phone, the one who hissed at me to get away from the window. But even though she had a new habit of bringing her phone outdoors with her, she was also capable of cleaning her motorcycle, oblivious of me, of the dog, of the problem our neighborhood was having with guns.

Not that we actually saw the guns, most of the time. We just heard them, runs of hard, hollow, heartbeats, their dusty after echo. I used to confuse gunshots with firecrackers, but not anymore. By August, any sort of bang made me stop and listen hard—the hammer of road repair two blocks away, a car door slamming, a man using the heel of his hand to pound on the door of a house with no doorbell. I knew when it was guns. It was the way the sound, familiar now, caused my skin to lift just a bit and bristle with electricity, the way it caused my heart to stop dead then start again, rushing to catch up.

Yet I did love that neighborhood in the summer. The flashing fan blades in the windows of houses without air-conditioning. Stray cats stretched out on front stoops blinking at traffic. The high and low notes of lawn mowers buzzing into the dusk. Dogs who nearly levitated from the force of their own barks when I passed by with Patsy. People walking so slow through the watery air, as if the city itself, a wet dome, a toppled lake, cradled them upright, allowed them to float.

That neighborhood is a mixed-up place, full of old South Minneapolis white lefties with teenage grunge kids and Che Guevara banners in the upstairs windows, next door to African American extended families who barbecue on the front lawn on summer Sundays, next door to lesbian mixed-race collective households who hold their picnics in the back, next door to Mexican immigrants who call out to each other in long breaths of fast Spanish, next door to a brownstone three-plex with a black avant-garde jazz musician living in the attic, a Jewish lesbian novelist living in the basement, next door to hip-hop Southeast Asian American kids with parents who relocated here from postwar Cambodia, next door to white gay men who are renovating, next door to a crack house. I hated it when people called this a bad neighborhood. When they said it to my face I froze up, looked away over their heads, or turned to flick an invisible piece of lint from my shoulder. Stuffy, tight-ass, white-flight assholes are the words that swelled in my mind as I felt my jaw joint start to throb.

One night, a few weeks before the shooting on our block, Linnea and I walked the dog together through one of those too-green evenings before the mosquitoes became completely impossible. The water in the park lagoon was honey in the falling dusk and we craved a snack, something cold and sweet. Usually I walked Patsy by myself, and when I walked I tried to think about my life with Linnea. Whenever she was out of my sight that summer I was afraid she was slipping away. I couldn't picture her. I couldn't recognize the life I was living as my own. But when Linnea walked with me, it was completely different. I didn't think. We walked in synch, our muscles storing the memory of every other walk we had ever taken in the previous nine years. On that night we walked slowly along the park's edge and pointed to houses we liked. We imagined living in this one or that one, someday, if we could ever afford to buy. We tied Patsy to a bench outside of the little natural foods co-op. The dog watched us through the plate glass as we went inside. A kid from the anarchist center across the street rang up our sale. One side of the young woman's head was shaved, the other side a short scruff with long, neon extensions, and I wondered where else she would get a job if the rumors were true and this co-op would close soon. Linnea paid for her ice-cream bar and my dairy-free Rice Dream sandwich, just as Patsy began to yip. Outside we sat close on the bench looking out onto Bloomington Avenue, where traffic was light, the air golden and still. Patsy crawled under the bench and licked my ankle. We let the cold white cream melt in our warm mouths, licked chocolate from our lips, and I felt all my body's molecules go still. My thigh fell against Linnea's thigh, my heartbeats pulsed slow, bluesy, bebop. We whispered. The day seemed to roll sticky over our skin, puddle at our feet. That's when we saw it.

"He's got a gun," Linnea said in a low, alarmed monotone. Her eyes were fixed on a crowd that had materialized in the middle of the avenue, a group of five or six young men. They couldn't have been more than thirteen years old. They piled out of a bronze-colored car rusted around the wheel wells and stopped at the red light ten feet in front of us. The gun was a big semi-automatic, stuffed partway inside one of the boys' jackets, a jacket it was too hot to be wearing. They tumbled from the car to the street to the front of house, just two doors from the anarchist's storefront. *I am just beginning to notice you, my teenage neighbor with a gun.* I reached under the bench to hold Patsy by the collar. My body's molecules were moving again, too fast now, everything in me was vibrating too fast. The gold bled too quickly out of this evening. I clutched Linnea's arm, squeezed it hard. I imagined the gun-sputtering fire, imagined Linnea spattering apart even as I held onto her. As the old bronze car squealed away, the boys gathered in front of an old white stucco house with a battered front door.

"Can you see the address over there?" Linnea whispered.

"Don't look," I hissed. "Don't let them see you look."

~

On a day, like this day, when I was getting ready to walk the dog through an afternoon so hot and capped with blue, I wondered if it was the guns I had actually seen and heard that I feared or if the neighborhood gunplay had pulled to the surface an older, more personal tremor. Then I looked down at Patsy's furry blond face. She was so anxious to get moving and have a pee along the avenue that I tried to stop thinking about it. "OK, let's go," I said to her, as we stepped out onto the sidewalk. But walking brings on thinking I can't contain. As Patsy and I rounded the corner and lost sight of Linnea my thoughts blipped back to those boys with the gun we had seen a few weeks earlier. And then my thinking wandered even farther, to another time, years before, when my body had tried to shake out of itself on that very same street corner. That was a very different story, when I was just twenty-two years old, waiting for a rented school bus. I had no longtime lover then. I was always half-flinched, ready to duck, waiting for something to blow. My companions that day were forty lesbian separatists and we were on our way to Michigan for the annual Womyn's Music Festival, an all-female weekend of thousands who crowd the outdoor concerts and run bare-breasted through the fern-carpeted middle Michigan woods.

The long hair and billowy denim skirt I wore back then were not the lesbian separatist style, and I was afraid those women with their shorter than crew-cut clips and their rules for proper lesbian speech would not talk to me. I was scared my breasts wouldn't look good, couldn't stand up before 20,000 eyes, even though I knew it was incorrect for a lesbian to care. I was terrified that the woman from Illinois I was meeting there would disappoint me. I thought about her every day, her pale face and lank hair falling out of a cheap barrette, her long legs and full butt, her ridiculous love of cloudy days, and her favorite lunch of meat loaf with macaroni and cheese. Was she really just a friend? But most of all, I was scared someone on the open road would notice us, a bus full of lesbians with our shirts still on. I was scared some guy with a prickly blond crew cut would throw a hand grenade or shoot a bazooka or simply gun us down with one of those rifles he kept in the back of his pickup truck.

Whether or not it's a real gun hanging on some guy's truck rack, or bulging out of some little boy's jacket, or just the TV version I play in my head to help me understand a feeling, my body responds the same. The inside takes flight, lunging down the block before the muscle and bone even have had the time to twitch. Still, I've always been the type to go ahead anyway. In the case of the Michigan bus, I was right about some things. The most serious separatists didn't talk to me. The ones who did were instructive: a lesbian wearing a skirt is trying to pass as straight; we shouldn't call ourselves women but only, always, lesbians; we should separate from anything to do with men; we needed our own colleges, our own nursing homes, our own Laundromats.

I nodded a great deal on the long drive there and back. My hair was hidden in a man's felt fedora I had picked up in a vintage clothes shop back in Minneapolis, my legs were tucked up inside my long skirt, my heart was beating at once too fast and too slow. The woman from Illinois had come to the festival with a new lover. She hardly met my eyes, touched me only with the tips of her fingers when she passed me a joint, spent most of the weekend in her new girlfriend's tent. The lesbian sitting beside me on the bus ride home had a round, sunbeam face that quivered when she told me, "At home, in my bedroom, I have a bookcase full of books and they are all written by women."

"You mean lesbians?" I asked. I leaned against the glass as the late August sun cut through the bus windows. I stared at the hard-muscled arms of the lesbian driver, one of the ones who ignored me. My luminescent companion had told me about that bus driver, how she lived on lesbian-owned land, tried to do business with lesbians only, how she had stripped down her name, both first and last, to V. Just one letter. V for Victory? For Vengeance? I found myself holding her one letter in my mouth. I sucked on its hard pointed lines. I felt voluptuous next to it. Her square back, her roughly turned-up sleeves—she wore her clothes like a guy on the way to build a house. Even though I knew she would not approve of me in my long skirt and name full of syllables, she stirred me up, made me fantasize. *I lean over your hardwood back. I offer to help you steer.*

The slanting sun exposed me to myself. I wanted more than to eat macaroni and cheese every day with my most loved friend. I had admired a lesbian for her manliness. This sort of attraction was certainly not allowed in the lesbian separatist rule book, was not palatable to any noticeable faction of feminism in 1981, unless you counted the sado-masochist lesbians who led each other around the festival grounds on dog leashes and nobody I knew back then approved of that. It was another, deeper, snap of awareness to realize it was not just boho experimentation, not just radical feminist politics, women loving women—as the lesbian songs said back then—simply for women-loving's sake that made me as queer as any bristle-headed separatist on that bus. It was sex, pure lust, which seemed more serious, more immutable, more worthy of gunplay. And so I worried even more about a bus bomb, a gassy blast, shattering glass. But there were no guns, no explosions, and the bus dropped me off just where it had picked me up, on a quiet South Minneapolis corner, a block from the park, in the part of town where years later my beloved and I walked our dog.

~

Most days of the year, the days without gunshots, this neighborhood is just another geography of wood and brick homes clustered around the wide avenues of an upper Midwestern city. When I moved to Minneapolis in the early 1980s, five years before I met Linnea, I had trouble imagining this place as a city at all. The streets seemed so roomy, the sky so open and wide and such a sharp shade of blue. Urban danger required tighter quarters, I thought, thinking of all the cramped, smashed window, graffiti-littered neighborhoods I was instructed to stay away from when I was a child growing up under the sooty blue industrial skies of Chicago's southern regions.

On the night my love affair with Linnea began, I lived in a two-room studio in a twelve-unit red-brick apartment building just west of the freeway that tears South Minneapolis into halves. The two ruined edges along the 35W retainer wall are a little jagged. The streets there resemble keloid scars of poorly stitched stomach surgery. Two weeks later, before I knew I'd be needing room for Linnea soon, I moved to the other side of the incision, six short blocks east of the freeway, into a big Portland Avenue corner duplex a friend was vacating. It had the lowest rent anyone I know had ever heard of, even for that part of town. It had deep cherry woodwork, pocket doors, two porches. When I sat on the side porch on sunny afternoons I could almost pretend the traffic noise on Portland Avenue was really the sound of waves, water battering the shore, the even, thumping beat people hear on windy days along the lakesides in nicer parts of the city.

Nine months passed before Linnea moved in with me. Nine years later we lived there still. So much of Linnea's and my life together happened in that apartment.

Once Portland Avenue was the showcase side of town. It was lined with immense Victorian mansions for the city's lace-curtain class—turn-of-the-century bankers and lawyers and store owners. But it had been decades since this was a respectable place to live. Now the rent is cheap, the races are mixed, the mansions are cut up into apartments and duplexes. Our old place was at least thirty blocks from the city's famous lakes and landscaped Mississippi River bike paths, but we had Powderhorn Park, eight blocks square, a big green bowl scooped out of the flat city. The small lagoon at its center, too dirty for swimming, was the summer home to ducks and geese and even, according to my resident bird-watcher Linnea, the occasional egret or blue heron.

It was the Fourth of July, the summer before Linnea moved in with me, when I first noticed something new in this neighborhood. The park that night was crammed full of people waiting for fireworks. As I walked down into the bowl to find my friends, I noticed there were guys hanging around the corners and against the brick walls of buildings, calling out to me, commenting on the shape of my ass, *whattsa matta baby, you won't talk to a black man*, in that way smart black street guys know to rattle a white girl who doesn't want to come off as racist. I grew up with all of that, every time I walked through a Chicago commuter train station or any other city place where guys had nothing to do but hang around. I was surprised to run into it here, in squeaky polite Minneapolis. I was sorry to realize how out of practice I was, as edgy and tongue-tied at twenty-eight as I had been at sixteen.

Just after dusk, a crowd of kids who had been hanging around the old cement bandstand just north of the lagoon tumbled into a mob fistfight, the type I had only seen before in televised hockey games. This was the time in the late eighties when the newspapers were reporting an influx of gang activity from Detroit, Chicago, and Gary, Indiana, but the Minneapolis chief of police, a gone-soft former New Yorker, announced there was no gang problem here. Others with good intentions insisted that talk of gangs was just racist panic, the twitching nerves of the predominantly white populations of the Twin Cities in the wake of a big African American migration from Gary and the South Side of Chicago. The migration was a fact. Some African Americans did move here, in spite of the reputation for arctic winters, to escape the gangs and drugs of those rougher places. And, more than a decade later, it's common knowledge that there are plenty of Minneapolis gangsters who were born here. But there were some who painted the demographic changes as a diaspora of freeloaders and criminals, drawn here, the rumors read, to cash in on Minnesota's liberal welfare system and a wide open drug market. Even if this more cynical scenario were a tiny bit true, it did seem wrong in the beginning to believe any of it.

But whatever the city leaders were saying, it was clear in the park that steamy holiday evening that there were people on the scene who hadn't been here before and some sort of turf skirmish was developing. The police just made things worse by sweeping the area with a high-beam searchlight, bright as a knife blade. The rest of us—circles of lesbians, black and white parents with little kids, noisy gatherings of Southeast Asian immigrant clans—lounged on old sheets and blankets, stretched out on our backs, and waited for the fireworks. But we felt it as well, that too bright slash. Whether it was gang-related or just gang-wannabe play, something was going on down there at the bottom of the hill. The searchlights didn't stop the fight. More and more kids ran to join the brawl with fists in the air, voices hoarse and rattling.

Later there were other kinds of warnings—visible drug dealing in the streets near the freeway, the newspapers renaming the area two blocks from our house "Crack Avenue," the multiplying city murder statistics. But that night in the park was the first sign of trouble I saw with my own eyes, the first time Minneapolis felt like what I had always understood a city to be. I walked home with the sense of having been nudged into an awareness of an old familiarity, hyped-up racial edginess, the possibility of wandering into violence. As a child, I had repeating nightmares of getting lost on some mysterious Chicago street, bleak and shadowed by tall brick buildings with no windows. Night after night, this dream woke me up sweating. Ever since then I had rarely been able, at least while sober, to shake the feeling that something was about to go wrong. On that Fourth of July I finally had evidence that these weren't just neurotic dreams. The world really was what I remembered it to be, a park full of gathering tension like wind around a translucent funnel. There was more here than just my pumping imagination.

Perhaps my little parcel of dread was what was left of a small person's fear of the improbable safety of tall buildings that arch up too far into the sky. Or maybe it was just the everyday racist distrust all the kids learned where I grew up, the warnings to watch out for those other ones, in the next neighborhood. It might be the reasonable residue of a childhood full of Chicago TV news reports on presidential assassinations, gang shootings, murdered nurses, tornadoes that squashed whole suburbs, antiwar demonstrators with their heads cracked open in front of a downtown hotel. Or maybe I grew up fearing what my life would become, a departure into the dangerous neighborhoods depicted on the jackets of paperbacks I wasn't supposed to read. Dim-lit worlds of inverted sex, shadowy companions, female husbands. I didn't hear gunfire when I was growing up in the first ring of suburbs south of Chicago. The only shots I heard rang from inside my imagination, if I were even to think the word lesbian.

By the time my new city turned into Murderapolis, it seemed my life had become everything I had grown up primed to avoid. But I had worked hard to get where I was. I was deciding for myself where to walk, where to live, who to marry, despite my training. I loved the way I was always aware of what room Linnea was in and what she was doing, the way I could spot the ugly pea soup green siding of our house from a block or two away, and the way my heart would noticeably pulse as home pulled me closer. It was only during these bad months at the end of summer that I hated my neighborhood. But no, it wasn't the whole neighborhood I hated. It wasn't even most of the neighborhood. It always started with one house, even one apartment, sometimes on our block, sometimes a few blocks over. The nexus of the nervous nights. The season-long street quarrels. We never knew exactly what else went on, maybe turf wars over the price of crack or police violence or scene stealers just in from Detroit or Chicago or the desperation of some addict with a gun, all conspiring to raise the temperature.

It was this constant waiting for the water to boil over that made me walk the dog a little bit more quickly than usual on that deepening afternoon, the day just after someone tried to blow away those two little boys. As Patsy and I walked we passed by the porches of Portland Avenue and peered into the windows of parked cars. I listened to each breath in, each breath out, my breath and the breath of the street, watching every movement, flinching at every sound.

I had been avoiding trouble for so long by then, ever since I gave up drinking and getting high and started living on the clean side of the veil. I appreciated things I had never noticed before. In July it was the speckled orange petals of the tiger lilies planted along the foundations of some of these old homes and springing up by surprise in our own yard. In August it was the purple coneflower blossoms in perennial gardens along the avenue, echinacea, the same plant used to make the herbs I took to build up my immunity in the years when Linnea and I first got together and I was learning how to take care of myself. But whenever we heard it again, the pa, pa, pa of bullets three, two, one block away, the curtain was wrenched open again and I was reminded of another kind of life.

These were the times when I understood the motivation of the men and women who sat outside our windows incessantly drumming the dashboard or eating lunch, fast-food burgers and fries, while they waited for a buddy to come back from the drug house around the corner or down the alley or across the street. My drugs were different, but I used to wait, too, for those moments when the wine caused my molecules to spin out and happily tumble, fears gone, poof, replaced by distant laughter. When the toke took away the shape of things, everything re-opened to giddy interpretation. I remembered cravings. I could even feel the edge of its old after-flush as I picked up the phone to call 911 or the police crack unit, because in our last years on Portland Avenue we had come to assume that where there were drugs there were guns. I used to live for the thrill of not knowing what was next, but no more. After all these years with Linnea, I had become accustomed to believing I could steer my life, keep myself safe, keep Linnea safe, too, by the things I chose. Stay sober. Don't get high. Do good work. Eat right. Walk the dog every day. Watch for happiness, and embrace it. Then pa, pa, pa and the world flipped over again. I couldn't tell anymore if life on my block was as bad as it seemed when the guns fired, or as fine as it seemed when the guns were silent.

The night I sat on the bench outside of the co-op in the honey dusk with Linnea there was a little part of my body that expected a gun even before we saw it, despite the syncopated stillness, the sweet cream on my tongue, and the hard support of Linnea's thigh next to mine. But I was always a tiny bit wary when Linnea and I were together in public. When we are visible as lesbians it's easy to fear that hatred might materialize as the worst of what I can imagine—a hard crack, a sharpshooter from the carpet store across the street appearing as a glimmer in the window before he takes us out. But if I linger in the wrong kind of fear I might choose a bad moment to duck. *I was just beginning to expect you, my thirteen-year-old neighbor with your boxer shorts showing and that gun cradled, an infant against your stomach.* The gangsters in my neighborhood have money to make or drugs to pick up or a buddy to impress or an enemy to kill. They wouldn't even see the ones who got in the way.

~

But all of that was on a bad day. On better afternoons, I was happy to look up and down my wide block, the type that used to be shaded with a canopy of branches in the years before Dutch Elm disease. I saw neighbors carrying groceries into their houses, standing on ladders to paint the third-story trim, walking together in clumps toward the park with baby carriages and toddlers pumping to keep up. On that afternoon, walking the dog, I saw that my block was a roller-blade track for a narrow little girl with long, lank hair and an even younger boy following behind as any baby half-brother would, the thick brush of his hair shaved into a neat fade, both their sweatshirts tied around their waists.

I saw Dorothy, the old woman who lived on the corner just across the narrow side street from us, crawling across her lawn that evening, pulling weeds. Her hair and her cotton blouse, her loose cotton pants, were all the same shade of yellowish white. She sprouted out of the grass like a summer mushroom, on just the spot where several years earlier a man in a faded denim work shirt was hurled from the out-of-control convertible that crashed into her front stoop. There was not even a dent in the earth where that man lay waiting for the high white cry of the ambulance. We didn't see his actual flight, but I remembered it as if I had. I could see his blue-shirted body gone for a terrible moment, blended into the still summer air. Linnea ran out of our kitchen and across the street to help him. "His shirt was open," she told me later. "When I placed my hand on the bare skin of his chest, I felt his heart beating."

But on that day, walking Patsy, what I saw instead were two women across the street, lugging flagstones over their sloping front lawn. We didn't really know them, had only met them once. They looked like the lesbian separatists I knew in the early 1980s in their baggy drawstring pants, their short hair cut in no particular style, their radical feminist T-shirts. I always felt younger than women wearing stock lesbian clothes, as if I were still twenty-seven, newly in love with Linnea, suspended in my hip-dyke post-music-festival stage and dressed in denim miniskirts and studded, ankle-high boots. Those women across the street looked as though they were from a decade past, before rainbow flags, lesbian sex magazines, out lesbian mass-media rock stars. But actually those women were of the 1990s generation, much younger than me. They kept dogs, a big sleek brown mutt with a friendly face and a smaller, shaggier sibling. I always waved when I passed by with Patsy.

On that day, my neighbors were not building walls but a front garden of rocks, wildflowers, and pink plastic flamingos. In the old days, that one-lettered bus driver V had renamed herself, trimmed her identity down to just one sound, because the rest of her syllables, the rest of the world, seemed to be waving a gun in her face. She wasn't the only one who talked nationalism. Even I had moments of wondering if it would be better to just go away from the others to protect myself from the same thing that scared me still, the bullet homing for the visible lesbian breastbone. But separatism had always seemed too much like running away, leaving the mess for someone else to clean up, which might be the same instinct that drove the people I started out with farther and farther from the center of the interracial city.

But these women on my block didn't seem to be backing away. Their hair was not shaved back to the skull line. Their names were not shaved back to one letter. A rainbow flag trumpeted from their front window. In this center city, the queers lived in a scattered site fortress. Gay men flew their rainbow flags flamboyantly from front-porch flag poles, their lawns clipped as close as those old lesbian separatist haircuts. Linnea's and my flag was pasted in Linnea's study window. The translucent rainbow sticker let the morning light shine through and announced our residency, one skirt-wearing lesbian wife, one hard-backed lesbian husband. Those horizontal stripes of primary colors, the bumper stickers and jewelry and colored fabric that wrinkled and flattened in the wind were the mid-nineties queer insignia, a holdover from the diversity slogans of a national lesbian and gay march on Washington. At first I disliked the image. It was a little too subtle to promote visibility, I thought, like a secret handshake only the initiated knew, too appropriated from Jesse Jackson's presidential race, and too close to the kind of cute tchotchkes displayed in New-Age unicorn stores. But after a while, I got used to recognizing it as a marker of my people, and in the neighborhood they comforted me, telling me which doorbell I'd be welcome to lean on, if it ever came to that.

While the women worked across the avenue, Patsy and I passed around the front of our house where Joe from next door, our landlord's son, was driving a thirty-year-old riding lawn mower he had reconditioned in his backyard. The machine looked like something out of old TV, *The Man from U.N.C.L.E.* or *Dr. Who,* a bolted metal box on wheels with metal switches and blinking red lights. Joe was not wearing a shirt and his bare shoulders were glistening like the bald spot on the top of his head. He had some sort of dust-filter muzzle strapped to his face. He lived alone next door and his home was a warehouse of rusted washing machines, lawn-mower parts, and police-band radios. He could fix almost anything without ever having to go to the hardware store. He had told us enough to reveal that he hated the federal government, dark-skinned people, the city housing inspectors. Over time he learned that we didn't want to hear about it. We never asked him personal questions; he returned the favor. Even though we hated what he believed in, we came to almost like him. On this day he jostled by, his shoulders, back, thighs, jiggling along to the mower's low throttle, and I couldn't help but wonder how his breathing must sound in his head as it rasped in and out of his filtered leather gag.

I walked Patsy north on Portland that day so soon after the shooting, just two blocks, past the red-brick mansion that seemed to keep changing tenants, past a big wooden Victorian painted such a bright shade of pink Linnea and I called it the Pepto House, across two alleys and two side streets, past a big green duplex with a screened-in deck and gorgeous tile interiors that we walked through once when it was up for sale and we wondered if we could afford to buy a house yet. The hair on Pasty's neck bristled as two Huskies who had been asleep behind the deck screen leapt awake and barked down at us ferociously.

Down a couple blocks Patsy and I walked past the church where I had tried not to pay attention one February afternoon when a famous rock musician got married. After hours of the chop, chop, chop of a helicopter hovering over my roof I gave in, put Patsy on her leash and slid down to the icy corner to stare with the rest at what turned out to be nothing but a white limo attached to a canopy tunnel, and a few sharp-dressed security guards who looked so fine they put even the most puffed-up neighborhood pimps to shame. Nothing much was happening at the church that summer evening as Patsy and I passed. A few young boys in oversized jerseys were bouncing a basketball in the parking lot. It was still a couple of weeks before the annual evangelical block party, featuring wailing soul music, outdoor services, and haranguing preachers who so loudly condemned the poor homosexuals that Linnea started calling it the Soul Irritation Festival. Up from the church toward home was the house we called the brothel, a brown-brick and pink-stucco palace with an upstairs full of tiny bedrooms. One of the ever-revolving household of gay club boys who lived there took us on a tour once, and told us it had actually been a brothel at one time. "Sometimes it still is," he said, as a bleary-eyed man passed us in the narrow hall with his boots in his hand.

This wasn't the longest walk we had ever taken, but Patsy was happy, smiling that doggy smile she saved for the last half block before home. At the brothel, we were just across the street from home, and after we crossed I could hear Luis in the alley behind our house playing loud Salsa music. His four little dogs and his neon green parrots in their silver cages were barking and squawking in the yard as one of his boyfriends helped him wash his red BMW. Some of Luis's paying visitors were thin, silent white men with leather upholstered cars, receding hairlines, cell phones. This day's guest was more intimate. Luis and this boyfriend talked in streams of Spanish as the garden hose let loose cool rivers of water over the smooth surface of the car. The boyfriend was missing two of his front teeth; Luis called him Mr. No Teeth when he was not around. Mr. No Teeth always smiled at me when I passed. His hips swayed almost imperceptibly as if he were about to ask me to dance with him across the gravel and ground-up glass. Luis explained it several times to Linnea. "These Puerto Rican guys, they like the girls with this," he said, slapping himself hard on one of his buttocks. "But I told them," he said, "You watch it. Her husband has a big gun."

Linnea doesn't own a gun, but I liked how he recognized her right away as an old-time type of butch dyke. I liked it that he saw me as Linnea's wife. There was a time when I'd have been offended, but I had come to like that his Latino boyfriends flirted with me, even if it was just to cover up what they did with Luis when they disappeared into his basement. On this day, Mr. No Teeth was with his young wife, a new red henna in her long dark hair, their six-month-old baby strapped across her stomach. She chattered along with them while stroking the baby's head with one hand, polishing the silver chrome hood ornament with the other, a remarkable ability, it seemed, to believe in her husband's gap-toothed grin.

As Patsy and I headed back toward our porch, Luis's car-washing party filled out the background of our yard, but the foreground was full of Linnea, massaging the silver gas tank of her motorcycle, smiling to herself. The yard where Linnea stood was mostly dirt with a few grassy highlights. The rotten fence around her was reinforced with the chicken wire we had stapled up to keep the dog from squeezing out between the loose planks. Linnea's Kawasaki 750 was the altar of her best prayers, the act of polishing the silver tank her meditation to living in the moment. She took off her big silver rings so she wouldn't scratch the paint. She rubbed the thick white lotion in regular circles as the fence boards creaked in the muggy breeze.

A few summers earlier, Linnea almost had a fight over that fence. There used to be some teenage boys who lived close by, walked past every day, and kicked in the rotten boards along the sidewalk. Those boards were so old, so precariously nailed, that it didn't take much strength to kick the wood right through. The landlord should have rebuilt that fence, but he never did. It was one of the reasons the rent was so cheap. The kicking began before we put up the chicken wire. Every hole was a spot for the dog to squeeze through, run down the alley, and eat garbage until she was sick. I would cry and moan, "I'll never see her fuzzy face again," for hours until we finally found her. And every wounded board was one less barrier between the street and Linnea's motorcycle.

Every time those boys kicked the fence, Linnea repaired it with whatever scraps of wood were left. With every kick she got a little more pissed. It became a flash point for her. The familiar splintering sound. Her face flushing red. Her fingers springing back into hard, knobby fists.

It was a Saturday afternoon, high summer, when three or four of those boys stood out there, swaggering and cursing, this time with girls to impress, this time with Linnea staring through the blinds, waiting. She spun around when she heard the first splinter. "That's it. I'm calling the cops."

"Don't do it," I begged, swaying behind her. We hardly ever called the police back then. We had heard so many stories of friends whose straight-A basketball-star sons got shoved around by the cops in our neighborhood. "They'll just pick up the first black kid they see."

"Then what am I supposed to do?" She was fuming, her back was hardening, her skin paling, every muscle in her arms, shoulders, visibly stiffening.

"Isn't there some way to talk?" I said, clutching for something to calm her, to make this moment pass. "Can't we just talk to them?"

"You want me to talk to them?"

"You think the police care what happens to a couple of dykes?" I said. We had heard stories about that, too. Cops who shove butches around. Police who tell people in this neighborhood that they deserved whatever they got, living here.

The next splinter was louder. "That's it," she said again as she barreled out the door. I was surprised at how calm her voice was. She must have taken a breath first. "Could you guys stop it. Please. Don't kick the fence."

By the time I followed her out, one of the boys was yelling, "Bitch. Honky Bitch."

I shadowed her in the doorway, my arms crossed stiffly over my chest. The young man waved his long fingers toward her face; his oversized Oakland Raider's jersey swung loose under his outstretched arms. It felt as though any second everything solid would slip out from under us. He stepped forward with each taunt; the muscles in his face were clenched as tight as Linnea's fists. When he saw me standing behind Linnea his taunts changed.

"Bulldagger bitch."

"Stop kicking the goddamn fence." She was yelling now, too.

"You need me to fuck your wife? You need me to fuck you, dyke?"

These boys were our neighbors, but we spun in different worlds. Linnea and I don't want to separate from the city, not like some of my cousins who have fled Chicago for Indiana, not like those gays we read about, the new homo homeowners of suburbia. *But we don't know you guys, you fence kickers. We don't know your mothers.* Living here didn't seem to bring us any closer. The targets of their kicks had changed. We felt them in our stomachs, between our heartbeats. *Just as you meant us to.* If we waited for any one of them to come closer the fight wouldn't have been about the fence.

I opened the screen, pulled Linnea in by the elbow. "Maybe we should have just called the cops," I whispered into the bristled hairs of her hard wet neck as I shut the door on our neighbors.

$\sim$

Our old neighborhood was one that some called historic, some called diverse, some called bad. When did the place we lived become a spot on the map that showed up highlighted yellow on TV news reports about the rising murder rate? When did we start to expect to hear gunshots at night while we fell asleep, gunshots in the yard in the afternoon while we hung wet laundry on the line, at least one run of gunshots every single summer day?

Yet for so many years we stayed, both of us living in that apartment longer than we had ever lived anywhere. Everything about that place sang home to us. It was the same for everyone around us who might have left, except that they had always lived there, or they owned their home, or they couldn't afford to live anywhere else. People in our neighborhood were medical assistants, office workers, bookstore clerks, poets, welfare recipients, alternative schoolteachers, part-time graphic designers, musicians who performed at local cabarets. We figured old Dorothy across the street must collect Social Security, along with the rental income she got from Evelyn who lived in her upstairs apartment. Elena upstairs from us was the editor of a magazine that published only work by people of color. Her girlfriend worked at a Latina battered women's shelter. Mickey two doors down, who fixed up one of the houses Joe used to own, was one of the city's first out lesbian firefighters. Nearby, there were crack dealers, probation officers, bus drivers, taxi drivers, drivers of semi-trucks. There were graduate students, sign-language interpreters, part-time college instructors, card-shop clerks, coffee-shop-counter workers, and young girls who worked the corner behind the body shop off Lake Street.

After she finished graduate school, Linnea taught college, but she wasn't tenure track and never knew from year to year if she would be rehired. I had so many different kinds of jobs while we lived in that apartment—switchboard operator for the power company, university civil servant, adjunct teacher. Nearby there were mothers who met their kids at the bus every afternoon. Three former lovers of mine lived in the blocks around the park. We had close friends there, too, people we had loved for over a decade, at least one near each of the park's four corners. The friend who watched Patsy when we went out of town lived just six blocks away. Across the street there was an apartment full of guys we thought were selling drugs. Someone who hunted deer every fall lived on the street behind us and left the carcasses hanging overnight from his back balcony, where they swung, reminders of lynchings in the too-white dawn. Behind Dorothy lived another woman well past retirement age who wore squeaky-soled shoes, had parlor-set hair, kept a perfect garden, on the same corner where those two boys were shot from their bikes.

The good things and the bad things existed at once, alternate universes occupying the same place and time. Where I grew up, we learned a neighborhood was either good or bad. No in-between. Now I see that this is probably not true, but I'm not the only one to gravitate toward something being one thing or another. I had friends who lived near us in our old neighborhood who complained as a kind of joke, "ooh, we live in a bad neighborhood," but I couldn't accept those words as the truth without seeing all of what I loved blotted out. The tiger lilies. The luster of the Victorian woodwork. The cheap rent. Arty neighbors who kept their lights on all night. Linnea's and my hearts beating in tandem as we made dinner, cleaned our house, fought or kissed good night before falling off to sleep. The low growl of the occasional early morning car headed home down Portland Avenue.

~

That gun we saw in front of the food co-op, swaddled against that young boy's stomach, could have been the same gun that wiped those boys from their bikes. It probably wasn't. I never knew how many guns there really were. On my worst days I expected a gun on every corner. I expected a shot to fire from every curtained window, the glass to shatter out of every speeding car. I heard one shot and it echoed through me 500-fold. On the better days I hoped it would all just end, that we could stop it, like any war, that documents would be signed, peace declared. On better days we called 911, called our neighbors, laughed because 911 was busy, so many of us were calling. On better days we tried to help, watching the street outside of Linnea's study window while some African American guy was frisked over the hood of his car, was folded into the back of a squad, to bear witness, in case the cops got mean.

But more often those last summers I heard the guns all the time, when

I was in the shower, in my dreams, even in motel rooms far away from the neighborhood. These were the days when I was out of control. My fear expanded exponentially. These were the days I felt connected to the people we watched on the nightly news, bustling with their daily business along the streets of Sarajevo or Tel Aviv or Gaza or London or Oklahoma City. People who paused in doorways, but finally, simply, went on with their lives as if they hadn't been presented with the evidence of how it will all blow apart, splinter into smoke and rubble and spinning lights.

Yet most days I still tried to believe that if I did the right thing it would get better. Like that night at the co-op. On our way home, we were relieved to see a park-patrol car pulled over on the grass a few yards from the lagoon. We ran to him, forgetting our usual fear of uniforms, anxious for anyone to take control, tripping on the damp grass. Patsy was grinning and nipping at our heels, thinking the sudden trot was a game. The patrolman was alone, eating his dinner. He had a wide, clear, nice-guy face. His hair was cut close so that the naps lay flat against his scalp. We pelted him with a hailstorm of words, the address of the stucco house, the size of the gun, the number of boys, the color of the car. He was park police, not regular city patrol. He set his submarine sandwich on the seat next to him, wrote notes in a steno pad while he creased his brow, nodded his head slightly. He didn't seem to know what to do. He probably just wanted to finish his sandwich and watch the ducks skid across the deepening gold surface of the lagoon. We told our story. We walked home. There was nothing more to be done. The gun hadn't even fired and already that sweet evening was completely rearranged, not so much honey-colored now but molten purple, swollen, throbbing like a sock in the eye.

∼

We will never know who held the gun that night the boys on our block were shot. Five bullets, pa, pa, pa, a pause, then pa, pa, two more. At the movies, when you see a gun in the first scene you tense up for the rest of the show, waiting for the pop. So it was with us.

We crept out on the porch the night it happened. The sirens shrieked too close to the bone. The streaking ambulance beams cut in through our kitchen windows. Elena came down from upstairs wearing cutoff sweatpants and a wrinkled T-shirt. Her blunt-cut hair was rumpled on one side from reading in bed. Linnea still had her jeans and boots on, but I was not dressed for the street. I wore canvas slippers and a little cotton tank dress that looked like pajamas. We stood together on the side stoop, bent over to see what was happening. Do you think someone was killed? Can you see any bodies? Slowly we inched to the sidewalk toward the street that pulsed with red and ice blue ambulance light. We heard the crunch of Joe's steps in the alley.

"Maybe Joe heard something on his police band," I whispered to Linnea. She nodded and broke away from us to meet him at the end of the fence. The soles of her boots scooted over the loose stones, glass shards, and empty fast-food bags that littered the sidewalk. My body felt hollowed out. A newspaper car careened around the corner and pulled over a few feet from where I stood with Elena.

The reporter who eased himself out of the car was a sloppy dresser. His khaki pants were wrinkled, his blue-striped shirt only partly tucked in. He looked as if he hadn't shaved in a while. It turned out he was a guy Elena used to work with when she wrote for the city paper. He stared at her ripped sweatpants, seemed surprised to see her there. "Elena?"

"How's it going?" she nodded.

For a minute the reporter seemed to think Elena was there to cover the story. "Have you figured out what's going on?" he asked.

"Naw," she said. "I just live here."

He stared at her for a moment, his eyes blinking in tandem with the whirling lights. "Oh," he said, as he turned and ambled down the street toward the action. He didn't seem in any particular hurry and I wondered if he was the best they could find.

Linnea was trotting, a little breathless, when she returned to report. "Joe said they were kids. Thirteen or fourteen. On bikes. They're still alive."

"I wonder who they are," I whispered.

We knew so many of the people around there. Joe, who mowed our lawn, unplugged our sink when it was clogged, vacuumed out our furnace every fall. Dorothy, who always waved to the shape of us, that nice girl and her young husband across the street, our outlines all she could make out with her hazy eyesight. Jo, who painted and performed in a drag art-rock band, married to Laney with the bright blond hair and fabulous handmade hats. Luis, across the alley who we knew was gay from the first day we saw him out there in his short shorts, his tropical bird-print shirt, his real tropical birds cawing and squawking out the open windows. *But you*, the young men who kicked our fence, we don't know which houses you lived in. *You*, the young boy who died earlier that summer in another drive-by shooting a few blocks south, we never talked to you either, but always slowed down to read the sign on your streetside memorial of flowers and a scrawled cardboard sign—REMEMBER OUR SON. STOP THE VIOLENCE. *And you*, the young man who lived across the alley, mentally slow, the paper said, killed in front of your home when you didn't know to flash the right gang hand signal, we never met you, only read about your short life in the Sunday news. There was a line through the middle of our old neighborhood. It was not always a color line, or a class line, or a we-are-from-here-and-you- are-not line. This border was harder to discern. On one side were people of all kinds and colors who don't carry guns, don't have to hold the heads of the dying in their laps, who only watch and wonder what to do, and sometimes who leave.

On the other side are the boys and sometimes the girls on either side of the guns. *I want to wail for everything I will never know about you, wail for your mothers and for your little beating hearts and for your big brothers who walk four abreast in the middle of the street by my old house because they want someone to be afraid of them and for your negligent landlord who lives out of town, and for the cops who live in the suburbs, too, and hassle you for no reason at all. I want to wail for the drug king-pins and their urban underground corporations and for the crack dealers from Detroit and Gary and Chicago and Minneapolis, and for the white guys from the suburbs who drive real slow around the block looking for a connection, and for the local addict, twitching and tossing cigarette butts and hamburger wrappers out onto the curb, wait-ing in a car on the side street where I used to park my old Pony, and for the thing that is missing in all of you, wherever you live, the cavity that craves the drugs that are cash in pockets of the ones who bring guns into all of our old neighborhoods. And no matter how you feel about women like me and my lesbian husband, I want to wail for you boys sprawled in the street and for how few prospects you see, young black men from this neighborhood, and for how goddamn stupid it is that you have been shot off your bikes on a hot summer night in the Midwest.*

Two neighbors passing by from the Chicago Avenue bus stop joined the little group gathered on our front stoop. Chicago Avenue is a straight shot from the hospital, and these women were still wearing their medical technician smocks. It was almost midnight, so they must have been on the three-to-eleven shift. Elena rocked from one foot to the other. The old reporter in her wanted to know what was happening. We all did, but I didn't want to get any closer. I wanted to cry, or throw up, or scream fuck you, fuck you. I felt like smoking cigarettes and chugging wine. Instead I paced, three steps forward, four back again. Finally Linnea broke up our little mob, walked over to her truck, unlocked the door, and leaned in. The pulsing lights played over the rectangle of her back, lighting her up like a stadium scoreboard. When she came out she was holding surgical gloves in one hand. She motioned to Elena and they started walking.

"Nea," I called, my arms crossed over my chest, holding my dress close to my skin as if I were cold on this hot night. I was overcome with my usual internal newsreel. With every step she took away from me I saw her explode again. I saw her dear cells dispersing, red smoke streaming away in the shrill twirling wind of this fucked-up evening. But I knew it was useless to tell her to stay back. That is why she carries those gloves in her truck, in case someone is bleeding, in case no one else is taking care of things.

"They probably don't need your help," I called out to her.

"I know," she said, turning to walk backwards and raising the hand with the gloves as if to calm me. "Just in case."

She was still holding the gloves in her hand when they came back a few minutes later. "I don't think they're dead," Elena said. "The bikes are still lying in the street," she added, as if that could comfort us.

The reporter followed a few moments behind. "Did you find out any-thing?" he asked Elena.

"I don't think they're dead," Elena repeated like a prayer, a mantra into the fidgeting night.

The women standing with me were shaking their heads. "Getting so dangerous everywhere," one of them said. Her straightened hair was pulled back into a tight, dry, ponytail. Her laminated hospital ID glistened like an extra eye from the top pocket of her smock. She must have walked by our house every night she worked, but I didn't recall ever seeing her before. I couldn't quite make out her name in the dark. Rochelle something. The other woman had a head full of braids held off her face with a wide white scarf. She held onto that scarf with the tips of all the fingers of one hand, as if a wind was blowing off the scene down the street and she had to hold on or lose it. "Maybe we should get out of this neighborhood," she said.

Maybe we should all get out of this neighborhood, I thought. I could live without this. Those women on my stoop weren't really talking to me, but I joined the conversation anyway. "Do you think there's someplace safe to go?"

"I don't know, I don't know," the ponytailed woman said, and we all laughed low humid sounds that swirled, smoky into the spinning lights of the departing emergency vans. As the light faded, that woman's badge stopped glistening, became just a tiny Polaroid of her face. I could leave this place I thought, as those women walked away, their thick-soled nurse's shoes making no sound at all on the gritty sidewalk.

The article in the next morning's paper read, "Neighbors at the scene reported that the young men were wounded, but survived the shootings." That's all we knew.

～

When we did leave the neighborhood, the following summer, it wasn't because of the guns.

One Saturday morning we saw our eighty-six-year-old landlord, Joe's father, shuffling up the side porch steps. He paused briefly to glare at the shabby porch furniture, then used his key to come into our hallway. We knew something was up. Henry never just stopped by. He thumped and coughed until Linnea, in her robe and still wet from the shower, opened the door about a foot. Henry shoved his head in and croaked at us. "The housing inspector called and he's coming by here, and I don't want any of that, so I'm selling this place. Do you want to buy it?"

Linnea laughed and tried to pull the front of her robe closed, while I sat behind her at the kitchen table, sipping my morning tea. "No," she said.

"Well, I'm selling. Cash only, " he said. Then he turned, poking his way out the door and back down to his car.

We knew we had to make plans fast, that whoever bought this old heap for cash was going to have to either tear it down or renovate or the inspectors would be after them, too. And we were right. The guy who bought it took just a five-minute walk-through, despite the inspector's report listing hazardous plumbing, treacherous electrical outlets, rotted floors, deteriorated windows, unsound porches, and downpours of loose plaster. It was our home. We hadn't let ourselves see how bad it had gotten.

Our latest upstairs neighbor was a good friend we had known since he was seventeen. Elena had accepted an unexpected job offer in Detroit. Nik moved in that January and the new owners evicted him by the end of June. This was just a week before we moved into our new house, not too far away, just the other side of the park, but on a street where people were still surprised when they heard gunshots. Less than a month later, all the woodwork we loved so much was carted away, the stained glass was gone, the wild lilac bushes were shorn, and the siding was painted a flat shade of gray.

Life went on along the avenue. The papers say things are better now. The murder rate is dropping; the gang leaders are in jail, but Jo and Laney told us they found a bullet lodged into the windowsill of their porch. Then we drove by and saw what had been the window of Linnea's study boarded up, and Mickey told us that our old place had become the house on the block most likely to get shot at. One night the crack team raided, breaking in through the front window. "We sure miss you," everyone told us. "That corner is gone."

The summer we moved, the governor ordered state-patrol helicopters to hover over the worst neighborhoods. No one knew quite what they were supposed to accomplish. Patsy growled when she heard them coming. We could see them most nights through the skylights of our new bedroom as they ascended up out of our old neighborhood.

❧

Our old Bohemia, even at its worst, must be only a sliver of what it was like to live through the wars in Zagreb, or Beirut, or Beijing, or South

Central L.A., but still, it amazed me how life went on. That afternoon after the boys were shot, as I stood on my porch contemplating if I'd be able to leave Linnea in the yard and walk the dog around the block, the street was beating slow, a loose-limbed syncopation. Patsy was a furry top of pure want, a whorl of nothing at all but that blue beating moment. Linnea stroked her bike in the yard below us. I watched her solid back, her tattooed arms, her wide legs. Life was going on, right there before me. Linnea polished her bike in rhythmic circles, her face lit up bright as a holy card Madonna. Full of love for her, my molecules spun.

Before I stepped off the porch and down onto the sidewalk, I listened hard, but didn't hear anything but the usual scrape of car tires, the thump of big back speakers, the shriek of children chasing a runaway puppy who zigzagged across a scrawny front lawn, kitty-corner from Luis's stoop. I know I've said enough to convince anyone otherwise, but I still can't call this a bad neighborhood. I refuse to leave it at that. It is a neighborhood with bad spots, hard moments, dangerous surprises that spring up like potholes out of the otherwise solid pavement. But in every house, hearts are beating, while traffic pounds by like waves.

Once we left Portland Avenue, I felt the difference. At first I couldn't sleep in the quiet, and for a while still heard the dusty blasts in my dreams. I missed the porch furniture I had painted with Barney. It was too rotten and full of carpenter ants to move. I missed the rattle of Elena's Yahtzee dice audible through our old kitchen ceiling. I missed my usual turn onto Portland to get home, and sometimes, by accident, I turned there anyway and got teary as I slowed down past our old address. Before the new owner tore it apart, I'd pull over to stare at the sloping bones of its big pea soup facade, the face I had always put on the life I shared with Linnea. Our familiar countenance had vanished. What would we look like now, without this curb to park our cars against, without the key to open this door, without our shared attention to the noise outside to define us? Then my muscles relaxed, my ears changed focus, and even my tremors subsided. When I hear shots on this side of the park, maybe three or four times in the course of a summer, I'm not sure they are shots at all. Maybe firecrackers.

But even in the old neighborhood, fear did not make every moment. That was what I relied on, while watching Linnea's motorbike devotion, while watching Patsy who seemed to actually taste the air with her big open-jawed grin. Sometimes I miss our walks down Portland Avenue with the leaves barely rustling, just a hint of a breeze, maybe the first cough of autumn. Patsy heeled on the way down our old steps, her ears alert, looking up at me with her doggy smile. When we got back from our walk, Linnea would still be there. Her bike would be shimmering, her heart pumping, waiting for me to tell her the story, an anecdote with lots of high notes. She would say, how was your walk my love? I would tell her how happy I was to walk Patsy in the summer, because I will have nodded at neighbors, and answered the questions children asked like yes, she's a German Shepherd and Husky mix and no, you better not pet her because little kids she doesn't know make her nervous. I'll have decided that I was safe, Linnea was safe. There was no one aiming a gun barrel at the lesbian bus that day. My heart will have been beating and the dog will have been smiling and Linnea will have told me she's glad we are home.

Crazy Diamond

The air where I grew up in Chicago is not the same as what I breathe these days in Minneapolis. Chicago's breath is yellow, a kiss from the lips of someone who can't stop smoking. As we approach from the western tollways, Chicago glimmers green through the smog, a skyline mirage, the Emerald City. I always cough as we approach; my lungs bristle, the air harsher than the plain blue Minnesota air I've become accustomed to. About the time we see the giant red-lit lips of the Magikist carpet-cleaning sign at the western edge of the Chicago city limits I am rubbing my neck, aching from the seven-hour drive. I stare out the streaked window, my lips parting, my tongue moving aside, my throat swallowing every gritty electron of a landscape I have tasted hundreds, thousands of times before.

This was how it was when Linnea and I drove back for my baby brother's wedding. Paulie, the youngest, was the first of three kids to go through the ritual, the first to book a church, hire musicians, order a catered meal. But he was not the first to marry, not the way I see it. He wasn't the first to commit, to promise love, honor, and monogamy, not the first to live with the love of his life. I think it happened just the way it should. Me, the oldest, the only daughter, I was the first. But I had no embossed invitations, no aunts and uncles traveling seven hours of smoky highway to attend, no banquet with chicken Kiev, potato and vegetable, no disc jockey, no Croatian musicians from my dad's favorite restaurant on the East Side, no white-frosted, six-tiered, sugar-rosed wedding cake.

None of this was a problem until I started to make comparisons.

When I held our lives next to each other, my brother's looked more like a pretty diamond, mine like plain gray rock without facets, and I was left feeling stoney, unwilling to sing for my baby brother's happiness. Which is not how I felt about his wedding.

I knew that Linnea and I could get married if we wanted to. Lesbians do. It's not legal, of course, but since when did dykes let that sort of thing stop us? I had read whole books about lesbian relationship ceremonies—weddings, holy unions, commitments, trysts. I'd seen photos in silver frames on friends' fireplace mantels and bedroom dressers. I'd even taken a plane all the way to Seattle to watch my first woman lover marry her current woman lover in a pagan ceremony on a green hillside that overlooked a wavy, lapis blue lake. So what was stopping us?

That's the question I asked as we drove back into Chicago. Why didn't we get married? During almost every trip I fantasized out loud about the sort of wedding we might have. My ideas were bright and spun fast like a movie that gets shown in omnitheaters, the screen on all sides and overhead, a galloping picture of the inside of a tornado, or maybe a star exploding. That's how big I wanted our wedding to be.

On the drive to Chicago, on the way to Paulie's wedding, I couldn't stop talking about our wedding. Our invitations will be comic-book style, I said. Linnea just listened, just kept her eyes on the road. Like the old comic-book soap operas, Mary Worth or Brenda Starr, I said. Exactly like Brenda Starr. A beautiful woman in some kind of emotional pain, holding her head, clutching her long, bouncing tresses with manicured fingers, her mouth oh, oh, ohhhing in alarm, her dress too tight, her cleavage busting out of her low-cut blouse. Her Wonder Woman blouse. A tight red femme fatale lesbian superhero blouse. The invitation will say LESBIAN WEDDING across the top, in big bold italics, a comic-book title. Wouldn't it be fun to send an invitation like that to Aunt Cecilia? We'll kidnap a priest, make him marry us. I'll wear a red leather wedding dress.

Linnea just kept driving, chewing her bottom lip as she concentrated on the road. I don't think she took me seriously. The inside of the car we rented to drive to the wedding was clean, uncluttered, so unlike the car I really drove then, a rusted Escort with rosaries hanging from the rearview mirror and statues of the Virgin Mary glued to the dash. The upholstery in the rental car was plush and soft and the seats fell back flat when I wanted to take a nap. The ashtrays were not full of pennies and old Kleenex and crumpled-up cough-drop wrappers. The glove box had no broken pencils, no old hair clips, no rusted screwdrivers, no pretty pieces of raw amethyst from a Lake Superior shoreline rock shop, no scraps of paper with mysterious phone numbers I'd never called. There was nothing in the glove box but the manual. All that clean space. There was room in that glove box for another whole life, a life that might choose any number of weddings.

Linnea always drives when we rent a car. I wonder sometimes why I always let her, wonder if I'm kissing up to some weird notion of what the wife does, what the husband does, old-time pressures to be the rider, not the driver, to be the woman my mother would rather I be. It hardly matters; Linnea is not that sort of husband. If she really were the man passersby sometimes mistake her for, I'd never let her drive. When I dated men, I was an impossible girlfriend, a she-wolf, refusing to bend for anyone. But with Linnea I can relax; I can let her sit behind the wheel. She really wants to drive. She feels safer when she's behind the wheel, and all I really want to do through most of Wisconsin is lay the seat back and sleep.

But that afternoon, the day before my little brother's wedding, it pissed me off that Linnea was driving. She was always driving.

"You never let me drive," I said. I felt the blade in my voice. I didn't like talking to her this way, but I couldn't stop it. I was pinched, squeezed in from both sides by some surprise of geological pressure, too narrow to contain my own insides.

Behind the reflections of the road in Linnea's sunglasses, I could see her eyes pop open too wide. Where did this come from, I could hear her thinking. "I didn't know you wanted to drive." She tried to sound apologetic, but I could tell she was annoyed.

"How can you not know that?" My voice was reaching into its higher registers, almost squeaking. "You know I LOVE rental cars."

"I don't know you love rental cars," she said. "You never told me you love rental cars." I watched her as she talked. She never understood my attachment for things such as rental cars, strangers' living rooms, roadside supper clubs, all the things that help me imagine myself a different person, with a different car, different history, different fingers, nose, lips. Linnea's not like me. She doesn't have to work to keep herself from ghosting away and reappearing as a shadow in the mirage of other people's lives. She always knows who she is. I watched her gaze flatten, her attention to anything but the road dissolve away, like deep green Wisconsin behind us.

Sometimes when I see her focus fall back this way, the skin across my knuckles, behind my lips, gets tighter still, and I keep poking for response. Eventually she will speak again. *Fine. Whatever. If you want.* She will talk, but I won't be satisfied. It could go on for hours. But this time I watched the fog waver around the edges of the approaching lit-up city and I knew I wasn't really mad at her.

What I was really mad at was waiting for us on the other side of downtown Chicago's hazy spires, not visible, then visible again in the wavering distance. I was mad at all of my aunts and cousins and uncles and all of my parents' friends and colleagues and all of the children of all my parents' friends and colleagues who were about to gather under the fat tones of the elevated organ at St. Michael's on the North Side, all them insignificant and gray as little granite icons beneath the five-story marble altar writhing with devils and angels and the long gaunt body of God. They were going to gather and they were going to sing and they were going to pray and make speeches and line up along the carpeted aisle with their tongues extended to accept the host, inviting that long gaunt body into their throats, while Linnea and I would stand back, she in her lavender suit, me in my rose palazzo pants and scoopneck tunic and wearing the little ruby and diamond-dust ring Linnea got down on one knee to give me when we were first in love. We would stand in the back and watch and cry and love Paulie and Mitsuko like crazy, even as we tried not to get in the way.

If we ever did have a wedding of our own, Linnea wanted a picnic. We could rope off a few tables by Lake Nokomis, she said. We might have been in a car on the way to Chicago, or at home sitting on our turquoise sofa, or out at our favorite restaurant in Minneapolis sharing sesame noodles and steamed dumplings. Wherever we were, she always said the same thing. We could grill. We could barbecue chicken. And potato salad. We could play Frisbee with the dogs. Then what happens,

I always asked. I wanted to hear the about the climax, the shivering crescendo, the part where all the lights are up and the sequins sparkle. Nothing happens, Linnea said. We just eat with our friends.

No, no, no, I always told her. I wanted to rent a hall, a place they usually have a show, a storefront cabaret. I wanted to begin with Chinese appetizers and karaoke duets. We could sing together. Maybe "I've Got You, Babe." I wanted our friends to dress up, in drag if they desired, or at least very, very fancy. I wanted my family to come and her family, too, but I didn't want to hide anything. I wanted to kiss right in front of them and I wanted our friends to tell funny stories about us. I wanted Linnea to wear a new tuxedo. I wanted a dress made out of burnt amber lace. I wanted one of my ex-alcoholic hairdresser friends to do my hair, all bouffant and blond as a queen. I wanted to look more like a queen than I had ever looked before, with jewels on my eyelashes and strung through my hair. I wanted to play Tony Bennett songs, and I wanted our dog Patsy and one of her dog friends to be the ring bearers. I wanted pirogi from Kramarcek's on the North Side for my family and I wanted pasta from Delmonico's for Linnea's family and I wanted a lesbian polka band at the end, and I wanted everyone to polka with whomever they wanted, dykes with drag queens, biker babes with my mother. I wanted to lay our whole lives at my family's feet like a stream of crazy jewels, and I wanted them to laugh and be mesmerized. I wanted to see their amazement glimmer in their pupils. I wanted them to say, *your life is beautiful, it really is. We're going to tell everyone.* That's what I wanted.

Linnea always laughed when I told her this, even if we were on the way to Chicago for my brother's wedding and I had been a bitch for hours. She laughed the kind of laugh that tumbled out of her mouth like amber nuggets, the kind of laugh that means she's happy, that she loves me. But at the end she always said the same thing. Honey, that sounds too expensive. Wouldn't you rather take a trip?

As we drove into Chicago for Paulie and Mitsuko's wedding we passed under the Hinsdale Oasis, a glass-enclosed bridge over the tollway all lit up with the golden arches of McDonald's, a greasy, glittering truck stop in the sky. The office buildings of the western suburbs glowed gold in the twilight, and I wondered if they were built to shimmer this way on purpose, to tell people that here, in this distant satellite of the bruised city, here it is rich, golden, here there is money to be made and property to own and here is the place where you will finally crest that hill, the same hill that has been just out of reach, over the horizon, flickering on the other side of the mirage. There's always a mirage. For my parents, it has been me, the mirage of a regular girl getting married to a regular husband in a church on the South Side. We'd have supper at the Knights of Columbus Hall, chicken or ham, potatoes and carrots. I would be thin as a steak knife and wear a poofy white dress. My husband would smash the white cake into my open mouth and I would laugh even though I really wanted to saw his head off. They would tap water glasses with their spoons and we would kiss with dry lips. We'd have a honeymoon in Hawaii if we could afford it. If not, maybe somewhere in Florida, maybe St. Petersburg where I was drunk for three days once when I was in high school. We'd come back and live near them in a clean brick apartment building with white walls and all new appliances. In this mirage, I can't see any more kissing. I can't see my body, not my breasts nor my fingers nor my nose. I can't see the face of my husband. The new baby has no name, just flickers in her crib like a TV show with bad reception. In this mirage, my parents are proud of me.

On the drive back into the air of my childhood I said to Linnea, I don't want to get married. I want to be lovers, always lovers. I want to say the word over and over again. Lovers. LLUUUVVVERS. Do you see the way it falls out of my mouth like a big old shining stone? We are lovers, like the artists in the 1920s and '30s, the ones who lived in Paris in rickety lofts overlooking the smokestacks of the teeming city. We will live in slanted rooms that look like the inside of a rhinestone, painted watery shades of mulberry and bittersweet orange and aquamarine. We will live on coffee, eat when we can, and never, never, go bourgeois. We will stay together because we have to, because our bodies crave each other, because when we are apart, all of the colors fade. People will see us in coffee shops and nod, blow us kisses, but they won't bother us. Everyone will know we are the greatest lovers of all, and don't want to be bothered with their idle chitchat.

Linnea said what she always says, both hands on the rental-car wheel, slowing down behind a semi in the afternoon airport traffic. The west side Magikist lips kiss the grimy, half-lit air over our heads. I rub my neck and cough uncontrollably. Honey, Linnea said, aren't we already married?

Not officially, I whispered back, wanting more from her, from this moment, from the world. So let's go to Las Vegas, I said. Let's elope. My voice was froggy from all that coughing, but I kept on. Let's get married in a drive-through wedding chapel like movie stars on the lam, under a sign that promises thirty-minute service. They won't be able to tell we're two women. We'll stay in the car. They'll only know us by our outfits. Do you think they'll check our drivers' licenses?

Linnea's face lit up like a box of glass beads. I go on this way just to see that look. Yeeeees, she said laughing, drawing out the sound of it, filling the word with all of her breath. A neon drive-through wedding chapel. Like ordering at Taco Bell. We'll say, I do, into a tinny speaker.

Better than Taco Bell, I said. We'll have a certificate for the wall. Married in Las Vegas.

We could rent a white Caddy, Linnea said.

I could wear, I said, a leopard wedding dress.

I reached across the stick shift to squeeze her knee as we laughed, as Linnea laughed, her face bright as a casino marquee. We pictured it together, the neon streaking like bottle rockets over our heads as I lift my dress so I don't muddy the hem when we run across the color-washed plaza on our way into the Four Queens Casino, the sounds of change chinking, of ice cubes clinking, the sound of falling fountain water. Then we laughed until I started coughing again. I let my head fall against Linnea's shoulder. Even if we couldn't pull it off, I said, it would be a fun vacation. As we drove into the Chicago Loop, the tall banks and insurance buildings reached up over our heads, the lit tip-tops gone into the smoky smog, a mirage of the way into heaven.

As we entered the city's center, I let myself fall into a waking dream. In it my brother's wedding is my own. I can be a diamond. Mitsuko's dress is tight across my hips; her garter squeezes my thigh. I dream my mother's cousins rush up to kiss my cheek. The smell of their cigarettes lingers on my skin. I dream my mother cries and can't look Linnea in the eye when she thinks of us on our honeymoon. I dream Paulie and my cousins pass around a beer, guffawing at some joke I don't want to hear. I dream my middle brother Benny borrows the DJ's microphone, sings us a

Frank Sinatra song. I dream there is a silver-draped table in the corner piled high with gifts and flat white envelopes full of cash. I dream the dancing is heady and hot, the hardwood floor rumbling, and even the waitresses in their plain dresses and splattered aprons joining the whorl. I dream Linnea in her long-tailed tuxedo holds me against her chest under the disco ball as the sworling light leaves shivering constellations across the facets of her face. I dream my father stands before the silver microphone, tells jokes about how much he likes Linnea, tells everyone that I have chosen the same husband he would have chosen for me. I dream my cousins and high-school girlfriends tie cans and ribbons to the back of the rental car, giggle as they pelt us with stinging handfuls of bird seed. I dream we drive away in the rain, the mud splattering out from under our tires, as my father smiles and waves sadly, as my mother's bottom lip quivers in the spotty parking-lot light.

This was just too much of a dream, a mirage so filmy, so hard to grasp, I didn't even dare dream it under the cover of night. I could only make it up in the sinking sunlight at the fading end of a day with the blue-gemmed towers of downtown Chicago looming behind our heads as we swerved around the grimy Loop, as I coughed while we passed under billboards that read DA BULLS or featured three-story portraits of Mike Ditka's face. Further south, past Comiskey Park where the White Sox play, I noticed, as I always do, the spot where the South Side Magikist lips used to stand. *Kiss your carpets Magikist clean.* Those giant lips had been colored in with little glittering bulbs that flickered on at dusk, along with the streetlights. This airborne kiss is how I used to know I was almost home. Now, remembering it, my coughing subsided to an occasional sneeze. I was adjusting to being back, in my own body, not diamond, not coal. I'm another kind of jewel that my relatives can't see, the lesbian daughter arriving home with her husband, diamond-backed like a snake, the patterns covered by my clothes. An old song came on the radio, a favorite from my druggy high-school days, "Shine On, You Crazy Diamond." My baby brother was about to get married, was about to live as I do, with someone who is not from our family. His life would be cut into new shapes with exposed planes and surprising shimmers, part of his old life lost. The windows of the rental car were spotted with

Chicago grime and muddy splatter from the damp March expressway. Kiss, Kiss, Kiss, said those crazy jeweled lips, an echo from long before I met Linnea. I was home now to dance at my little brother's wedding. Shine on, shine on, you two crazy diamonds. I hope you are as happy as my lover and me.

Our Muddy Bodies Longing

I cried at my little brother's wedding. I cried before it started. I cried off and on throughout the fragrant and bellowing Mass. I cried at the end in the dim church foyer, as the relatives filed out into the rain and the wedding party filed back in again for photographs.

The bride and groom and dazed attendants wandered back toward the altar as if hypnotized, following the orders of a mumbling man with a camera in his boxy hands and two more slung over his shoulders. I watched, teary-eyed, while the lamp of his flash lit up the hollow cathedral dome over our heads in staggered milliseconds, bright posed moments frozen into the space of a heartbeat.

What was it that pulled the water from my eyes? I wasn't sad. Yet tears flowed, smudging my eyeliner, wetting my cheeks. I am not the type to cry at weddings. I never played bride as a child, never daydreamed about inching down the aisle swaddled in white tulle, never scratched a new name into a denim loose-leaf binder, Mrs. Eddie or Ronnie or Jimmy So and So. These days I watch my young nieces play. These long-haired daughters of Linnea's little sister yelp with glee at any mention of a wedding. They spin ecstatically across carpets in long skirts their mother stitched for them from her old prom gowns as they cradle naked baby dolls in their arms, chanting, keening, *mommy, princess, here comes the bride.*

I don't remember this kind of play in my childhood. My uncles often called me princess, *oh what a princess you are with all that long hair,* having had no idea of what else there was to say to a little girl, their first niece. So, I was interested in princesses, how they wore their hair, the color of their party gowns. But I never imagined my princesses getting married. I had dolls, but they were more literary than anything else, named for the saints, Catherine or Bernadette. Sitting together on a bench under my bedroom window, they wore looks of repose, as if they had an active interior life. I never imagined being their mother, never thought of them as the children I would have after I married. I wasn't interested in the dolls with soft fleshlike skin and bald heads who cried when you tipped them over and wet their diapers when you squeezed a bottle of water into the hole in the center of their heart-shaped lips. I preferred the ones with apartments and convertibles and downtown jobs, like Barbie, or the ones with language skills, like Chatty Cathy (whom I renamed Bernadette) with the tape recorder hidden in her chest, the on/off switch disguised as a red button. I was looking for someone to talk to, and was certain the domain of wife and mother would not be the place to find what I wanted.

Not that I was immune to expectations. I knew about gravity, that boys and girls were supposed to end up in magnetized couples, the plusses and minuses electromagnetically matched, an audible, elemental buzz that echoes through the ages. I had no problem living inside the prevailing current, building elaborate snowflake valentines for my first love, Ronnie Brink, a skinny, disheveled neighbor boy with a shock of blond hair over his forehead and a gap in his front teeth, whom I liked mainly because someone had whispered that he liked me. On the playground the boys chased me down, dragged me by the wrist to Ronnie's side, pinned us both against the chain-link fence on the corner of the elementary-school blacktop. A boy named Stevie played priest in this mock wedding that felt more like a trial. I wriggled, pulled, even tried to bite myself out of their grips. My heart pounded for hours afterward, my breath hard and hysterical, as if they had been holding my head underwater.

By the time I got to high school, my romantic goal was to remain always fleeing and unfettered. Maybe I would drive around the country on my own, like the hippie chicks harboring draft dodgers in James Michener's *The Drifters*. Maybe I would live alone in a ramshackle shack on a beach somewhere, smoking pot and watching the waves until I dissolved into disembodied enlightenment. Whatever my life would be, I was certain I would live it alone. All those women who watched a wedding with water falling down their faces as the bound-up bride minced down the long hushed aisle—I didn't understand. Weddings seemed old-fashioned and implausible, like Beaver Cleaver's mother. Like virginity. I laughed at marriage, spat on marriage. Why should I tear up at my little brother's wedding? Salty bubbles skidded down my cheeks as I snuffled quietly into my sleeve. Camera flashes brightened the stifling air like lightning, and Linnea, my real love, my unexpected and chosen, the one I talk to, Linnea noticed, as she always does, and fished a hanky out of the inside breast pocket of her suit jacket.

~

The rain beat down steadily on the day of Paulie and Mitsuko's wedding. The sound of it sunk in under our skin. Rain has a way of bringing on the body's sadness, the continuous sound of falling water pulling everything down, down. The weight of gravity. Old melancholy comes dislodged, courses down.

Not that I was sad about Paulie and Mitsuko's wedding. Not at all. Yet on the day of the wedding with rain pummeling against the windows of the room where Linnea and I slept, I woke up sad. I was weepy with memory, with the faces of all the girls I hadn't seen since high school. Where were they now? Probably married, or divorced and remarried, and some of them, the ones who were pregnant before graduation, with children old enough to be married. Rain misted the freeway all the way downtown to the wedding Mass at St. Michael's. My whole life was caught in my throat, the way it always catches there when I come home, when my past and present collide into one immense breath, impossible to swallow.

Under the dome of a Catholic cathedral incense has a wallop it holds no place else. Inside an enormous stone-vaulted chamber, where the air is woolly with holy aroma, where a multitude of candle flames writhe and sputter at Mary's marble feet, where the polished wood pews are watery with shadows, where the blue-violet and umber and forest green beams of half-light through stained glass wash the flat planes of our faces into watercolor, where the stations of the cross repeat the same circle around us all, the inevitable march, the story that gets told and told again until it is more than a story, until it is the underpinning of all we believe, all we assume is as necessary as the blood and water circling through our veins and capillaries—here in the church, incense becomes the body. The body becomes incense, becomes the church, and we all become one organ-thumping organism. I squeezed Linnea's elbow as we walked into St. Michael's. Already I was starting to tear up.

And then I was thirsty, all of a sudden, despite the rain outside and the itchy, teary corners of my eyes. I knew there was not enough water in the city to quench me. There was a prickling in the back of my throat. My dry tongue made a scraping sound when it nudged the back of my teeth.

"I need water," I whispered to Linnea as I gazed at the still pools of the holy water fonts, cupped and beckoning in the arched doorway to the main chapel. I have always imagined that holy water would taste like perfume, like lavender water from an old-fashioned crystal bottle with a squeeze-pump spray. I pulled Linnea away, toward a side door, holding her tight by the elbow of the long black leather dress coat I'd given her years ago, the first Christmas we lived together.

"There must be a drinking fountain somewhere," I whispered. She nodded, her face focused, as intent as she always is when I ask her to help me. I felt her open palm and the bands of her wide silver rings against my back as we stepped through the door into a shadowy alcove filled with busy bridesmaids, Japanese and American. The stiff material of their dresses scraped as they hurried around us. There were other women too, some Japanese, Mitsuko's well-dressed sisters and cousins just in from Japan. My relatives came with bags and sacks under their arms, some looking only vaguely familiar, my half-forgotten aunts and third cousins wearing the various faces of Eastern Europe and the white South Side of Chicago, shaking out umbrellas or moving unruly piles of coats from one wooden bench to another. In the corner was a shock of fuzzy light. A holographic dream projection. Mitsuko in her wedding dress.

She was the kind of bride you see in a bridal magazine, the sort that would send our nieces careening into spins and yelps, *bride, bride, bride*. My experience with American bridal magazines is too limited to know if the models are ever Japanese, but everything else matched the standard image. The creamy makeup. The too-smooth-to-be-real skin. The rolled and tendriled hair. The white cloud of a dress. She was a soft-focus, gauzy vision. I gasped for a moment, sputtered in spite of myself. "Oh, you look so beautiful."

It had been years since I'd been that close to a bride. The last time had been 1979, at the wedding of Wendy Wosinski, my high-school synchronized-swim-team pal. I'd been to three funerals in the five years prior to Paulie's wedding, but no weddings at all, not a one, in the last fifteen. I lived too far away from my cousins and childhood friends. I was immersed in the early AIDS-era world of young gays and lesbians, where massive ritual gatherings were more likely to mark that another young man had died. Weddings were a heterosexual thing, a custom from another country that had nothing to do with me, a thing that happened in history or in the movies but not in my life. But that wasn't the whole reason. I lived only eight hours' drive from so many of these family pageants. The truth is that I'd avoided weddings for all these years, as if I were avoiding the memory of a near drowning, and so weddings had become strange to me.

Fifteen years earlier I'd arrived at Wendy Wosinski's wedding late. The congregation was already seated, the first strains of the bride's music already begun. Wendy stood in the back with her arm crooked around her father's elbow. Her long narrow gown fit her like an opera glove. She seemed in a trance, unaware of anything but the first mincing step she was about to make down the long gold-carpeted aisle on her father's arm. I stood back near the weighty wood doors, stunned by the heavy thump of the organ and the tendrils of incense that had made it all the way to the back, and I was stunned by Wendy. She was so relaxed and coordinated. The long contoured train of the dress billowed behind her while centuries-old organ music wrenched between the dark slanting walls of Holy Ghost, a wide, one-story 1950s-style church just a couple of blocks from where we both went to high school. Wendy belonged in this moment. She could have been a statue carved out of the polished mahogany beams, another among Mary and the saints.

Not me. In my madras wraparound hippie skirt and with long raggedy hair woven back in an everyday braid, I was alien, an intruder, even though I used to live here, too, used to eat the host here every Sunday, used to fake my confessions on Saturday afternoons in the coffin-shaped boxes in the back, and used to crouch on the hard pew kneelers afterward. I had seethed and twisted with my own inability to just say my ten Hail Marys and be done with it, to simply believe and leave.

Wendy Wosinski's wedding happened at one of those moments when a girl like me is twenty years old and certain that if I turned right I would have one sort of life, if I turned left I would have another. Now I see that this might not be true, that people make heart choices, make sex choices their whole life through. Off the top of my head, I can think of three women I am close to today, lesbians, who were once married to men and didn't come out until they were past thirty. And in this same instant I can think of at least three more who are "has-bians," women who lived a lesbian life for years, and now are married to men. What's more, I know men who were once women, women who lived whole lives as men. There's a person in my city who lived sixty-five years as a man, had a career in the air force, and today is a woman who calls herself lesbian. I never would have thought, at age twenty, that the charge pulling me to any one desire, any single static comprehension of self, could be stashed away, saved for later when I would be free to choose again. Decide or die, that's what I thought.

Before Wendy's wedding I had been hovering, afloat between gravity and flight. At twenty, the urge to claim an identity can be as bodily and craving as thirst. I'm glad I quenched myself, glad I found lesbians, came out, had my first few disastrous affairs while I was still young enough, romantic enough, to avoid acknowledging how sloppy and awkward romance can be. I am relieved that I didn't drag the debate out for ten more years. I am glad my thirties have not brought on an abrupt identity shift, with all the re-visited adolescence that naturally accompanies any coming-of-age. I am glad of so many other choices as well, glad I didn't drug myself to death on a driftwood beach, glad I didn't tour the country in a pop-top van, because now I know what trouble those girls can get into. What I found in the late-seventies, late-disco-era, college-town bars in my drunken years did damage enough. Yet my young deportation from all that was expected of me, even if self-imposed, had consequences. Once the choice had been made and I began to flap away from heterosexuality and its rituals, it was as if some sensory organ shut down. An organ that would have allowed me to keep identifying the shrinking landscape inching away below me—my family, Chicago, all my cousins' weddings—the world I had abandoned.

How many family weddings did I miss in the fifteen years since Wendy Wosinski's nuptials? They were all probably a lot like Wendy's big day, a lot like Paulie's, too. First the Catholic church is filled with the blood-beating pulse of the organ, the fluttering candle flames, the giddy fog of incense. Next a meal in some rented hall, and a band or disc jockey as the aunts and uncles from the old East Side neighborhoods circle the room in a big, bobbing, polka wheel, then split apart to dance free-form to the kid's rock and roll, all elbows and gawking grins. My cousin Antony, whom I have known since one month after my birth, is the closest thing to a generational echo I have in my family. Three times he has waited by the altar for the slow measured steps of his bride. I could have gone. I was invited, expected, but something about the turnabout view from which I hovered kept me from even considering it. The first time I didn't even remember to return the reply card.

If gravity has a sound, it would have to be that of rain, the constant, inevitable, pummeling, pushing into, under the earth's crust. The force that causes the rain to fall down instead of up, that causes the bits of bricks loosened by storm to drop and the rain collected in the gutters to run downhill, this is the same force that holds the Earth, the sun, the stars together. It's what holds the planets in their orbits. It's what keeps the big rock of Earth from breaking apart. We tend to think the same of our customs, the rituals of common culture. Without the nuclear family, our politicians tell us, without that fundamental thing, the one-man-one-woman marriage, our shaky organization will break apart, our insignificant bodies will no longer be held to any ground, our limbs and hair and lost shoes will spin through space, a cubist collage of all we hold dear. The thing we celebrate at almost every one of these cultural pageants, these things we call weddings, is our contract with nature, our agreement to behave as we believe the authority of gravity demands. But gravity is the least understood of all the elements. Suction, a helium balloon, helicopters, super glue, a dollar bill let loose in the wind, all defy the gravitational field. If the politicians, the morning commuters, the crowd at the baseball game would just look up, if the wedding parties, the mothers and fathers of the bride and groom and the guests in their party clothes and polished shoes would follow the wave of the organ bellow out the heavy church doors and up into the heavens, they might all see the rest of us up here, alone, in pairs, in odd-numbered clusters, unbound and flapping, proving that nature is always more complex than we want to believe.

But what do I know about nature, about weddings? I am the unnatural one who flew too high, was too giddy with my discovery of gravity's loophole, the one who like Icarus was free until I took it too far, who thought my escape proved not complexity but reversal. There is no gravity. There is no craving for the old Earth, for the deep cushion of ancient culture. There is no other world than my own, up here, where I do what I want, where I soar and skirt the sun. I didn't feel my feathers melting away, didn't notice until too late how they spun and glittered on their way back down.

The noise of gravity was constant on Paulie and Mitsuko's wedding day, but Mitsuko seemed oblivious to all stimuli. No sights, no sounds registered on her carefully creamed face. She and Paulie had been up all of the night before, searching for her sisters' lost luggage, and she was already exhausted from the weeks of preparation for the Big American Wedding, the wedding that had turned out even bigger than she had imagined, once the gravity of my family had taken hold. (Family priest, or funny Father Keena from St. Michael's? The rude organist from the home parish or someone who doesn't have to commute all the way downtown? And who should sit with whom at the reception?)

I knew about all of this, all the pressure, all the family quirks that Mitsuko and I like to whisper about in less formal settings. Still, all I could think to say when I saw her there, all lit up, a dream of herself, was "Oh, so beautiful." There she was, draped in the trappings of every Rodgers and Hammerstein musical and Shakespearean comedy, every princess fairy tale, every Walt Disney movie, every question my uncles had ever asked me when I was small—*and who do you want to marry someday, little princess?* I knew she was just Mitsuko, my almost sister-in-law, whom I had loved since the first time Paulie had put her on the phone to talk to me. ("You say it, Mitsuko. Pronounce M, then *it's cold*," she said.) Still, in that moment, she was an icon to me, a light-filled globe of marriage.

I was so thirsty my throat itched, but I stood and stared anyway.

What was happening was something I had not expected. My grief for what I had left behind was a sudden plummet, a hard splash into the frigid, undrinkable sea. Mitsuko barely moved a face muscle to greet me. Her maid of honor, a thin woman with permed blond hair, Mitsuko's best friend from her college years in Ohio, leaned over her, touching up the rouge, the red lipstick, intent on the tiniest details of her canvas. The wide skirts of Mitsuko's dress, supported by antebellum metal hoops, bounced like a slinky down to her ankles, and her face was so powdered and smooth she looked like a living photo touch-up job. Just before I cried, I felt a slight vertigo. I was a loosened feather spinning toward Earth. I was a long-haired four-year-old in my mother's remade dress. It was all I could do to keep from spinning and keening—*bride, bride, bride*.

~

Adam and Eve were formed from two halves of a ball of clay. Once separate, their muddy bodies longed for each other. This is the story Father Keena told at Paulie and Mitsuko's wedding. The myths of creation march around us, endless, inevitable. Do we create the myths or do they create us?

Not too long after Wendy Wosinski's wedding I saw a puppet show. I had a boyfriend then but I was trying to leave him. I was in fact on a date with a woman, the second woman I had ever kissed on the mouth, the second I had slept with. She had a fresh scrubbed face, a short spiky haircut, a drum set in her living room, a job in a vegetarian restaurant collective. I liked her because she was funny and offbeat, but I felt no age-old buzz, no pull from the gut, no muddy body longing for the other half of itself. Instead I was dating her because I had to choose. Earth or air.

The puppet show was an old Italian folktale, full of birth and love and aging and death and rebirth. The usual circle. It was the love scene that made me cry. The puppets with their nodding papier-mâché heads and patterned clothing. The woman with a scarf around her hair, the sort my great-grandma from Poland used to wear. The man's dashing and bare papier-mâché head both virile and vulnerable. In the love scene they spun around each other, their limp puppet feet just grazing the dust that surfaced from the floor. They spun and glittered, an inevitable twirling, *love, love, love*. And then they were married.

I could not explain to the nice woman I was dating why the puppets made me sob. She knew I had a boyfriend I was trying to leave. She may have thought I was crying for him, and perhaps I was, a little. He was an older man, a mentor, the sort of liaison I don't approve of now. I was trying to leave a good friend, trying to leave a parent/lover, trying to rise up against all the spinning forces of history that seemed to me to be so beckoning, so undulating, so likely to drown me. That nice woman wanted me to tell her why I was crying, but I couldn't. It was a sloppy, choking date, our last.

My muddy body longs for Linnea. Her muddy body longs for mine. But Father Keena never really suggested magnetic mud, physical melding, that being too bawdy for the Catholic church. No, that's the part I added in my mind. Father Keena said that Adam and Eve were formed from one body of clay and I thought, yes, my muddy body longs for Linnea, our clay forms spin and glitter, and we are married.

But we are not married, not in the eyes of this congregation, not in the eyes of Father Keena, although I can imagine talking to him about it. He seemed so nice with his cragged beaming face, his arms open before the congregation, so amused when my Aunt Vera and Grandma Rose marched up to him in their satiny hose and party pumps, before the service, to asked if this rainy Saturday afternoon wedding Mass would take care of their Sunday obligation.

It was raining, too, the night Wendy Wosinski told me she was going to marry the boy across the street. The rain needled against the cracked window of the old Dodge I was driving. For a while it came down fast enough to flood the glass with tiny light-filled droplets. Then it slowed, dropping noisily, pin by pin.

Most of what we had in common, Wendy and I, was water. It was those long nights of swim-team practice, chlorinated laps of first arms only, then legs only, then the eggbeater kick, to make our thighs strong. I was best at the underwater distances. How long could I glide under the heavy bricks of water without coming up for air? Half a lap? More? I worked up to two, and it was my favorite time, alone in the blue-tiled depths, the silence complete, arms and legs suspended but still moving. As long as there was air in my lungs I had to fight to stay low, the tips of my breasts just grazing the pool floor, gravity reversed. There were hours more after that, the slow work synchronizing show routines, the perfection of the tricks, vertical spinning descents or arched-back circles around invisible rings, but it was the underwater reverie, the defiance of water, the whole body breath control that I remember best. In the showers afterward we slouched under the running spray, the sticky Lycra of our suits smacking against our skin as we pulled the fabric back and let it loose again. I envied her narrow thighs, her small but firm breasts. She envied my height, my naturally long eyelashes, my eyes that changed color in certain light. Like me she was olive-toned, the type to tan quickly in even the slightest sun, without burning. We could have been cousins.

Wendy, oh Wendy, I was better at literature. You were better at math. We were both planning to leave, me to read books, you to collect numbers in your head like colored marbles. He was a guy who used to tease you when you were a kid, a guy you used to spray with a hose on Saturdays when you stood in your driveway in your bikini, sudsing up your father's car. Did you feel the Earth's flat geographical plains shifting along a fault line when you kissed him? Do you spin and glitter through the sudsy water together, shouting, we are married, married, married?

When you told me, that night in the car, your face glowed like a polished pear. The rain pricked against the dashboard, your face fell into and out of the golden beam of the streetlight and you told me that you had stumbled across the thing we are all supposed to be seeking, the center vein, the precious metal corridor to the main ventricle. You faced me. You talked. Your face was like my face, the face of a South Side girl with Eastern European roots, the face of girl who had made her choice. Your face shone like the night-light I'd kept on my dresser since I was a kid, a woman spinning in ruffled petticoats, bright from the heat of the bulb beneath her skirts. You shone and you shrunk as our bodies pulled away from each other, smaller and smaller, until we were both specks on the way to another country.

As I stood in the foyer of Holy Ghost, late for Wendy Wosinki's wedding, I wondered if she still carried numbers in her head. Was she counting the beats leading up to her first measured step? Then her heavy veil swung around and she saw me. She broke her pose for a moment and waved, wildly, a girl from another time gesturing madly from the deck of a steamer ship. I was shocked and almost forgot to wave back. I had broken into a holy diorama, a sacred scene, and now here she was, the lead statue, waving at me. *Good-bye, Wendy. Good-bye.* Then the heavy thumps of the bridal march sounded and she snapped back to attention, and I watched the long pull of her train as she took her first steps down the aisle.

When Mitsuko did the same, all these years later, I cried as I hadn't cried since that whirling puppet show. I wasn't the only one. As the watercolored outlines of the stations of the cross splintered over all our heads and the even thump of the organ matched our heartbeats, eyes were welling up right and left. My mother was smiling a little, tight-lipped, but water was spilling out over her cheeks. Mitsuko's sisters were wiping their eyes with handkerchiefs. My cousin Dino, always dramatic, looked as if he were about to fall back into the pew and let out an ecstatic wail. I could see that even Linnea had a little pool welling up in the corner of one eye, if I looked close.

The incense wafted, spirits rose from the feet of the saints, and the music made the rafters of our bodies shake. I had been so thirsty, so salt-water drowned, and never did find a fresh-water fountain, but now my thirst was spotting away as I cried along with the rest, and kept crying until the photographer's strobe lit through the incense clouds like storm current. I might have been crying just because I was supposed to, the sputtering candle smoke, the incense in my eyes, the great marble altar with St. Michael pinning the devil to the dirt with his great stone heel, all conspiring to bring forth my feeling. I might have been crying because my baby brother was grown, was making his choice, was living a life private and precious, apart from us. I might have been crying because I so furious at the way Paulie and Mitsuko got to spin and glitter in the gravity of family, within the gravity of this big bellowing church, that they got to and I didn't, their union universal, mine and Linnea's a fragment of gravity's collapse—loose pieces of what some will always see as one of nature's black holes. I might have been crying because I had left, because this was my family, my people, and yet their customs had nothing to do with me—but I don't think that was it, not entirely. I might have been crying, finally, not because I had left but because I had returned, my head and heart graced with this day's holy water, my muddy body longing for Linnea, her muddy body longing for mine. We had returned, both married and not, to the city where my Polish great-grandma spread a babushka over her hair on the way to her Sunday obligation, in the country where Linnea's tattooed Italian grandpa married the one his muddy body longed for, his bare head virile and vulnerable. We had returned to the place where our long-haired nieces reel with dreams of growing up into love, the scene of my ingenious escape and my teary plummet home, my choices still standing, my questions never answered, my wax-and-feather wings at once drowned and rising, both of this country and of another, skirting the sun and spinning, glittering in the mud.

Boom

And then there was dancing. At Paulie and Mitsuko's wedding there were the gentle, bobbing turns of the slow dances, the women's ringed fingers clinging to the men's suited shoulders as Sinatra sang out from the DJ's stereo, the men's big hands circling tight around the women's dressed-up waists, the sway right, sway left, as if the wind caused them to lean together, so smoothly to and fro. There were fast dances, too, the latest rock and roll, the young ones swimming and spinning, the women's bare shoulders dappled in disco light, the men's dress jackets tossed aside, the parents and aunts and uncles dancing too, ties and clip-on earrings flapping and jiggling, chins bobbing to the hard bass DJ beat. There were the usual traditional numbers, the shuffling polka wheel, the swing lindy, the cackling chicken dance. There was that public/private moment where the groom locked eyes and waltzed with his dazed bride. There was the sobbing bride's dance as Mitsuko wept in the arms of an uncle she hadn't seen for years, here all the way from Japan. There was the dizzy free-for-all, the garter tossed, the bouquet caught, the Japanese sisters and cousins giggling through a crooked kickline. Mitsuko's hoop skirt spun like a lace top. Paulie tossed off his jacket to reveal his confetti-print party shirt. Everyone danced.

Everyone, except a certain few. By the looks of goings-on at most big family weddings one might assume that gays and lesbians don't dance, at least not with each other. At this wedding, for instance, my cousin Dino and his boyfriend Danny, along with my love Linnea and I, spent too much time huddled in our seats. One night in a gay bar would reveal the truth, that homos can and do cling and spin, bob, squawk and glitter, fueled by the booze or the beat or the excruciating urge to touch in public. But not here, at our brothers' and cousins' weddings.

Sitting it out on the sidelines, Dino and Danny seemed at sea. My cousin used to bring a fake girlfriend to these family affairs, someone known in the gay world as a *beard*, because of how she appears as proof that her date is really a he-man, capable of growing stubble on his chin, able to attract a female. Almost any female will do, as long she is what a girlfriend is supposed be, testosterone's opposite, a real woman. I have heard from my mother that Dino has put on a great show at weddings, catching the garter, slipping it up just a little too high on his date's thigh, swinging his faux beau around the dance floor with a theatrical gusto that only a masquerader can muster. My mother asks me, "Are you sure about him? If you could have seen him at Frankie's wedding . . . "

Dino and Danny were invited as a couple to Paulie and Mitsuko's big night, but they would have brought women this time, too. Danny would have been passed off as a friend, just Dino's roommate, except that I got so mad when I heard their plans. Dino called me a few weeks before the wedding, from Chicago where he lives still, in the thick of our family. "Of course, we're bringing girls," he told me. He must have heard the boom of disapproval in my voice, safely righteous so far away in Minnesota. It's not that I didn't understand what he was afraid of. It's just that he brought it up so casually, as if he assumed Linnea and I had made similar plans. As if it were even possible, boxy Linnea dressed up as a girl and passing unnoticed through the throng of our family, or me faking it with some guy, as if I would prefer to jack up the hopes of all my aunts and second cousins. "Is Barrie next? At last?"

What I said to Dino were the same few words, repeatedly. "Why would you bring girls? Why do that?"

"The aunts. The aunts," he said every time.

"But it's humiliating, to pretend."

"But we'll be so much more comfortable."

I don't know for certain if I was the one to change their minds, but that was the last I heard of their girls. Once I was there, however, on my old home ground, I wasn't as certain of what was best for them. Dino and Danny were not so comfortable, sitting out most of the evening in the shadows, sipping drinks and whispering. Tranquil Danny with the

WASPy movie-star features was always quiet anyway, but Dino, such a big-mouthed Italian, was boisterous all through dinner. Then he swung a few jitterbugs with Grandma Rose and the great aunts who didn't stop dancing to comment on whom he'd come in with. But later he was subdued. Beardless. A gay extrovert with nothing to do at the wedding but watch the straight people dance.

∼

The hall where Paulie and Mitsuko held their reception was out where there used to be farmland, but you would never know it now. These days it's a freeway plain, a constant parade of grimy, rumbling trucks bellowing black smoke. The soot in this place settles into the air, imperceptible unless you notice that everything is a shade duskier here than it is farther out, away from the semi-truck exhibition and the northeast Indiana mill emissions. It wasn't until I left and came back again that I was aware for the first time how perception changes the shade of fact, how the air of my childhood had a slight gray-eyeglass tint, noticeable for only a moment before it disappeared. The wedding ceremony had been in a cathedral on the other side of the city. Incense and altar art. Votive candles flickering at Mary's feet. The glass-busting wail of "Ave Maria" trembled up to the rafters and down into our stomachs. But that was thirty minutes north of the sooty South Side freeway plain where I really come from.

Some people are the same wherever they go. Linnea's that way. Her speech patterns change a bit when she has been around her Italian mother and grandmother, but other than that she is the same person wherever you put her. Not me. Places get under my skin and I get confused, forget my lines. I mutter to myself when I lose my place this way. This ground where I began is not so different from any other industrial settlement of the blue-collar descendants of Eastern European immigrants. (Urban New Jersey reminds me of this place. So does the grimy port side of Superior, Wisconsin, and Tacoma, Washington, and Queens.) When I am back here on Chicago's South Side and lower suburbs, my corpuscles pop with the stench of truck fumes and the billows of mill sulfur I remember from childhood. I feel a slight dimming, a stretch of the shadows I don't always recall when I am at home with Linnea in Minnesota.

The old barn Paulie and Mitsuko booked for the reception was just past the Tinley Park Mental Hospital, across from a trailer park, adjacent to a fake lake. The building had been renovated especially for weddings, complete with a restaurant kitchen, two bars, a disco ball for the marvel of after-dinner dancing. The wood inside was chestnut-colored, polished bright, and the overhead beams were bare, the ceiling open all the way up to the arched barn roof. It was unique and sweet; I understood why Mitsuko, who grew up in Japan loving American country quilts and *Little House on the Prairie* novels, would have picked such a place.

But the mirror-backed bars, one on each floor, the stiff white banquet tablecloths and heavy white plates and coffee cups, the waitresses in pale orange uniforms and square-toed white shoes, and the heavy butter and meat smell coming from the kitchen were all too familiar to me. It was that supper-club smell that reminded me of all the restaurants where I had worked while still in high school, and again after I dropped out of college. I had prepared for everything in the weeks leading up to this wedding—the days off work, the rental car, the fresh haircut with deep edges that left the nape of my neck exposed. I'd thoroughly thought out my outfit of palazzo pants with a scooped-neck, bell-sleeved tunic, patterned with the faint shapes of roses, and my arty silver and green turquoise jewelry. Linnea and I decided that she would wear the crystal pin I gave her on our first Valentine's Day instead of her usual dress tie. What I didn't plan for was a smell that would hurl me back to the days when I could not have even said the word lesbian, not to mention shown up at my brother's wedding with my female lover in tow.

The only thing I remember about lesbians from when I was growing up was the response I once felt to the very thought of anything homo, a shock wave in the pit of my stomach, the lip-twisting revulsion. This is not something I recall being explicitly taught, although it's not hard to see where it came from. Today I go out of my way to read gay histories and attend screenings of documentaries that catalogue all the ways lesbians and gays used to be pictured in books, in movies, on television, but it's not so much the obvious images that shock me into memory—not the ridiculous lisping men in pink kerchiefs, not the rough-hewn women's prison matrons. Rather, it's all the spaces between the spoken words that I ran into long before I knew how to think about such things. The unutterable revelation that deteriorates into a shadowy camera angle. The zoom shot in on lips too shocked to speak.

Given the cultural climate, it's no surprise that we never spoke of such things when I was a girl. I didn't know anyone in our 1960s neighborhood of steelworkers and schoolteachers whose parents filled them in about much that had to do with our bodies. I think of the time I asked my mother where babies came from and she nervously handed me a mysterious pink pamphlet, published by the Modess company, with silhouetted drawings of ovaries and tubes and a gourd-shaped uterus. Then one day at school, during the time we usually had gym class, the boys and girls were separated without warning. The boys hooted and whistled as if we had all suddenly lifted our skirts and showed them our underpants. The girls filed down to a polished wood hall that usually housed volleyball nets, gymnastic mats, and fold-down lunch-room tables. We tittered nervously in stiff folding chairs while we watched a movie about once-a-month blood, about a girl whose mother let her have a yellow dress she craved now that she was a woman, and the stigma of VD depicted as a white X drawn across the abdomen of this bobby-soxed girl, that letter-sweatered boy.

None of it quite explained how the baby gets in the girl's body, despite the cartoons of sperm fish endlessly throwing themselves at the placid hovering eggs. That night I had a dream that men have an extra thing hanging between their thighs. Not the *pee pee* I had seen on my brothers, but another tube, a hose for the sperm. In my dream a man put that tube up into my secret hollow, out of which the blood was supposed to flow, and I was pregnant. That's the way I thought it went, for months. I considered it on the way home from school, shuffling over sidewalks covered with the little brown seedpods we called whirlybirds. The sky shuddered from another sonic boom and I walked faster. No matter how often I was told that the blast came from a very fast plane that had broken through what adults confidently called "the sound barrier," sonic booms seemed to me a Cold War warning, as ominous as bombs.

Those whirlybirds with their thick round heads and spinning tails looked like the cartoon sperm I had seen in the menstruation movie. I kicked them with my toes, crunched them with my heels all the way home from the school bus. Then I suddenly knew, for no reason at all, that there wasn't an extra tube hanging like a garden hose between men's legs. It was all one thing, the *pee pee*, the penis. That was where babies came from. A gust of wind blew a clattering shower of whirlybirds down from the maple trees and I thought I heard the thin whistle of another fast plane on the smoky horizon. *Boom.* So that's how it was done.

I was not so obviously intuitive when I asked my mother about homo-sexuals. I was reading the *Chicago Tribune,* the *Ask Ann Landers* column. A woman wrote in complaining that her husband was a homosexual. I was sitting on the nappy green front-room couch with the grimy paper spread across my lap, when my mother walked by in her work clothes— slim-cut sweatpants, white polyester polo shirt, a whistle on a long white cord that swung like a pendulum between her breasts. Her mahogany hair was ratted into a sensible bouffant just above her bangs. My mother was a Physical Education teacher in a high school one district south from the one where we lived. Although she's only acknowledged it once or twice, I know now that she must have worked with lesbians, every-day, in the gym, in the locker room, in the Women's P.E. teachers' lounge with the picture window that looked out over a basketball court. But I hadn't heard much about lesbians then. I only knew that whatever their off-hour proclivities, there were two kinds of women in my mother's whistle-bobbing, clipboard-grasping profession—the ones with big hair like my mom's and the other ones who did not wear lip-stick and whose hair was not so high.

My mother backed up a full step or two that sunny afternoon in our green shag living room when I asked, "Mom, what's a homosexual?"

"That's a man who hates women," she said, without even a pause. The twist in her lips was not quite visible, but I could hear it in her voice. "What are you reading?"

She snatched the paper off my lap before I could absorb Ann Lander's reply to the poor wife with the husband who hated her in some new way I hadn't heard of before. It wasn't the words so much that stuck with me.

I knew somehow that they weren't quite the truth. Rather it was the twist in her tongue, as if she were sucking a bitter Life Saver, and the slight shudder in her step as she swept out of the room.

~

It was this same shudder that began to follow me the moment I smelled that South Side supper-club smell at my brother's wedding reception. I had forgotten all about it, and now here I was among my people who had surely grown up inside that same collective spasm. How could I know who had shrugged it off, whose body still jangled in its wake? I noticed a shadow, and then I noticed Linnea, how she looked that night, so handsome in her violet suit, her pale green shirt, the crystal pin that gleamed from her top button. She stayed beside me during the cocktail hour of the reception where my family stood and sipped as the low murmur of their voices rose and fell between the cedar beams like one breathing body. I looked at Linnea and saw the illumination of love. What did they see?

My father's brother, a college teacher, one of few in our family to have left Chicago, shook Linnea's hand. His caterpillar eyebrows rose and fell like an inchworm as he asked her questions about where she taught, how she liked her students. Dino's little brother Frankie, the most sweet-tempered of my cousins, walked right up with the wife I had only heard about on his arm and said, "Why is it we never see you around here anymore?" So far so good. We were safe, it seemed, as long as we didn't say much.

Yet to a few others it was apparent that our presence there together broke right through the sound barrier. I introduced Linnea to one of my father's good friends, a high-school English teacher like my dad. He was someone I had always liked when I was a kid because he listened to rock and roll and danced with his wife, at sit-down parties, in restaurants, right in front of everyone. When I was in my early twenties, he wrote me a letter, asking me to suggest names of books by woman writers he might want to read, and I sent him back a list in which I asterisked novels written by lesbians, and so I thought he knew about me. But when I said to him on this night, "I would like you to meet my lover Linnea," his face whitened a shade or two and he actually began to stammer. I was too stung to stick around to find out if it was the word "lover" that flustered him so, or if it was just the fact of Linnea and me.

I didn't do much better with the wedding photographer. "I'm the sister of the groom," I told him, when it was clear I wasn't on his agenda. "Please take my picture with Linnea here, because we're together." The photographer was a big guy with droopy pants, and the heavy cameras hanging from his shoulders caused him to stoop. He stared at me in incomprehension, as if I were one of the wedding guests trying to speak to him in Japanese. In his photograph of us, Linnea's face is too boxy and pale, and I look wide-eyed and puffed as a blowfish, as if he had managed to capture on film exactly how we appeared to him.

I wonder if we look different in different places, if my flesh changes as I step onto old ground, if Linnea's body changes when she comes home with me. What is common, normal among our friends and daily acquaintances, becomes a phenomenon, a curiosity, a wonder. I know this only because I am from this place, too. I remembered another self when Linnea whispered, "Those people over there are staring at me."

People gawk when they are curious, when they are scared, when they are disgusted, when they are in awe of a thing that astonishes—a movie star, a car wreck. I looked to where she nodded and saw the smoky corner where my mother's cousins huddled, staring at Linnea or peering toward the table of Mitsuko's relatives from Japan. These watchers were my relations from the side of the family I don't often see. Their bodies were wider than before, their hair grayer, harbingers, perhaps, of the body mine will become. They came to the wedding in pastel-print dresses or good spring jackets, Sunday pumps and polished dress shoes. My mother, true to gym-teacher form, was a virulent antismoker and had wanted to make this a no-smoking affair, but if she had succeeded, it would have been her relatives who missed out, tittering and puffing their way through this wedding's after-dinner hours.

I felt a jolt in my chest when I saw all these faces I hadn't had even a glimpse of for years, and I wanted go to them for kisses and questions. Yet so far I had walked a wide berth around their table, afraid of what they would think of Linnea and me, worried about what I might want to say to them in return. When I saw how my great aunts and second cousins stared, I wanted to get all up in their faces about it. I am so quick to disdain the attitudes of my relatives, even when my father, one of few I knew growing up who insisted it was wrong to be prejudiced, has tried to assuage me by saying, "They can't help the way they were raised," or when Mitsuko shrugs and says, "My marriage to Paulie, it's not for everyone," and especially when Dino proclaims, "Why would you want to say anything that would pull you away from the family?"

Unlike Dino, I have already pulled away. When I return, I can't tell which is more important—the heart flutter I feel when I recognize another face I have known since the week I was born, or my other constant, the continual seething of a body dead-set against the countless things that are not so much the ideologies of the people I grew up around as what they have always known. Most of both my parent's aunts, uncles, and cousins are average, working, white people from a dirty city with a not-too-distant immigrant past. They don't read many books. They don't know any foreign languages. They have not undergone diversity training or sobered up or stopped smoking. They tend to think the best of anyone related to them. They tend to hate what they know nothing about.

My father told me, just after Paulie and Mitsuko got engaged, that he remembered how the movies of his adolescence, during World War II, depicted the Japanese as the yellow menace. They were lunatics in bomber cockpits. They had evil squinty eyes and deranged smiles. They were not human. The Japanese are a people he can finally see, he said, but only because his son is marrying Mitsuko. "Those movies, they were just propaganda," he tells me now, shaking his head as if he can't believe he fell for it.

People do fall for the first big cultural charges they encounter along the way. I suspect that too many make themselves into the people they will be just once, around the time they come of age. Whatever infiltrates their belief system in that crystalline moment strikes an alliance with what they were taught—in school, by their parents, at the movies—and then never leaves them. I was formed by mumblings about the omnipresent Iron Curtain, by TV reports of civil rights marches and corrupt presidents, by the Vietnam War that everyone knew was wrong. And the dubious ideas that drugs were good, sex had no consequences, and home was a place to get away from. And what I learned when I did leave home—that nothing could really stop me from living a life that ran counter to everything I had ever heard of before. What my parents' generation heard of was hard work and a better life for their kids along with yellow devils in kamikaze planes, the shock of Pearl Harbor, and uncles and cousins who never made it back from the good war. Homosexuals were never mentioned by either generation, except in whispers, which led to an image as potent as that of the World War II newsreel Jap. The queer was a creepy-crawly shadow figure, vaguely like a communist, but worse. A body that hides because it's defective, turned inside out.

Yet there are gradations all along the scale between the farthest reaches of my family and me and I am hardly the confluence of my family and my generation, but rather the one among my siblings and cousins who is most extreme. I complain when Linnea holds back, letting rude comments slide, intending to make her point at some later opportunity that may never present itself. I go too far the other way. I am impatient with all the ways people don't push themselves beyond what they have heard. When those people are my family, and I see them stare at Linnea, it's hard not to lose my cool.

People who have never been stared at for some unpopular fact about themselves—the ones who blend in well with the prevailing scenery and never question their right to belong—don't understand what it feels like to be other. The kind of stares I speak of are not benign. Linnea and I have come to recognize them on our skin, that same shudder, the same smirk we have seen on the faces heckling us from passing cars when we've walked down streets holding hands, the same slight twist of the mouth I saw once on my mother's lips on that day long ago when I asked her to tell me about homosexuals.

Besides, I remember living here. It's not so hard to guess at the contours of this terrain. Didn't one of the uncles who used to call me Princess turn away in the rainswept cathedral parking lot when Linnea and I tried to say hello? Didn't my cousin Frankie's wife have the nerve to tell my mother that Paulie and Mitsuko's future kids would never be allowed to play with her babies? She didn't want any children of hers, she said, to start talking Japanese. And didn't my lovable little Polish grandma, my mother's mom, complain unceasingly for months about the seating arrangements at the reception? My father, she insisted—who just placed her at the table he thought she would like, with her sons— had banished her (the Polack) to the undesirable side of the hall, back near "the Japanese." And what I don't have on good authority I read in the newspaper, the research just in, homophobia showing up as bigotry's last stand in families such as mine.

And so I sat or stood or walked around my brother's wedding reception and wondered just what it was my relatives saw when they looked at Mitsuko's narrow-boned uncle and his round and tidy wife with a sprayed Western hairdo, bowing and smiling at any approach. Did they see Mitsuko's giggling cousin in a beige, tailored pantsuit and silk blouse? The cool and organized sisters of the bride, one with long hair pulled back in a clip, the other sleek and bobbed as a magazine model, a head-turner in designer earrings and shoes? The junior bridesmaid, Mitsuko's shy and pretty niece in a frilly purple prom gown, who dropped her eyes when anyone tried to speak to her? How many of the older generation of my relatives saw each individual face instead of just "the Japanese," a flock of foreigners who reminded them of smoke tails building and dissolving into a too-blue day, bombs falling from silver bellies? Did they see humans connected to them now by a wedding or did they only notice the myth of a face, a story they believed just because it was the only one that had ever sunk in?

Mitsuko's sisters lined up their visiting family in various configurations, just themselves or with the bride and groom, snapping photos while the party buzzed and beat around them. The Croatian musicians my brother hired were strumming and singing old European folk songs, the waitresses were running for more cocktails, my mom was pinballing from table to table and enjoying her status as mother of the groom. My mother's aunts and cousins were finally pulling me aside to kiss me on the cheek. Their dusty face powder filled my nostrils with memories of childhood Memorial Day picnics and Easter visits. "What have you been doing up there in Minnesota?" Did I appear the same to them as I looked in the bathroom mirror, as I looked in the lens of Linnea's eyes?

The same great aunts and second cousins who grabbed my hand with such loving pressure leaned close whenever Linnea walked by. Cigarette smoke curled up from their ashtrays as their heads knocked together like resin balls on a tavern pool table. What had they just seen? Her boxy shoulders, her sturdy torso, her wing-tipped feet, her square shining face—was that a woman? I saw Linnea, her handsome body more cubed than curved, the matte shimmer of her suit picking up the mirrored light from the dance floor, the hem of her pants dropping casually over the polished black wing tips. On this night I wanted to yell and hiss at how they treated Linnea, staring that way, and yet I was engulfed in that supper-club smell, and so remembered there was a time I when I gawked and shuddered, too.

~

We straight girls sat together in the college cafeteria and stared, our billiard-ball heads clunking and chiming. We gawked at the couple who lived in our freshman-year dorm. The real lezzie was the dark one with the rough-cut face and short hair, we all agreed. The other one, the tall blond might be pretty, if she could get away, if the lezzie would ever let her go.

I had spotted the lezzie before, in old quarter novels I'd fingered, laughed at, tossed aside. She lurked in the background of late-night movies I didn't understand and B-side pop songs with seedy suggestions that seventies rock-and-rollers tossed in to scare people when they got too high. There was so much that was never said about her, her portrait never fully shaded. She was a specter that took on flesh only in the collective imagination—bumped and gnarly orange-peel skin, a brown suit and a striped tie, lips too red, as if she had just eaten a blond girl alive.

I saw the lezzie for real one night when I was wasted and sitting on the floor of a bar, watching the colors slither and slide. This is a story I have told repeatedly, and yet I am still not sure it really happened. There was a person with a stubble of blond hair, an air-force tie, sharp creases in a buttoned-up jacket, who smiled at me so sweetly that I smiled back, ready to be scooped up and carried away. I will never know for sure just who he or she was. Some flyboy transformed by booze and pot into a figment of my imaginings? Such things happened. Some military dyke who picked up drunk straight girls? She exists. Some nice butch who wanted to help a lost girl up off the floor? She exists, too. Some square-headed figment of my future? Visions do occur, although I haven't always believed what I've seen. When I heard her deep woman's voice, I ran away, to knock heads and titter and point with my dorm mates, who told me I was drunk and seeing things again.

But the one with orange-peel skin who would eat me alive did not exist. Today I can look back and shake my head, knowing that she was only another creation like the yellow menace, just propaganda. It took about two more years to figure that out. I sat on the teetering barroom floor. The semester had ended and I moved out of my dorm. I kissed a man who knew lesbians. I met my own lesbians. I met a lesbian I wished would kiss me. Finally I gawked across a bar, no wider than a hallway, dappled with mirrored-ball light and pulsing dance tracks, a bar not filled with box-bodied B-movie monsters, but instead with women like none I had ever seen before. They had magnificently cragged faces and wore slim-cut tuxedos and rhinestone rings on their pinky fingers. They were women I did hope would scoop me up in their strong palms as they would a pool of water in the desert. *Boom*. My sound barrier shattered. It really did exist, the noise I heard in my head, my chest, my heart. It annihilated, I thought, all that had lived there before and I knew I could never go home again. And I never have gone home, not as the girl who grew up on that steel-mill and freeway plain.

Yet when I do come back as I am now, I keep anticipating something different. I expect my relations to know Linnea when they see her, without the shadows, without the red traces of their niece's blood on her lips. What do I want from these people? I expect them to know us, but how could they? Where would they have ever heard of Linnea and me, before now?

~

The Croatian musicians were having a drink at the upstairs bar while the bartenders lip-synched along with "New York, New York." Dino had already played master of ceremonies with great aplomb, almost a moment out of *The Music Man*, as he introduced my parents and Mitsuko's aunt and uncle to the applauding horde as if they were visiting movie stars. He introduced Paulie and Mitsuko with a shout, "APPEARING FOR THE FIRST TIME." It was the sort of voice he might use to strike up a band, "MR. AND MRS . . . ," even though Mitsuko had no intention of taking her

American husband's name. All the hubbub had settled around who was seated with whom, and what ethnic marker waved from which table— the Japanese flag at the Croatian setting, the Polish flag with the Italians—my dad's seating-chart integration joke. Dinner had been served and cleaned up again. Aunt Cecilia, Dino's mom, had already leaned in to tell Linnea she wanted to come to Minnesota during the Winter Carnival to have a look at our famous ice castle and had already indicated to me that she didn't much care for my retro, cat's-eye spectacles. My slump-shouldered cousin Antony, Dino's older brother, had already let his new wife drag him out to the floor. She was the most current in an impressive history of cover-girl-lovely blonds who have been so wild for him. I was prepared to like this one. Everyone said she was steady enough to make Antony's third marriage the charm, plus I'd heard she was nice to Dino and Danny. Paulie and Mitsuko had already danced a slow one together. Mitsuko had already cried in her uncle's stiff arms, posed with her bridesmaids, thrown the bouquet, tossed the garter, and with Paulie, had already cut the cake and kissed when the relatives tapped their spoons against their water glasses. My middle brother Benny had already sung his signature toast to the tune of "Oh, Canada." My father had already announced that his son and new daughter-in-law had made him the proudest he had ever been, and my mother had already fumed because she hadn't had a chance to use the microphone. My parents had already danced the wedding polka, had already sat down to have a few cocktails with their friends, college buddies and fellow high-school teachers, all married, all with kids at whose weddings my parents had danced, had cocktails, and recollected their own weddings. The disc jockey was playing a fast one, and I watched as my aunts and uncles picked up the pace, dancing apart the way they must have had to learn just for nights such as these.

Linnea and I spent some of the wedding hours next to each other, some on opposite sides of the room, as we do at any gala. I noticed her sitting alone at the edge of the upstairs level of the hall, where my brother's college friends were seated. She looked down over the swelling, frothing scene like a tourist watching an ocean view. She was leaning forward in the folding chair, elbows on knees, a loose, easy smile on her face. I couldn't imagine what she was enjoying so much. Certainly part of it was the Scotch. She'd polished off at least three drinks by now, more than she ever has in one stretch. I abstain from booze because I know that a sip of any intoxicant might open the trap door to a long fall, but Linnea has a drink or two now and then, maybe even three or four if the occasion calls for it. This is as drunk as she ever gets. Her skin was rosy, blushing, her face a lamp of friendliness and goodwill toward everyone.

I stood on the main floor. The wedding billowed and chattered around me. The DJ's music was tinny and bass heavy in the cluttered disco twilight. "What are you doing?" I mouthed to her.

She waved and motioned for me to come up. When I got there, she beckoned me closer, ear to lip, so she could whisper. I expected a blurry, *I love you,* or *you looked so pretty down there, I just wanted to touch you.* But instead she said, "I feel . . . ," and then paused for a long booming moment.

"I feel," she started again, "like a big queer."

The edges of her ears were burning red. "You're drunk," I whispered back to her, and she laughed and threw her arm around my shoulder.

"I feel like a big queer," she said again, still laughing and beaming, and I could see she had figured out the landscape of my family. She was laughing, so I laughed, too. She was, after all, exactly who she is, wherever I bring her, a big old queer at my baby brother's wedding, and no matter what we did or didn't say or do, everyone knew it. About her. About me, too.

"I feel like a big queer," she said, "and I want to dance with you here." And why shouldn't she want this? I wanted it, too. What was this wedding, any wedding, but a thundering festival of the thing itself, the big promise to love and honor, the big hope for the passion to make it stick? Linnea and I held that promise between us as much as any of my relatives did, just married or remembering fifty years.

I looked at her lit-up face, her square hands clutching a lowball glass as she jangled the cubes in her drink. Her brown eyes stared at me, until I remembered where I had been since I had stopped living in this place. All the lights boomed alive in me, and in that instant I stopped trying to see her through the grimy lens of a landscape I had left so long before. Instead, I saw her as I usually do, her face the face of my own marriage, her hands the holder of my pulse, her square feet in her special-day wing tips as familiar and usual and dear to me as any husband's feet are to the woman who has loved them for all these years. I watched her sitting there next to me and the plains of my heart shifted back home. Of course I will dance with you, darling.

∼

But that's not what I said, not yet. My grand jetés between the self who loved Linnea and the me who used to live in this place had given me vertigo. I led Linnea back down the stairs to the edge of the dance floor, but I did not dance with her. Instead we sat down with Dino and Danny. The disc jockey called out, "This one is for all the married couples here," and the four of us sat that one out together, cracking jokes across the empty banquet table. *Don't you hate it when they flaunt it? When will they announce the special dance for gay couples?* Linnea winked at me, and I whispered, "Not yet."

I was working on my courage. I was tasting meanness at the back of my throat. Why should we be the only ones who stand out here? Why couldn't the boys do it, too? This was the trouble with remembering my new self in this old place. When I let the landscape seep in too far I was in danger of drowning in memory, and I couldn't fathom the blathering monster I must seem in some of my family's eyes. But once I regained myself, as I had, off and on through the night's festivities, then I couldn't comprehend who Dino and Danny were, and why they preferred to stay so mute. So I nudged Danny and asked, "Would you ever have a wedding, with Dino, I mean?" Danny shuddered and shook his head. "Oh no." Impatient, I leaned over the table toward Dino for my next question, even though I already knew what he would say. "So are you guys going to dance tonight, with each other?"

"No, no," he said, with just the edge of a laugh, as if he wished he had the nerve. Of course not. Never. Even though they lived in the chichi North Side of the city, had illustrious careers and money and more property between them than all my mother's aunts and cousins combined, Dino would never be comfortable enough. "Why should I put a wedge between me and my family," he has said to me over and over again, "like you did?" And he never has. Not like me, who had to leave before I could even ask such questions. I needed a wedge of at least 350 land miles to be so comfortable.

The dance floor was still packed and the DJ was playing another fast one. "Dance?" Linnea asked Danny, and I had to laugh at the sight of it, the two most masculine among us four twisting and turning in their wedding suits. Then Linnea danced with my father's relatives—white-haired Grandma Rose, her light-footed daughter Aunt Cecilia, and even Aunt Vera, the wife of my father's uncle, a retired brassiere saleswoman with neat ear-length permed hair and one eye always looking out for her Alzheimer's-dazed husband. These were not the ones who had stared at Linnea. By this time most of that side of the family were on their way home, and even Dino and Danny were getting up to leave. The ones who danced with Linnea were the relatives we saw more frequently, the ones getting used to seeing us together. These were women who grew up dancing with one another because they didn't have a partner, because there weren't enough men at the party to go around, because the boys had gone away for the war. Who would suspect a couple of jitterbugging dames of lesbianism just because they were dancing, especially when such words never passed anyone's lips? And yet they knew when they danced with Linnea that they were hot-footing it with a big queer. It was toward the end of the evening and they must have been feeling vaguely tipsy, slightly naughty, even a little bit loose. Aunt Vera pulled Linnea behind a wood pillar and whispered, "Nobody knows what we're doing over here."

Of course, all they were doing was dancing. Linnea dipped and swung the ladies, one after the other, and her dance partners had the most fun they would have all night. They lay their heads back and laughed, relaxing into Linnea's facile dips and turns. For Linnea the body is a basin of love. Dancing is what makes its waters ripple, each undulation a message, a cry, *I love breathing, I love feeling, I love being here right now*. Not even my relatives could resist a turn around the floor with her. Then Linnea danced alone, rosy and winded, back to our table, and I couldn't resist her either.

Still, I grimaced a little as she led me out to the middle of the pack. I clung to her square-suited shoulders. I could feel her pulse through her fingertips. So there we were. Dancing. I laughed and felt my muscles loosen. Linnea danced. I tried to keep up.

We were so near the close of this pageant of love, and although I was the only one there who hadn't been drinking, even I felt the room's giddy tilt-a-whirl. The DJ's speakers warbled with Sinatra's late-night attitude. Linnea's feet whirled so fast below all I could see was a blur of bright motion. Like eggbeaters. Like a helicopter blade. That's how slow I felt in comparison. Don't look down, is all she said. She is a much better dancer than I am. I didn't know how not to look. I didn't trust that my feet could feel their way across the floor unless I watched them do it. So I looked down and watched myself stumble.

When I looked up again, past her droopy-eyed smile, past the couples huddled and swaying around us, their faces mottled by mirror-ball light, past the dance floor and over the stained banquet tablecloths, I saw Antony and Frankie, the married cousins of my generation with their party-garbed wives, watching us. It's a particular phenomenon, to be stared at not only by newcomers but also the ones who have known me my whole life, yet have never seen me before. Four faces, flat and round as nickels, white as golf balls, insistent as searchlights piercing this freeway plain. Their faces hovered there, four hazy planets, four round splotches of shock. I watched them watching, and stumbled again. My love, she caught me, cinched me closer, waist to waist, my lips to her ear. *Boom.* She held on, through the shudder. I held on, too. We spun for Paulie and Mitsuko, for marriage, for all the extravaganzas of love, and I watched nothing but the shape of the motion we made.

The Summer of a Certain Rain

There was just one thing we wanted that didn't belong to us when Linnea and I moved out of our old apartment. By the time we left the duplex where we'd spent our first decade, we had collected so many things. Not just drawers full of snapshots—of surprise birthday parties, of grinning weekends in lakeside cabins, of the dog and cats gnawing open their Christmas gifts. Not only our stories of trips back to Illinois and Wisconsin to watch our siblings marry or to meet our new nieces and nephews. Not just the files of love letters, not only the lyrics of all the swinging Sinatra ballads we had danced to so many times in our sunny living room. There was also our motley accumulation of stuff. Toys. Statues. Home art projects. Refrigerator magnets. Postcards and posters. Most of it was coming with us, of course, but the thing we most yearned for was an object we feared we wouldn't get to keep.

It was our massive oak dining-room table, too heavy for one person to move, stained a dense mahogany, darker still from extreme age. For ten years, we lived with it at the center of everything. Except for the tiny bedroom in the back that looked out over the alley, our whole apartment had the feel of one big room. We could cordon it off when we chose. The elaborately carved pocket doors, when we could keep them on their tracks, would close tight, shutting off our studies from the living room, or if we preferred, we could open the rooms to the afternoon light; the doors would slip away into passageways in the walls. Most of the time our apartment was a bright open wheel around the hub of that table.

The table was in the apartment already the day Linnea helped me move in what was then just a few things—a futon and a disassembled bed frame a friend had made for me, a few boxes of books and papers, clothes, one young gray cat, one old auburn cat, and a turquoise wagon-wheel couch with a saddle stitched into the Naugahyde. Nine months later, when Linnea came to live with me, we shoved that table out of the noisy room that looked out over Portland Avenue and into the center of the apartment. She needed a study for her books and desk and computer so she could finish her dissertation. She needed a window ledge for her crabby black Siamese who hated all of us and was happy to sleep the whole day through, or stare out at whatever was going on out in the street, or gaze back in toward the middle where the rest of us were doing something or other around that table.

By then the table had become another one of our pets, a creature who helped host every celebration, the spot we put up a small Christmas tree every December, the display for jack-o'-lanterns the October we had a pumpkin-carving party, the place we had guests set up their offerings one Saturday evening in November when the theme of our party was the Night of a Thousand Pies.

If we could have figured out how to get it apart we just might have taken that table with us when we moved, without bothering to ask. After all, it was the landlord's fault his property had fallen to junk. It was not our choice to get out in such a rush once he decided to avoid the inspectors and unload the place. Why shouldn't we take it? We had always been nice enough to comply whenever the landlord's son Joe stopped by to ask us to please not answer the door when the inspectors came knocking. OK, we always said, quickly adding, you know, that broken light fixture in the closet has really been bugging us, or, say, could you help us put up a ceiling fan? We would get a day or two of his tools and attention before the walls and window sashes would resume their downward slump unimpeded. So it was easy to figure they owed us the table, even if we doubted they would agree. But the trouble with that table was we could never figure out how to get it apart. How had they gotten it in here, we wondered, every time we tried to find a way to rearrange the furniture to accommodate it.

We might have had more room for the table if we hadn't kept filling the apartment up with every little thing we adored. A box of origami nuns we bought at an art fair. The macaroni Madonna, made by our best friend Peter at a Christmas-tree-decorating party. A punching nun puppet, a gift from my brother Benny. An old mirror I dragged down from the attic and set on painted cinder blocks where we placed every sort of Our Lady artifact—holy cards, candles, Mary statues, shell sculptures, medals, rosaries, booklets, holy water bottles—as well as other items that looked good in our gallery of femme sanctity and kitsch sacrilege, such as a doll in the image of *Star Trek* ship's counselor Deanna Troy, a brass statue of Kannon we brought back from Japan, a glittery Plexiglas tube filled with sequins and little toys and a tiny hiding Elvis Presley in gold lamé, wands Linnea made out of metal tubes and leather and feathers she found on the side of the road when she toured around on her motorcycle, crystalline growths of clear purple stone we brought back from an Ontario amethyst mine, a gold plastic charm in the shape of St. Lucy's missing eyes, no bigger than my pinkie fingernail. Our decorating themes, such as they were, rotated over time. For a while we had processions of plastic dinosaurs arranged across the fireplace mantel. When visitors inquired I used to tell it was a Dino-Rama, metaphor of the extinct spirit trudging toward a female image of god, referring to the way I had so artfully arranged the little plastic stegos and brontos and duck-billed platypuses across the nineteenth-century cherrywood ledge, trekking endlessly toward a pottery Madonna with a ceramic drawer under her feet. And there *was* something spiritual about our compulsion to fill the living room with Madonnas. For me it was a remnant of my Catholic upbringing combined with a craving for that which was bigger than our bodies. For Linnea it something close to what a gay pagan friend of hers said the first time he stepped into the center of our home. *Ah. The goddess in chains.* But we kept the rest simply because it made us laugh, ridiculously, sitting on the floor of a toy store elbow-deep in a bin of plastic dinos, or unveiling a hand-painted Madonna-faced clock Linnea spent hours creating one weekend when I was out of town.

Even after we packed up the dinos to keep for visiting nieces, boxed up our collection of Pee Wee's Playhouse dolls in case they might be worth something one day, retired the Madonna piñata when the painted paper legs and arms started to disintegrate, people new to our mélange would stand stock-still in the center and stare. "We're thinking of opening up a gift shop," I would quip and most would exclaim at how much there was for the eyes to take in. "I hope you are never planning to move."

Amongst all of this was that table, every scar and water ring as familiar to us as the moles and freckles on each other's bodies. The table didn't belong to us. Still, we lived with it every day. We would put the table in the archway between the pocket doors leading into my study. Then I would need to close the doors and the table would be in the way. We would put it against the fireplace once it became clear it was too dangerous to send flames up into that broken chimney, but then we couldn't see the green-mottled fireplace tiles. It never quite fit, wherever we placed it. The corners stuck out and caught me at the thigh, or blocked the view when we had friends over to watch videos.

More than once Linnea threatened to chop it up and haul it out into the alley. More than one friend with carpentry skills climbed underneath to try and figure out how it was put together, so at least we might take it apart and store it in the attic until we wanted to use it again. Each time our volunteer crawled out again shrugging. How did they get it in here? Through the window? Or was it built in here?

But Linnea would never have cut that table up, because we loved the curvacious carved legs, the heavy scratched and stained top that was strong enough to stand on when I dusted the holy candles we kept on the high top shelf of the mantel. It was strong enough for dancing had we ever felt the urge. We loved the built-in leaf that revealed itself when Linnea and I stood on either side and pulled. No searching in the basement or in the back of the coat closet for the missing table piece before Thanksgiving or Christmas Eve dinner. And, once extended, that table was long, nearly nine feet, which is what gave us the idea to start inviting all our friends over for Thanksgiving dinner.

Linnea and I have always resided at the center of a troupe with unconventional ties to their families of origin, and so we are often surrounded by quirky personalities. What's more, our friends are frequently free for the holidays. So they have all come to our house for dinner, as many as we've been able to fit around that table, sometimes twenty, sometimes more. There were years when we had to add a card table at one end. There were years when everyone laughed at the same jokes and shone with affection for one another by the end of the evening, and other years when someone's new boyfriend pissed off all the lesbians, or some diva we hadn't invited before grated on all of us when he announced he *never* helped clean up.

One year there was a fire in the borrowed upstairs oven at the same time there was a plugged-up kitchen drain downstairs. While Linnea was upstairs fanning out the smoke, I dragged Joe over from next door to fix the sink. Our dinner guests got into a debate on oral-sex differences in butches and femmes in gay versus lesbian bedrooms. As they shouted and exclaimed about who put what mouth where and when, Joe stood, a few feet away with his sleeves rolled up and his plumbing snake disappearing down the drain. I paced, wondering where Linnea was, worried that Joe would never return to repair our pipes again. But Joe seemed to enjoy the discussion and later we found out some of the men at the party, with more expertise than Linnea and me at identifying male proclivities at a glance, assumed he was one of the party guests. We had always wondered just what it was that Joe was into, living alone over there. His scruffy male mechanic friends visited late at night and there was never a woman in sight. "Who knows?" we said. "Maybe," after sending him home with Thanksgiving pie.

Thanksgiving around that big table turned into a tradition our friends came to count on, so much so that when we tried to cut down the list and neglected to invite a person here or there, because they had drifted to other circles or had turned us down the year before, we would find, the next time we ran into them, they had trouble meeting our eyes. Sometimes they even challenged us. Why didn't you? Don't you know what it means to me? It was exhausting to calculate every year who was still part of our chosen family and who had spun off into another, who had broken up with whom, who could realistically sit across the table from one another. Some years we left this kind of trouble for our guests to work out among themselves; other years we tried to engineer the dynamic. One November our ensemble of friends were so badly split over an ugly divorce that Linnea and I didn't want to eat with any of them, and so we escaped with Patsy out of town to a snowy Lake Superior resort and ate Thanksgiving dinner at a restaurant. But most years we had the party—free-range turkey and cornbread stuffing, fresh cranberry sauce, sweet potatoes mashed with orange juice, colossal salads and vegetable stews, and in the years die-hard vegetarians were among us, the addition of mushroom quiche and spinach lasagna. And there was pie. Pumpkin pie. Sweet-potato pie. Squash pie. Pecan pie. Apple pie. Blueberry pie. Chocolate pudding pie. All of it served from that table.

As soon as we found out our landlord was selling our building we knew we wanted to get away with that table. He wouldn't notice, we figured, if he hadn't missed it for the ten years we had been living there, and the twelve more years before that when it lived with the people who gave us the apartment. But people's relationship to their property is funny. Once old Henry had put the building up for sale he was poking around all the time, pulling himself to the attic stair by stair, then scuffling around up there, counting things. Joe, for all these years, had only come over from next door when there was something to tape or wire back together, or to store his smelly collections of broken-down lawn mowers in the basement. Now he tramped up and down the steps day and night muttering to himself, ticking off all the barely remembered things that belonged to his family.

$\sim$

When Joe decided to clean out the attic, there was a solid deluge around our home. It was too much trouble to carry everything down the slippery hall stairs. Instead, Joe and one of his scruffy cousins took out a window and threw it all into the yard. This went on for weeks. I would open the back door to put the dog in the yard and a chair back would sail over my head. Or a bag of fabric scraps. Or a handful of paperback books. I had to remember to look up before I let Patsy out. I worried about our green glass yard ball that had survived blizzards and hailstorms but had no experience with a rain of old furniture. Linnea worried about her motorcycle and swore under her breath whenever she watched a box fall and break open a little too close.

This was the season of emptying out, for as anyone who had ever visited our apartment had feared, the job of packing up our lives and moving it to a new place was immense. For ten years we had accumulated, and when we got down to sorting through it all, we were startled by what we found. In the basement was an old vacuum cleaner that was broken when I moved it to this address and was broken still. Nearby was a ripped box full of snakes built out of chicken wire and plaster of paris, each longer than one of my outstretched arms, waiting to be adorned with beads and tempura and little things I found around the house. Our friend Peter had made them for a serpent-decorating party he threw, years back, in celebration of St. Patrick driving the snakes out of Ireland. I carted a box full of blank viper canvases home that night and in the next few months embellished a few, home therapy while I was in chem dep treatment. I'd always intended to do more with them, but after so long in the basement they were spongy and brown with mildew. So, we carted them, along with the vacuum, out to the yard and into Joe's trash pile.

In the attic, Joe was sorting years of junk into piles of what to keep, what to toss, what to sell. We did the same. There was a cotton yard hammock I'd carried around for years because we never did find a place to hang it outside, and if we had, it would only have been stolen. So off it went to the yard-sale pile. Boxes of books from both our bookcases went to used bookstores. I took hangers of vintage clothes unlikely to ever fit again, clothes I had worn on dates with Linnea, or on rendezvous with women who came before Linnea, including three leopard-print coats, to an Uptown vintage-clothes store where I had seen animal-print purses and luggage displayed in the window. "I hate to part with them," I said to the proprietress, who had saucer eyes and was wearing a feathered hat, "but they don't fit anymore." She ran her hand lovingly over the spotted polyester fur and purred, "Well, but our styles change as the years go by." My feet still fit into the red and tan cowboy boots with three-inch heels given to me by a former lover. They were rumored to have once belonged to a lesbian bluegrass singer well-known in the late seventies music-festival circuit, but they lifted me to what looked to be a foot taller than Linnea, and so they went into the yard-sale pile. I sold them to another lesbian old enough to remember that singer's particular blue twang. Linnea found a red teapot from China with matching cups that she forgot she owned. By that time we had found the house we wanted to buy, just a hair outside our old neighborhood on the other side of the park in the area I'd begun to call Bohemia Heights. So we kept the teapot for our new dining room, to put, we hoped, on the top of our dear oak table.

What could we do to get that table, short of sawing it down to pieces? I could carry it away in bits, one by one in my purse, but what good would that do? First we wrote a letter to Henry. We typed it on the computer, using a large typeface because he didn't see so well, and after all these years we knew if he couldn't read it he just wouldn't bother. We even offered to pay for the table, whatever he wanted. We sent the letter with our sixty-days' notice, and then we waited. Finally he called, in his usual manner, no salutation, just his gravel-road voice shouting from the other end of the line. "That table, I don't know, you'll have to ask Joe."

So we asked Joe, one afternoon, when the daily rain from the attic had subsided for a bit. Joe brightened when we mentioned that table. Oh sure, he remembered it. It was there when he lived in our apartment, when was that, nearly twenty-five years ago now. Oh, yeah, he loved that table. It had that great hidden leaf. He used to hide his money in there. Yeah, what a great table. No, he didn't think he could let that go. Let him think about it for a while, but he didn't think so. Probably not.

So there we sat, in the center of our half-packed junk, boxes of Marys and pretty beach rocks and Elvis clocks and books piled on top of and under the table. We were sad as we ran a finger or two along its dirty edges because it looked as if we were going to have to part ways. We had already thrown out the macaroni Madonna because the elbow noodles at the edge of her robe were starting to dissolve away into dirt. The inflatable pteranodon that had hovered for so long from our kitchen ceiling had sprung one too many leaks. The Madonna piñata was never meant to last. The snakes were contaminated by the basement. How would we remember all our early years, we wondered, as another clinking box of junk fell from the attic and scattered, like a meteor shower across the weedy yard.

≈

Joe must have felt bad about that table. He kept inviting us down to the permanent yard sale he opened down the block, inside and outside one of his empty duplexes. He had gotten into an heirloom-selling mood, and was emptying out the attics of all the buildings he owned and setting up the old furniture on the front lawn and in lower rooms of the house four doors down from our corner. From the looks of things, this duplex was in even worse repair than our old place. The wallpaper predated

World War II, the ceilings were stained brown from water leaks, the wood floors were worn and gray. Outside, Joe had put out rusted-metal farm beds, a wood buffet with missing drawer handles, a mirror we used to have propped up over the radiator in our bedroom, a Victorian end table we had eyed a few times in the attic but could never think of where it might fit, and a wide selection of dressers, some from our attic and others not, including the one where Linnea used to keep her socks and underwear. She wanted to keep the dresser, too, but finally gave it up to Joe in a fit of honesty, hoping he would change his mind about the table.

We followed the arrow on a crude sign that read *more inside,* scrawled on a piece of cardboard ripped off the side of a box, in search of Joe who promised he had another perfect table for us, one with matching chairs. We found him in the dining room fiddling around on his police-band radio. He did indeed have a dining-room table, dark wood with ugly Gothic legs and matching chairs with faded-red velveteen upholstery. It was a far cry from our old beloved, but we were so addled by all the boxes and the layers of dust that fell on our heads every time we moved something and the shoes and chipped utensils and rusted doorknobs that showered down from the attic every time we peeked into the yard that we actually considered it for a moment. Perhaps it was so ugly it possessed an inverted beauty. Perhaps we could recover the chairs, re-stain the table a lighter shade, replace the layer of wood on top that was peeling away like a sunburn. Joe and Linnea started to discuss it—whom you would call to help with a job like that and what kind of glue you might use if you tried to do it yourself—until I was suddenly overcome. I sighed loudly as I sat down on of those chairs that looked as if they came from a haunted castle. "I don't think so, Linnea," I said, causing her to stop talking and sit down across from me. She ran her square palm over the table's surface, then looked up. "No, I don't think so either." We both looked at Joe and shrugged.

Joe shrugged, too, and said, "Say, are you sure you don't want to buy the old place? The price is dropping."

We had already told him, weeks ago, that we were looking for another home. In truth, we had fantasized for years about buying that house from Joe and his father. It would be like saving a life, tearing down the gritty siding and restoring the wood, cleaning out the attic and making it into more rooms for us, a guest room, another bathroom. But even if we could have convinced Henry to take financing instead of cash, we could never have afforded what it would have cost us. A renovation mortgage too large for that neighborhood. Years of work rebuilding walls, replacing the roof, the furnace, the plumbing, not to mention the circa 1950 electrical. Then, what if Linnea finally did get a good teaching offer in some other place? We would have to pay money to the bank to get out. We finally decided we weren't the kind of people who could pull it off, who could dig in and stay.

"We bought another house," Linnea said to Joe. We could see the skinny shoulders under his dirty shirt sag a little. We understood why. Sure, he'd come to like us in his way, but more than that he was worried about who would move in after us. He hated so many kinds of people, we knew because there had been times in the beginning when he told us about it. We hadn't been his kind at the start, but we had turned out all right and he was accustomed to us. But in this neighborhood, the chances were high that some type he didn't like would settle in just over his twisted-wire fence.

The weekend paper was spread across the table he was trying to sell us and was open to the new home ads. *The Parade of Homes*, the headline read, an advertisement with colored pictures of fresh construction in the outer suburbs, circular drives beyond low stone walls named after spots in the English countryside. He asked us where our new house was, and we told him, fifteen blocks east, the other side of the park. That wasn't nearly far enough, he told us. Joe glanced down at the newspaper. "I was telling my dad that our houses on this block would sell for five times as much if they were just a little ways out. We should do it, you know? Just get out of here. Slide these babies onto trailers and drag them just a little ways out. Thirty miles is all it would take. Then we would have the real *Parade of Homes*."

Linnea and I locked eyes and I tried not to sputter. "That's ridiculous, Joe," Linnea said to him using the same word she had been repeating to both Joe and his father for years whenever they said something that would have surely caused me, had I been there alone, to lose my temper. Linnea just smiled and looked them straight in the face, leaving them to make out her meaning.

"No, come on," he pushed. "You gotta admit it. It's just this neighborhood, the bad element that moved in, you know what I mean."

I broke in before he could go any further. "C'mon Joe, you know how we feel about that."

"Yeah, yeah, I know," he nodded, his neck and shoulders sagging loose. He looked like a little boy arguing about why he shouldn't get in trouble for stealing the Christmas cake. The room we sat in smelled of dust and rust and damp things and the chairs creaked when Linnea and I shifted in our seats. "But the *Parade of Homes*, you gotta admit. Now that's a great idea."

Ridiculous, ridiculous we kept mouthing, because it was so far into stupid, and we couldn't stop laughing about it all the way home. White flight times a thousand to not only flee from the city but to take your house with you. We imagined together how it would look, all these creaky cut-up mansions wavering from trailers with bits of cracked siding swinging from rusty nails, windows shaking, glass breaking, old tables sliding around inside like the Zamboni at the ice show while dresser feet and picture frames and broken legs of dining-room chairs showered out the open attic windows. What a parade it would be, with Joe in front as grand marshal on his reconstructed riding lawn mower, the skin on his bare back jiggling as he waved like a beauty queen at the ones who stayed behind.

~

Linnea and I have slightly different memories of what finally happened to that table. I remember it missing from the apartment on our last afternoon there. We both recall the work we did that day. We rolled up all the fried-out extension cords snaked corner to corner from one or the other of only three outlets, swept up the dirt that seemed to re-emerge like a magic trick every time we turned around, dusted up the plaster sand that coated everything, as it must have for years. We had just chosen, until that day, not to notice.

"Honey, I don't want to clean anymore," Linnea said. "It doesn't matter. All this stuff is just going to get torn out of here." She was right. Our amateur slumlords had finally sold to professionals in the field. We were correct to expect that all the architectural antiques would be gone in a blink, the plate rails, the carved wood and ceramic-tiled fireplace, those exquisite pocket doors, the stained-glass roses, the archway of stained glass over the door out to the upstairs porch. It all vanished within a couple weeks from the day the new owner took possession. Which we knew was going to happen. So why was I cleaning? Just to touch every corner again, I suppose, trying to take our years in that place away with me on my skin.

Linnea kept complaining, but she understood. It was for me that she kept turning back to it even after the exposed plaster dust gritted up her hair, coated her throat.

Linnea remembers that the table was still there on that day. We both recall Joe and another one of his droopy-pants cousins coming by and trying to get it out, but ending up as stumped as we had been. But then I think they finally got it out the front. Linnea thinks not. Neither of us are sure.

So maybe it's still in there. Maybe it was strewn with powder and pipes that November night, the center of another kind of Thanksgiving, when according to our old neighbors, the crack team raided through the front window. But that seems unlikely. If the new owners could take out a fireplace surely they would have found a way to get at that table. Perhaps it has been refinished in a lighter shade more suitable to its oak-tree origins, and sits now behind the polished glass of an upscale Victorian antique store, downtown, in the gallery district. Or maybe Joe and his Mr. Fix-it cronies finally figured out how to take it apart, and did, and now it's set up in his dining room covered with mismatched screws and drill bits and pieces of ancient engines. Or worse, perhaps it was never reassembled and sits in another of Joe's attics, waiting for the day it, too, will sail out an open window that looks out over the alleys of South Minneapolis.

As for us, we let it go, as we did so many things the summer that rained old pots and dresser drawers. We were already exhausted by our accelerated house hunt, by figuring out what we had to borrow and beg to get a down payment, by endless trips to the bank and by going through all our old envelopes for proof of every dollar spent or saved. Once it was official, we could barely maintain a civil conversation with each other, we were so fatigued, and this was before we had even finished packing up all our stuff. But when we saw an ad in the morning paper promising old furniture we had to have a look. When we got there, we found what we wanted, in the basement, covered with boxes of Christmas ornaments, a little water-stained here and there, but the legs had a gorgeous deco curve and when we pulled it from end to end the center crease opened to reveal a hidden leaf. Sold—for only one hundred dollars. We loosened a few bolts to slip off the legs and took it away in the back of Linnea's truck.

The next week we found a deco buffet to match. Friends brought us a motley collection of chairs with a harp design in the back to match the table's legs and carved edges. We remembered that moody Victorian folderol was never the style we imagined for ourselves. In fact, on our very first date we had talked about how Art Deco was our favorite look, the sleek modern lines, the visual break from the weight of a heavier century.

And so, on that last afternoon in our old apartment, we mopped up the dust of a decade. If that table was there we might have placed an ear against its hard surface and hoped to hear the rising and falling voices of our friends. We might have pressed our noses against the mottled wood, to smell the stuffing and baked holiday bird. Ridiculous, but we might have been so maudlin. If we did or didn't, it doesn't matter, for I had finally understood that it wasn't the apartment we had loved from so deep in our bellies. Now that we were almost gone, I could see how the plaster sagged around the window frames, how the dust rained into my nose and seeped behind my eyes. That place was a wreck, not worth shoving onto any kind of trailer and dragging anywhere. There was nothing left to take away with us, so Linnea and I packed up our rags and our brooms and headed home.

Community Property

Most lesbians know the joke. What does a lesbian bring to her second date? A U-Haul.

Of course, it is not only gay men who love a random encounter. It is not only women who crave a common kitchen. Still, it does seem that the urge to share the circular breath of home comes early in so many woman-to-woman love affairs. How many times do our flocks of more rationally thinking friends shake their heads and call out from the neighborhood trees? Toooo Soooon. Toooo Soooon. And how often do we do it anyway, so eager to trip through new doorways together, to touch the strange walls and odd cracks between the bathtub tiles, to touch heads as we gaze into unfamiliar mirrors, trying to determine how we feel together in this new place. We breathe in and this fresh atmosphere seems to hold a protein we'd been missing. We breathe out and our spent air mingles, fogging the bathroom fixtures.

I wonder how the ground where we stand makes or unmakes Linnea and me. Was moving in together the equivalent of a wedding? Did we become more married, once we bought a house? My cousin Dino, who, unlike me, does not believe that public announcement is any way to honor homosexual love, has told me that he believes it's property that makes a gay marriage. We were standing on a sidewalk on the North Side of Chicago and looking up at the peonies growing in wide concrete planters that he and his longtime companion Danny had placed on either side of their polished condo door. He said the word property the way Scarlet O'Hara says, "Tara," in the scene just before intermission, when she holds the red earth in her palm. I could see that Dino's condo was a property it would be easy to love, a block from the Lake Michigan shore. His home had wide, shimmering windows that looked out onto the city, a dining room furnished with a long table and tooled leather chairs they bought in Mexico, a wall sculpture they shipped back from their recent vacation in Greece, and Dino's white baby grand that reminded me of how he was when we were kids together. He won piano contests when he was in grade school and acted in semi-professional shows until he graduated from high school. I thought he would grow up to work on the stage.

Joint property equals marriage? No, I don't agree with Dino's math. Collecting houses is one of Dino's passions, but I can't think that fact will ever make him more married. He made his pronouncement during the time when Linnea and I owned nothing but a bed, and so I laughed and said, "Well, we have a dog. . . " Then we changed the subject, to the potted peonies, I think, the brilliance of the pink blossoms and the fertilizer he used to help them bloom.

If I ever believed Dino's philosophy I would have to hurl myself into the cold plate of Lake Michigan visible from the roof of that burnished condominium. Whatever Dino does for his money, whatever we do or don't do to try to catch up, it's not likely that we will ever have as much as my cousin. Linnea and I rarely line up the cherries on the slot machines, and even when our work does pay us more than we expect, the dollars flap quickly out of our palms like origami birds migrating to some other household.

Dino seems to believe that the things he owns—with the man he sometimes tells people is his roommate, sometimes his business partner—are what keep him from losing his place in the flock of our family. I believe the family remembers me because of the way I flapped away and came back loudly loving Linnea. It may be that both our perspectives hover off opposite sides of the truth. But now that Linnea and I own a home together, I wonder if I can keep dismissing Dino's theories so completely. Signing the papers, shoveling the snow, and weeding the gardens, taking care of the walls and roof and old stone foundation that keeps it all steady, are a different sort of charge than simply knowing the press of Linnea's lips in every night's darkness. It's not that Linnea and I now have finally become one, but rather that we two are more interlinked, as are any community of roots or fins or feathers or human hearts. Our names are both listed on the title to a little bit of geography. We are written down together. There is a record of us where there was no mention before.

In some domains, they speak of the accumulations of the marriage home as community property. Whatever the political repercussions of the practice, I do love how the words sound. Linnea and I are not just two bodies in love, but a community of two, individual and dependent. We look in, toward each other, but also out at the rest of the flapping formations of our friends, family, neighbors. But didn't that begin long before we purchased property? Linnea did not bring a U-Haul to my door on the evening of our second date. We waited nine whole months before we began to share the same ceiling and floor. We considered shacking up sooner, at three months when Linnea's household of college buddies was breaking apart. Up until then, it was me who had always preferred living alone, but I was the one who sobbed when we decided to wait. The trees all around us shook with that toooo sooooon chorus, a message so much wiser than our immediate wishes.

And yet, by nine months we no longer cared what anyone else had to say. Even though like most lesbians we mark our anniversary from the first night we made love, it was when we started to live together that our community of two really began, and continued. A decade passed before we finally bought a house. By that time, we knew every curve of each other's bodies, knew the temperature of each other's skin in the morning, in the summer, in the moments we chilled to each other and in the moments we warmed up slowly under the grainy tips of each other's familiar fingertips.

We also know which of us forgets to turn out the bathroom lights at night. Which one always thinks the music is too loud, and which one always wants it louder. Which one never gets around to making the phone calls for the party. Which one forgets to turn off the flame and burns up the tea kettle. Which one leaves her papers all over the kitchen table. Which one leaves her key in the door overnight. Which one finally organizes all the magazines and recycles all the catalogues because she knows the other one won't. Which one wants more clutter, which one less. Which one pretends to sleep when the dog barks for her breakfast.

Which one hates the other's TV programs. Which one makes the tea too strong or cuts up the carrots too small or keeps the other one up all night with her snoring. Which one keeps secretly turning up the heat, despite the impossibility of the last month's bill. There are times when we laugh every day, and other times when our complaints amass, a variegated thunderhead, until one or another of us is lost in the fog, and so a squawk rings out—*you don't*, and *you don't*, and *you don't*. That's when the other's voice becomes a chilly hoot. *You don't know, don't listen, don't care.* In those close quarters it isn't our possessions that smooth the feathers and set us back into a happier air stream. It's the way we still recognize the orange and misty blue sun, setting on the edge of everything, the way we still know the lay of the land beneath our bellies.

There are communities of two who live as we do, but never buy a home, stay forever in their rented domiciles. We have friends in cities were it's not as easy to buy a house as it is in Minneapolis. Others tell us that no matter the price, they would never sign a mortgage paper again. We have lesbian friends in Chicago who used to live in an apartment building just three blocks away from my propertied cousin. One of the pair, Alissa, has told us repeatedly that she spent too many summers in the house she used to own in Minneapolis hip-high in basement flood-waters. Now she says she doesn't want to be bothered anymore, which I can understand. Oh, for a clean brick building, I think. Oh, for a city-scape view and a storage locker in the basement and a number to call when the plumbing is clogged. Two gay men lived upstairs from our friends, and habitated their apartment as deeply as anyone in any kind of home. Their rooms were decorated into every crevice—fabric and furni-ture, statuaries and stained glass, wall-sized paintings and window treat-ments for weeks. Draped and enclosed, dripping and swathed, the Palace of Versailles, our friends called it from down below in their spare and clean space with framed posters on pastel walls and Positano pottery in a glass pantry. It's astonishing that such different communities of love could exist within the same box of bricks.

But these couples were not their apartments. The men in the palace upstairs split up, had to divide the statues and draperies. Our friends had marriage trouble but worked it out, then fought with their landlord and didn't work it out, then moved their dishes and framed posters to the west side of the city. Their new apartment is a whole top floor, upstairs from nice landlords, a married man and woman with a baby, who have become Chris and Alissa's daily flock. My cousin and the man he calls his roommate bought a country house in Michigan right on the big lake, and another in the city down the block from their old condo. The last I heard they had stripped the city house down to the studs and rebuilt everything, including the gargoyles. Which of these couples seems more married? Don't answer. You need more information. The history of what they have or have not owned has far too little to do with it.

But then there is the case of Linnea and me. I broke into tears when Linnea filled me in on just what was involved with owning a home because I didn't know how we would pay for it all. It wasn't just the roof and the furnace and the pipes under the kitchen sink we had to worry about, but whether or not the kids who hang out in the alley would mar the fresh paint of our garage with graffiti, and whether the city sidewalk out front stayed intact. The city watches and issues tickets, Linnea told me, as I remembered Sundays in our old neighborhood after the city sent out drive-by inspection letters. That's when our landlord Henry came around, dragging a little tree branch from the front lawn to the alley, then poking his way back to the front to pick up another one, or nailing a swaying wood railing up along the front porch steps, then painting it a muddy beige that matched nothing solid on that raggedy house. We watched from the window and laughed at what that old man thought passed as fixed and what the city had the gall to call an inspection.

Now we were the ones with the responsibility, and after ten years renting a house constantly dissolving around our ears, we knew what would happen if we didn't watch out. The first year we had ice dams, frozen water expanding out of the gutters, opening up leak holes in between the roof shingles where the snow melted to a stream and flowed fast into the basement. Linnea paled when she saw it. Her body went sullen, brittle as the frozen trees in our yard. I had never seen her this way. Every creak and groan of the house is a noise she hears in her own joints. What I worried about was money. How would I make enough, if not this year then the next, or the one after that? I worried about keeping our nice house clean, vacuuming the carpet at midnight after working extra jobs, falling to the rug in tears the night the vacuum-cleaner wheel fell off. Once, we had stayed up all night sweating under each other's touch, calling to each other in the dark, but now I was sobbing over a broken cleaning machine. Is this what Dino meant about property making a gay marriage? Making it what?

Some time has passed, and we are no longer as stiff or hysterical. Our cave, our hollow, our nest, whatever it is right to call it—we were making it us in that first year. Now owning a house is just another among the things we do together. It matters some that we own it. Unlike before, we have a physical thing we could lose, a solid substance that could dissolve away between us like the red earth of Tara slipping through our fingers. I do agree with those who say that you can't really own places, that places own themselves, and the location of love cannot be so easily contained. But then I think of another friend, split from her lover of many years. After some time has passed it is not so much the lover she mourns but the property they shared, a hobby farm with acres of trees and a pond. Once she lost it, she had trouble feeling that even her own body was home.

I don't know if that is how it would go with Linnea and me. We are still so giddy in love with our house and are convinced it was waiting for us to find it. We painted our new living room a distilled shade of sunset, and I decorated the library under the stairs completely in leopard. We framed all the valentines Linnea has made for me—variations on a black-and-white bovine theme that began with a line from a poem Gertrude Stein wrote to Alice B. Toklas, *I marvel at your cow.* These cow-scapes hang now in our kitchen. Our rooms are the colors and patterns of how we adore each other, but they aren't what make us married.

Dino once told me he didn't believe the gay life was possible until he met two men who lived in a glass-enclosed house overlooking a sea coast. And yet, when I think of what really makes Dino and Danny, I have to remember back to the time before they owned buildings, when they lived in a rented garden apartment with Dino's baby grand. They invited Linnea and me over to announce what was already obvious to us, that Dino was gay, that he lived with the one he loved best. He made us dinner and talked about it, and later his friends stopped by. It was a coming-out party, a betrothal salon. Dino's special guest was Father Lenny, a favorite priest of our family and Dino's wavy-haired, gleaming-toothed confidant. Father Lenny brought his bashful sister, dark-eyed and narrow with a slow smile, and a gray-haired woman in sturdy oxfords who was either a nun or once a nun, with a nun's sort of name, Mary Catherine or Mary Pat. Father Lenny begged Dino to play the piano for us and since it was the week after New Year's, still the holiday season according to the ecclesiastical calendar, Lenny insisted we sing Christmas carols.

Dino is endlessly loquacious, but he finally shut up and played with fine-fingered flourish while the rest of us sang—quiet Danny, standing as he usually does, behind a couch, in a doorway, and Mary Pat Catherine tapping time in sensible shoes, and Lenny's speechless sister and Linnea and even tone-deaf me. A flock of queer squawking birds we were. Dino was the only one of us blessed by showbiz but all of us were trilling and flapping happily. Lenny's sister, we were told, had a woman at home. Mary lived in a residence of women and Lenny had his holy brotherhood. Dino had Danny. I had Linnea. What do lesbians bring to their second date? If they are lucky, four walls materializing on a smoky horizon, a hope for what might turn out to be a home.

Landscapes of My Beloved

Sin City

We didn't really mean it when we said we would get married in Vegas. It was a line Linnea and I tossed off at parties or whispered to each other in private. It was a tickle, a taunt, a metaphor, repeated because it made us laugh. But then our friends wanted to take a trip, a cheap week in March away from the chilly Midwest, and the neon desert beckoned. One of our chorus of friends was turning forty that year, and Las Vegas—pink-lit, pulsating—was where he most wanted to go.

It was Thanksgiving weekend that we decided, Chris and Alissa, Peter and Paul, Linnea and me, three longtime couples at brunch in downtown Minneapolis, together under the high beams of a renovated warehouse, eating eggs Benedict and pancakes and frittatas served by a kid from that pierced and tattooed generation that might be gay, might be straight. She seemed to enjoy waiting on our table of six committed homosexuals. We were four women and two men well past our dating days. We laughed. We teased. We told old stories. Linnea and I had the longest run of the couples gathered at our table that morning, yet we were the only ones who had never had nuptials of our own.

Chris and Alissa's wedding had been a simple ceremony, pulled together fast before one of the beloveds left town for graduate school. It had been summer and they set up in a park near the river, wore white pants and loose shirts, filled buckets with flowers from the farmers' market, and with good-old lesbian anti-authoritarian spirit officiated the ritual themselves, simple words of promise to remember, to love. The boys had a churchier affair, a college-campus chapel with windowed ceilings, both a radical Catholic priest and a Protestant minister from a gay friendly congregation downtown, hymns and prayers to the big Father, plain-pressed suits and flower-shop Bird of Paradise blossoms orange enough to part the gray haze of Minnesota December. First they did God, then they had a party for the rest of us—a potluck dinner and contra dancing in the gymnasium of a radical nun-run Catholic school.

You could get MARRIED in Vegas, our chorus of married friends sang, all through breakfast, and kept singing until Linnea, spurred on by coffee and our friends' laughing faces sprang out of her chair and fell to one knee. The high November sun pummeled in from the street and revealed how gray Linnea's hair had become in that past year. Our friends toasted us with forks and coffee cups. The waitress stumbled with an armload of dirty plates and righted herself again as she craned her neck to watch. "Please," Linnea said. "Please marry me." We looked into each other's faces. Hers is so familiar I don't always remember to look: her wide nose the same shape as her father's, the eyes behind the lenses of her glasses every year a little darker against her paling hair. My eyes were hidden behind spectacles too, eyes that Linnea has told me many times are shifting pools of green and gray and gold. We recognized each other there in the early winter light and laughed along with the rest. "Maybe we should," is what I said to my beloved.

~

So in our twelfth year of living in sin, Linnea and I finally decided to get married. Not that we were sure yet just what it meant for two women to use those words. Not that we hadn't already considered ourselves some kind of united, for years now, living together, traveling together, caring for a dog and three cats, buying joint gifts for our in-laws, attending weddings and funerals and holiday dinners. The only thing we had never done was walk down that mythic aisle.

But for all our asking and wondering and fantasizing over the years of what our sort of wedding might be, we never fully imagined that Las Vegas backdrop of bubbling lights and kerchinking coins. We never thought that our honeymoon entertainment would be front-row seats at a topless revue with a stage so bright it made the back of our eyes ache as chorus boys in leather loincloths snapped their fingers and tapped off tempo. *It's a gay men's chorus with showgirls,* I whispered to Peter across the nightclub table as we watched the big entrance of fifteen skinny women. Their nipples were tight in the breeze of the stage. They high-kicked gazelle legs up into cascades of headdress feathers while a dapper man in a glittery tux sang before a set that was no less than a replica of the Titanic, creaking and sinking into the electric sunset behind all those stepping and twirling feet.

We had, of course, heard of Las Vegas, but hadn't really pictured it. Acrobats in tie-dyed bodysuits levitated with pointed toes off silver poles. Amazing fellows in black tie and tails made whole sports cars disappear from a mottled stage. Caverns of blinking and purring slot machines made our hearts pump harder and our fingertips tingle as they stole all our silver. White tigers circled in a glass-enclosed casino zoo. Looking out over the traffic were truck-sized busts of two pretty-boy magicians whose best trick was an old-fashioned one, perfected years ago by Liberace, their obvious homosexuality so deeply unmentionable yet so essential to this boulevard of really big shows. Las Vegas was hilarious and over-lit, a drugged-up half-time at the football game, the Olympics of American Entertainment, but was it any place to get married?

Apparently so, judging by the avenues of wedding chapels. The sign before Wee Kirk O' the Heather insisted it was Las Vegas' finest since 1940. The Hitching Post was on the shadowy side of the boulevard— English, French, Polish, Russian, and Spanish spoken there. The Graceland Chapel, a wooden hut bathed in white and green light with walls full of photographs of the King, was the spot Jon Bon Jovi and Fernando Lamas exchanged vows with their brides. The Silver Bell Chapel featured its namesake in neon, a silent chime of gassy light, never ceasing in its claim that 300,000 happy couples were married there—no word if they were all still happy when they left. The Little White Chapel was the place where Joan Collins and Michael Jordan were wed, not, of course, to each other, and also the home of the $25 drive-through ceremony, a long driveway to a sliding-glass window under a canopy painted with bare-bottomed cupids and Frank Sinatra's voice piped through the outdoor speakers. The Sweethearts' Wedding Chapel advertised a $65 wedding pack. Burgler bars protected their plate glass so that the white lace-bound mannequin in the window looked to me like a bride behind bars, and I wondered how often it happened—women who were optimistic on their way into town but haunted on the way home by the edge of a sound, the tumblers in a lock turning, a gate shimmering shut to which she knows she has no key. *So happy they had to put her in jail,* one of our confidants quipped later, when we passed around the pictures.

When we tell people now about our wedding, we get one of two reactions. Either they laugh and stammer, *You did that? How fabulous.* Or else they look at us oddly, wondering, why, how, what could have moved us to do it that way? I wondered that myself on the drive in the rented Cadillac from the airport to our downtown Vegas hotel. The blue neon pulse of the pyramid-shaped Luxor casino ghosted our faces, on and off, sputtering moments of real and not real. A miniature New York City was scrunched into the space of a city block. This was more than some lunatic's daydream but a thing they really did build. And the people came to see it—Miss Liberty and the Coney Island roller coaster and the Chrysler building all rubbing shoulders. Vegas is not a real landscape but a fantasy that suggests our best memories can be recreated by remembering only the high points. If it muddies the romance, then leave it behind.

What could be the reason that Linnea and I would choose that trippy place to get married? It had something to do with the soundtrack we set behind our bliss, our lounge-music romance with another Las Vegas, the old one of swingers escaping to the desert to watch while the atom-bomb tests mussed their hairdos, of Frank Sinatra snapping his fingers on the stage of the Sands, of the clink of skinny-stemmed glasses, and of the way sequins catch and hold the glitter of artificial light. All this was one picture of what we were chasing, Linnea and I, pilgrims seeking the source of a distant glimmer, the light of what it feels like to be alive together. To get there, we had to be so happy they should have put us in jail, so sad they should have abandoned us there in that vacuum of cheap and expensive thrills, to give us a chance to at least try to stop endlessly thinking it all through.

Imagine it as if spotted from above. Two women embracing, not in that safe way girls learn in junior high, pelvises pulled away from each other, hands pat-patting each other's backs, but really embracing the way lovers do, skin and lips and breathing aroused and mingling. The tripping lights of the city gurgle around them, a peppering whirlpool of light and unearthly color. Beyond that are the suburban half-life developments of stucco and sod, and beyond that, darkness, under which the bare rocks of the desert shift along the planet's geological planes, their surfaces burnished copper and red. What do these two women need? How did they get here? Will it ever make sense? If there was a path that led us to this place, it was paved by these twin pulls, the fabulous human constructions of what is meant to look like happiness, and the parts that make and unmake themselves without our help. Both are what Linnea and I wanted at our wedding.

Home Ground

The winter we finally decided to get married was the second in our new domicile with the restored sun-ray engraving over the front entryway. The house is situated on a south side avenue named after a dead poet. Our realtor told us our miniature Queen Anne, built in 1909, had fallen to ruin by the mid-seventies when a guy named McKeegan bought it from the city for a dollar and rebuilt it from the foundation up. That winter we got married was mild, not like the one before when snow piled so high along the walkways I could run my hands over the top of a snowdrift without bending over. That was the winter we sent the dog out into the yard and lost sight of her almost immediately in the labyrinth of stacked snow. We had to dig a special path for Patsy so she would have a place in the back to pee, and another path to the garage for Linnea and me. That was the first winter we even had a garage, and two floors of house to keep clean, and a furnace to watch over. I remember all this now, the events of the year before we decided to get married, because it is part of the story, where it all began, the transition from one sort of life to another. It wasn't just that our names were joined on a piece of paper filed downtown, not just that it cost more to live, even though the house we bought was not on a fancy block, no more extravagant than the homes where other people in our limited circumstances lived. It was that we suddenly found ourselves immersed in an unfamiliar geography.

If I look out my window on a sunny September afternoon I can see the woman across the street who hosted the last block-club meeting. She sits on her front stoop. Her twin baby girls are spread out before her on a blanket and her three boys bang in and out their front door screen. Her curly strands of brown hair spring up around her head in the breeze. The widow who lives next door to us is eating lunch and reading the newspaper on her front porch. The guy across the street is still painting his house, as he has been so slowly all summer while his wife goes to her job downtown. It's afternoon, so in a little while he will walk with his son, too young for school, to meet his daughter at the bus and they will stroll back together. The girl has the same blond hair as her mother; her backpack hangs loosely from one shoulder. She looks so skinny in her blue-plaid Catholic-school uniform bought big enough to last her the year.

Down at the other end of the block are a lesbian couple with a son in high school and a gray dog who won a fight over a Frisbee one night in the park with Patsy. Across from them, live two men who used to be a couple, one short guy with lucid brown eyes who talks all the time, the other lanky, blond, and wordless. They lent us silver platters and serving spoons for the wedding reception we held in our yard a few months after we returned from Las Vegas.

One of our neighbors parks a yellow school bus in front of our house between her morning and afternoon runs. She is as round and flaxen as her husband is muscled and dark. Their children have a sandy cast. Last summer, they wove aluminum slats through their backyard chain-link fence, and Linnea and I wonder if it's so they don't have to see their neighbors, a lesbian couple we avoid too, ever since they cornered Linnea in our garage, pointed across the alley to a house where black people live, and said something despicable.

Across the street, a ponytailed and tattooed guy who reminds us of Linnea's brother has a lesbian sister, too, we know, because his kettle-drum voice carries over the grumble of passing cars. One afternoon I lounged on our front porch and listened as he explained to a friend why his sister put those rainbow stickers all over the bumper of her car. "She likes to advertise," he bellowed. On the corner where we always turn on the way to walk Patsy to the park lives a woman we suppose to be a lesbian, judging by whom we have seen stopping by. She wears floral print dresses, twitters to her cats through the screens, and gardens all the way out to the curb. Across the street from her lives a three-legged dog who lunges when we walk by, and a household of scruffy preschool white boys who wave sticks at us when we pass, shouting at Linnea, *you big, you big*, then stopping when they are unable to find the words for what kind of big they think she is.

Another kid from down the other end rang our doorbell one day. She's the daughter of Southeast Asian immigrants whose parents don't seem to speak much English. Her long hair hung loose to the center of her back and she spoke so low I could barely hear her. Her little sister was along, too. Her hair was cropped in bangs in front, to the lower edge of her earlobes at the sides, and her knees were a little dirty below the hem of her dress. When I tried to speak to the little one, she stared at me, and I couldn't tell if my words were anything more than random noise in her ears.

What Linnea and I have in common with our neighbors here is not so much the details of our lives but rather the ground of our living. This street. Our former block was a noisy bubble and we always had the same conversation—did you hear shots last night? This morning? Did you call? We've had that conversation once or twice on this block too, but have come to appreciate easier chitchat. *Such a nice day to sit on the porch,* and *are your daughters talking yet* and *how's that house painting coming?* It's the same between Linnea and me, the daily stories, the route I took this afternoon when I walked the dog, and how much damage the house took in last week's hailstorm.

In the absence of what used to be a constant flinch, that attention always paid to what was going on outside, we found suddenly that we were older than we had been before, that sometimes there was a silence around us we didn't know how to read, that new things would start to happen not just nearby us but also to us, and we would have to pay attention to new sorts of noises if we didn't want to lose our way. What fired the light behind each of our eyes? What did we need to do to keep it burning?

∾

It was that first winter, the year before we finally decided to get married, that we noticed parts of our pasts start to fall away. That was the season my old cat Artemis almost burned herself up in the furnace, an ancient boiler the size of a whiskey barrel that cycled on and off through the day's frigid hours. Artemis had been my tawny familiar since I was twenty, witness to all my distracted years. And she had been there through all my days with Linnea. She was a little breathing glimmer that reminded Linnea and me of so much that had passed between us. But at nineteen Arte was getting old. She howled randomly through the night, walked into walls, wet her own bed. Linnea stroked her ribby body. "What are you yowling about, old woman?" she asked her, and that is when we started calling her Grandma. We worried she wouldn't make it to the new address because she was blind and deaf and matted and living only for canned cat food. But the new house perked her up and she wandered more than she had in years, down into the basement and up again and in the summer even out into the sunny corners of our screened porch. All she needed near the end was wet cat food and a warm spot to doze.

Poking around the basement one afternoon, searching for a hot spot with only the sensations of her paws and whiskers to guide her, she must have curled up alongside the furnace while it cycled off. When it cycled on again there was a fire and I wonder if she even felt it at first, so warm, then too warm, then stinging. I noticed an odor, and I was at first just interested, a naive new homeowner curiosity. So this is the way our furnace smells. But then I smelled it in the wrong places, the kitchen, the bathroom, and felt the blood pump too fast through my chest remembering every odd news report I had ever heard about the sweet little house near the center of the city blown to dust without warning, a pressurized pop, and the neighbors gathering later at the property line, shaking their heads, their eyelashes starred with tears.

When I called the gas company, I remembered where I had smelled this before, when I was twenty-two, in my first cheap apartment in Minneapolis. The only heat source was a space heater with visible blue-yellow gas jets where I hung my wool socks to dry. The gas company wasn't interested in my memory reverie and told me to shut off the heat until they could come, and I did, but then I saw Arte, the remnants of what had been her amber mane now so tangled and matted beyond what we were able to comb out or cut away. She stood there dazed in a patch of sun, looking as she always did, and then she circled around the other way to hold her face up in the sunlight and I saw it, one side of her charred and sooty. I tripped over my feet running to her, and brushed the charcoaled hunks of fur to the kitchen table. She wasn't hurt, but big patches of her long hair had burned away. That was the smell I had remembered, the smell of my wool socks catching, going brown, shriveling away. Artemis had been a young cat then, still spending days outside chasing birds and begging food from neighborhood old ladies. Grandma and I had come full circle, our years cycling around a bad smell, but now it was more than my socks I was losing. This senile little animal, my watcher, my witness to the early years, was a wick alight and disintegrating before my eyes.

∼

As old Artemis faded, Patsy and I walked the ground of a new neighborhood. We weren't so far from where we used to live and I could have walked Patsy off in that direction, and sometimes I did, tripping down into the grass bowl of Powderhorn Park from the opposite direction. But now I felt like a visitor. I wasn't hemmed in as I had been before, between the park's wide swath and a streak of city-severing freeway.

Now Patsy's and my most frequent walks are to a park without a name. It's a green gully between alleys where there once were houses, all torn down after a killing flood in a summer remembered for one big dump, ten inches of rain in just three hours. There is a bronze plaque of an old man in that park, Mr. Burnside, a neighborhood guy who was killed when the flood collapsed his basement wall. The plaque tells the story of the rain that wouldn't stop, of the man who was swept away.

During the first year in our new house Linnea and I used the words, "Going to see Mr. Burnside," as code for letting each other know we were going to take the dog for a walk. But Patsy has pretty good verbal comprehension skills. She has been able to understand even the spelled-out letters of w-a-l-k ever since she was a puppy. Eventually she caught onto the phrase, "Going to see Mr. Burnside," the sound of it got her excited too soon. Once she heard it, she began to stalk us through the house, nipping at our ankles and even howling, until we hurried, got her leash, stepped out with her into the sun. So we changed the code again, this time to "Burnside-san," in memory of our recent trip to visit my brother and his family in the dense outer sprawl of Tokyo. Patsy caught onto Burnside-san, too, but by then it was the name the man in the park answered to in our minds.

Mr. Burnside's face emerges from his plaque in bas-relief, so much so that sometimes I forget he is not a whole bust cast in three dimensions, not a holy statue set on an outdoor altar. I forget his head doesn't hold all the angles of any human head, but is just the picture of a face, glowing in a way that remembers more than this moment. Judging by this rendering he was a bulb-nosed fellow, and at first we greeted him with sardonic commentary, figuring he was a guy who died on his way downstairs to get another beer. Then we met someone who used to lived nearby and might remember the family, so we decided we better knock off the jokes. It was a little cynical of us, to assume that the guy with his picture in the park might have breathed his last at the center of some less-than-heroic moment, but later we came to see that this was exactly the point. We didn't know him personally, but with his balding head and big square spectacles he looked like the guys Linnea and I both knew growing up, like working stiffs who built bars in their basements. My own father built a bar in his basement. We hiked to see him with affection, old Burnside-san, Mr. Regular-White-Guy-Grandpa in a part of the city where his kind are getting harder to find, a burnished signpost of the shifting times in our new neighborhood.

~

By the time we decided to get married, Artemis was already gone, a spot of the old life dusted way. It seems overblown to speak of the end of youth but that's how things were starting to feel. My old cat was dead. Her ashes were buried in our new yard under a seashell garden. Not that we didn't laugh at the way our middle age loomed. Before we left our old apartment, we piled everything we no longer needed on our front lawn to sell, and when prospective buyers stopped to finger my Annie Lennox poster or college photography equipment, Linnea's camping thermos or her old ice skates, we sang out "youth for sale," and the people who laughed with us were usually the ones who bought something.

My real grandma died the same year as Arte did. My mother's mom was a little Polish lady who shriveled once her children did what seemed best and moved her to a senior residence. Her old neighborhood was a block from the projects where she raised her kids. She lived on a city street lined with brick houses near the boarded-up steel mills, in the same apartment for thirty years. Nearby were stores where all the signs are in Spanish now, a battered park with gang graffiti decorating the benches and garbage cans where I watched fireworks when I was a kid, the buses that have driven the same route downtown for decades, and St. Kevin's, the corner church where both my mother and her sister were married.

They moved her to the far western suburbs, to a building I came to think of as the Grandma Warehouse, a high-rise with a parking lot in an avenue of strip malls. The building was filled with old women and a few old men. Some spent the day sitting on hard chairs in the lobby. Most, like my grandma, hardly ever left their apartments. I have a few photographs of my grandmother from the years when she still got around. In one of them, Linnea is sitting next to her in my parents' basement rec room, in the hours before Christmas dinner. Linnea is leaning over, listening to my grandmother tell her something, looking straight into Grandma's face and smiling, inviting her to keep on talking. And Grandma did talk to her. It was one of the moments, early on, when I noticed Linnea's instinct for locating the life in people. Look how good she was, paying attention like that to my little grandmother.

Once she moved to her new apartment, Grandma's stiff sofa and dusty wall hangings and silhouettes of robed saints looked out of place. I understood the family's concern. Grandma had to leave the old place because her landlord of three decades was dying. She had refused to move earlier on when there was still time for choices and my dad found her a nice set of rooms in a nearby city neighborhood. Yet I could see that she would not recover from the shock of feeling her familiar ground yanked out from under her. The look in her eye reminded me of lost wanderers pacing blankly down urban streets, muttering to themselves—immigrants

Grandma would have called "foreigners." They never adapted to the new territory. The temperature was never right against their skin. The pale green light that used to guide them had been extinguished.

The last few times I visited her, Grandma was gaunt and brittle with pain. She had uterine cancer that had metastasized. Her mind was still clear, but there wasn't much she wanted to talk about except Dr. Kevorkian, and there was little I could think of to say to convince her that life was worth the trouble. I showed her some photographs of my thirty-eighth birthday party and she paused at a shot of one of my friends, a gay man taller than me, his graying hair pulled back in a pony-tail, standing shoulder-to-shoulder with his lover. Grandma perked up for a second when she asked, "Is that your boyfriend?"

"No, Grandma," I said. "That's my friend John. He's very interesting though. He makes puppets for a living." Then I pointed to another shot, of Linnea with a platter of birthday cake from the natural-foods bakery balanced on her forearms, and I added, as I always do when my beloved has not come back to Chicago with me, "You remember Linnea, don't you, the one I live with?"

"Oh yeah, I remember," she said as she moved onto the next shot, a close-up of me with hair longer and blonder than it had been in a while. Grandma squinted at the photograph, then closed her eyes. "You look like your mother in this one."

Glancing around her barren apartment, I saw a few things I recognized, a lampshade, a chair. What was left to keep her here? I wanted her to talk about life. The charge of breath circling her bones. The wonder of holding some trinket in her hand and watching it open out into sound and smell until she could feel the burn of memory against her pores. There was another moment when she brightened, after I got her to talk about her youth. She moved to the city from a farm in Wisconsin where her immigrant mother spoke only Polish. She went out dancing in Chicago clubs, once even to a speakeasy. But after a few minutes, she closed her eyes and lay down on her sofa like a corpse, and I said, "OK, Grandma. I guess I'll go."

The next time I saw her, I asked again about her early days, but this time she said, "Oh, I can't remember any of that old stuff, see." A few weeks later she was gone. The last person she talked to was a Polish

nurse at the home where her children moved her for the end. "I don't remember no Polish," she had always told me, but according to what I
heard, the nurse and my grandma spent her last hours whispering in the
tongue of their mothers. Maybe the sound of it, the roll of nearly forgotten consonants, reminded her of some familiar green glimmer.

~

So this was a time of adding and subtracting. Linnea and I missed the
view out our front window of Portland Avenue, even the steady beat of
the traffic light on the corner. We gained a green grass lawn, and a
perennial garden, echinacea and black-eyed Susans and lilies. Neither of
us knew much about how to care for all of this, but we were learning. We
gained a new view, Cedar Avenue through the trees and the white-lit
sign of Matt's Bar, home of the Juicy Lucy, a greasy burger stuffed with
processed cheese, the sort of food I don't believe in but that Linnea tells
me is delicious.

Meanwhile, all our old domiciles were slipping away. Linnea's family
kept moving, one sister to a high-rise condo in downtown Chicago, her
mother and new husband to a house trailer near the Wisconsin Dells.
Her family had migrated away from the northern suburb of Chicago
where Linnea went to high school in a town known for its man-made
landmarks—a great curve of roller coaster that ringed the franchise
amusement park, a cement replica of the Sphinx. No longer could we
sneak away from her family gatherings to pay homage to these bulwarks
of Linnea's adolescence.

And my parents left Chicago for a late-life mortgage on a golf-course
house in Florida. My mother was learning to play the piano. She dyed
her hair blond and wore it pulled back in the ponytail I had only seen her
wear before in photographs taken the year she married Dad. And my father finally got his teeth fixed and bought a golf cart. Then my middle
brother Benny got married among the Baptists, foreigners as far as my
Catholic grandmothers were concerned, and settled in the center of
Illinois three hours south of Chicago. My baby brother Paulie is an air-
force lawyer and lives all over the world. His wife Mitsuko has not lived
in her hometown of Kobe since she was a girl. The streets of the district
where she grew up had been crushed and built over again after Japan's

last big earthquake. By far the most practical among us, Mitsuko told me she considered home the place she lived at the moment you asked. Still, when I told Paulie we ought to try and convince Mom and Dad to lighten their financial burden by selling the house sitting empty in Chicago's southern freeway and railroad fields, he bristled. "What are you trying to do, take away my home?"

But it wasn't our home anymore. We all had new homes, new families. All our histories were dimming while new stories took on light. Linnea and I lived without roller-coaster towers, without commuter trains, in a huddle of bungalows and miniature Victorians circling Mr. Burnside's face, where the end of day was noted by the shimmer off Burnside-san's copper-colored nose.

Shifting Ground

It was not only the places Linnea and I used to reside that were changing, but also our ideas of ourselves. This is why I linger outside the story of Linnea and my wedding instead of riding straight into that neon-lit day. The electric streaks over a desert horizon interest me the most here, yet I can't help but note the way any one thing is linked to its opposite and I always remember more than the bright points.

At the end of every year, Linnea and I had grown accustomed to looking at each other and laughing, *whew, that was a strange one.* It was as if we really believed that a year begins and ends on a concrete date, that if this one is rough, the one to come is sure to be easier. Is this how everyone's life feels? Even so, it does seem that the year of our wedding was both the best and worst.

The problem was Linnea's work. The news magazines spouted statistics, over a million "surplus Ph.Ds," meaning simply that Linnea was one in a cast of thousands unable to land a tenure-track teaching job. What a thing to absorb, that she might not become the English professor I knew her to be, that she imagined she was, that so many students called the best they had known. But despite pleas, petitions, student protests, the English department where she had taught on a full-time annual contract for over a decade was not going to renew her. It was "exploitation" according to the rule book, to keep an adjunct any longer and no one saw fit to make a permanent offer. Years of national job seeking yielded no better results.

I could always feel it when her situation thickened. "Hi Sweety," I would say, as I always did when she walked in from work, if I didn't look closely first, if I couldn't make out her eyes behind her shades. Then she would switch to her indoor specs, revealing the mud around the iris of her eyes and I knew she had received more bad news. Those were the sinking afternoons with Linnea slumped and speechless, and for a while I was unable to keep from sinking with her.

I must sound shrill when I explain it to people, unable to keep the blade out of my voice when I count out the reasons I think it matters that she has been so loved by the young people she has worked with over the years. Most of Linnea's students were, at least for a while, barefoot and ankle bracelet sorts of undergraduates, hyper-alert readers and critics, headed for either a job in the food co-op or graduate school. They are the ones who petitioned the administration, who published an open letter in the college paper, who marched in the city gay and lesbian pride parade with a placard that read *Save Linnea's Job*.

I used to dislike her students. The way the ones from wealthy families circled the globe on school holidays while Linnea and I, who couldn't afford to take an airplane ride together until we were over thirty-five, stayed home in our rattletrap apartment. Or the way they so physically identified with their little liberal arts college as if it were a ranch with their brand on the gate. I spent my early college years drinking up and dropping out of the anonymous plain of a state university. These fancy private college kids seemed spoiled and too lucky to me.

I changed my mind when I actually met a few of them. There was the witty gay boy with the thrift-shop wardrobe, his conversation was so sharp it almost hurt to listen, and the studious lesbian who looked like her father and held the same job Linnea had when she was an undergraduate, resident advisor in the women's dorms. But my favorites were the bruiser from Omaha with the black father and white mother who pulled himself out of gang life because he wanted to be a teacher, and the one who seemed just a few fingers wide, a girly lesbian with pale skin and a black cap of hair who loved to talk motorcycles and used to get by squatting in boarded-up houses. These were just a few of those attracted to Linnea's classes, the ones who wrote her letters, *it was you who have photosynthesized whatever I attempt.*

Of all the folks Linnea knew well in graduate school, only one has a permanent job in the field. Linnea's chorus of grad-school cronies wear a familiar pallor like residents of a town where the steel mill has shut down. Which makes me, I guess, a bit like an unemployed steelworker's wife, strangely the same role I may have found myself in had I married one or another of the boys, sons of steelworkers, I went out with in high school so near the abandoned mill plains southeast of Chicago.

I say strangely because I know there's got to be some way for Linnea to spend the education she accumulated through all those years of working her way through school, even if a cushy tenured professorate is beyond her reach. She must have a few more options than the average pink-slipped millworker does. Yet there have been days when the shape of Linnea's disappointment has felt to both of us just like those empty factories down the block from where my newly dead grandmother used to live—crooked structures without windows, surrounded by rusted piles of slag. And so instead of imagining myself married to some kind of expatriated pedagogue, a gloom for which I had no geography, I have pictured myself as that laid-off steelworker's wife, who is tight all along her arms and jaw and weary from dawn to dusk because she doesn't know what to do except nag about her husband's shoes in the kitchen, nag about dirty dishes littering the counter, nag about how her husband snores before the TV's static eye.

I understand why those students write her letters. It used to be that I could depend on Linnea, too. Her face was a box of light, a radiance from just under the surface that had come to look like living to me. For years I had depended on it. Then one day she said to me, "My lighthouse has gone out," as she fell forward into my embrace. I have not known what to do, except hold her there.

~

Who will hold me if I am holding Linnea? What light will I chase if Linnea's light is obscured?

Time and again I have turned to the chorus for help. When I speak of our friends as a chorus I refer to all the old showbiz meanings of the word. They are the ones tap-dancing toward a happy ending, the voices who support us singing harmony, the high notes who raise our rituals toward heaven, the lips who comment on the actions of our hours—as we will be sure to comment on theirs.

Linnea has friends among our troubadours, her Italian American lesbians, with ways of talking that remind her of her grandmother. They are women who cry at the sight of a well-made meatball. There is one among them, a Sicilian from St. Louis with a cacophony of black hair and a purse full of beauty weapons, who's always had a bent toward butches. *Linnea is my brother*, is what she says, referring to the way a girl wants to lean on Linnea.

Another member of the choir is a woman who worked for a while in a factory that manufactured props for impotent penises, and she liked it quite a bit, until Viagra pulled the bottom out of the business. This may seem like an odd job for a lesbian, but it was meant to be temporary, balm for her social worker burnout. These days she's a substitute teacher, but she used to pace the downtown streets with homeless adolescents who assumed her uncombed curls, her unraveling clothes, meant she was what she seemed, still a teenager herself. She knew how to stare kids down from the space of ten feet or so and then intuit how they were put together, and she has an annoying habit of watching her friends in the same way. After she watched Linnea, she said, "I think butch lesbians aren't so much a kind of man as they are a mother turned-up high. A sort of guardian angel."

When we were in Japan, Linnea and I came across such an icon—the image of a mother who is also a big brother. An Angel on High with weapons. There is a temple in Kyoto called Sanjusangendo that contains 1,001 Kannons under one roof. Kannon is a gender-ambiguous entity, male or female or both. Kannon sculptures are usually gold or brass-plated. Flat or cleavaged, her chest is often bare. She stands or she sits in lotus position with her lips pressed together, her eyes closed or gazing back out at whoever brings her devotion. Two of her square or delicate palms might be pressed together in prayer. If she has more hands, they clutch a branch, a blossom, a knife. Her fingers reach around her head toward the sky. The temple literature describes the central statue at Sanjusangendo, a 1,000-armed Kannon, holding tools "with which to remove the pains from the people and to bring joy to the people."

Linnea and I are not Japanese, nor Buddhist, so we will probably never fully understand the echoes of each bloom, each ax, each indecipherable item in Kannon's countless palms. And yet we were both so moved in this temple where dusky incense swelled our senses. One thousand pillars of two-armed Kannons lined up, rows of golden-comb teeth on either side of the centerpiece god who possessed a halo of illuminated fingers. There are people, we know them, who would not like it that we purchased a brass statue of a seated and robed Kannon in a Kyoto temple shop to bring home to our little statuary of Catholic Madonnas and Hollywood femme-fatale dolls. Our house Kannon has twenty arms. A crown of twelve more gilded heads pile up over her brow, and her eyes are closed in meditation. We mean no disrespect when we finger the tiny objects in her brass hands, one that looks distinctly like a wiener in a white-bread bun, and so refer to her (or him) as Our Lady of Hot Dogs with Everything. All we mean is that we feel so brightened by this idol, all the pieces of us, nutritious or not.

There are some who would demand that we leave all our home deities to the ones who know the full meanings of their prayers, and they may be right. But we haven't given our statues away. They are markers of worlds Linnea and I have encountered together. We don't know how else to acknowledge the way Kannon stripped us down to the blood, made our mouths and throats go dry. Our clothes, damp from the rain outside, stuck to our bellies and thighs the day we stood among the other tourists before 1,001 resplendent casts of face, "a wood of Buddhas," the guidebook read. Thousands of arms wiggling all at once, offering a hammer, a book, a ride, a conversation.

The temple literature says if you look long enough at Sanjusan-gendo's chorus of illumined faces you will find one that looks like yourself. I don't know what I would have felt had this been a golden prairie of bare-toed Madonnas. I might have loved it as much. But this calvalcade of Kannons had a wallop I had not prepared for. Did I find Linnea's face in the field of another people's heaven? Did I find my own?

When I left the temple all I could think to do was walk away through a waterfall of rain, off onto a block of food booths and fashion boutiques and finally into a Japanese beauty parlor. I always cut my hair when I want my life to change, but I had never before leapt into the stylist's chair with such unpremeditated fervor. I was on a mission; some part of me had to go. I pantomimed what I wanted to the woman working alone that day. I made a scissors motion with my fingers through my chin-length bob and gestured toward a picture on the wall of a Western woman with an inch of blond moussed up against gravity. The hairdresser nodded.

Linnea had abandoned me to this foolish quest, knowing how I get when my hair doesn't turn out how I want it to. I couldn't get her to believe that this time it didn't matter. It would be too much to claim that I had received a message on that monsoony afternoon so far from my home. I was no Moses on the mountain, no Bernadette greeting the watery shape of Mary under the proscenium arch of a country cave. And it wasn't long until I let that haircut grow out again. Yet something had entered me that day that had never resided there before. The light I chase is a glimmer off a forest of foreheads, a wild brush of arms. My arms. Linnea's arms. I was preparing to see us through a new prism as my hair fell to the tiles around the hairdresser's feet. So imagine it, no common syllables between a hairdresser and a client who lock eyes and grin in the silver field of the shop mirror. Some of what I had carried with me, over the seas, was falling away, would be swept up and taken out with the trash, burned or dumped or composted in a country not my own. All I knew was the earth was shifting beneath my shoes.

Clinging Ground

Members of our chorus have asked if anything has shifted between Linnea and me, now that we are married. After all, most marry in their early hours, and the two of us have been together for a dozen years already. Yes, I tell them. Something has changed. Our proximity to the bright lights of the world, and so our faith in each other's luster. By the time we stood together on that Vegas boulevard of budget nuptials we had some idea of what we were up to, but it was a long trudge before we could get so comfortable.

At the time we traveled to Japan, Linnea was still her old self. Yet we sensed the coming trouble. It wasn't that Japan was one of those trips that people like Linnea and me take in order to steal back lost pieces of ourselves, or at least we didn't mean it to be. Neither of us had traveled overseas before. We were awestruck by all that we encountered. But it was an accident that our first big trip occurred at a time when our lives had begun to look like a pilgrimage, toward what light we could not say.

The first thing Linnea and I do in a new place is seek out the ones that are like us. The only place in Japan where Linnea and I were certain we could make out the flickering of other lesbians was in a bar in the Shinjuku district of Tokyo. It was a tiny watering hole, three stories up a narrow cement staircase, a space not much bigger than our dining room. Japan is not a country where it's easy to find homos gathering openly, but the narrow men walking the six or so square blocks of the gay section of Shinjuku—Japanese boys with black hair bleached red and shirt-tails hanging over their belts, or the European fellows in tight jeans and T-shirts clinging to chest muscles—all eyed one another without wavering. Once Linnea put on her necktie the men eyed her, too, and as always I was amazed at the shortsightedness of gay men in drinking districts, such seasoned cruisers managing to miss the bulge of Linnea's chest and the lack of the same between her thighs.

The spots where women find one another were harder to locate. We had a hazy Internet street map to guide us, but even so we had to ask at a little corner sex toy store. The slouching boys hanging out with the cashier pointed us vaguely down another narrow avenue. The place we finally discovered was packed with fifty or so compact bodies. A couple of the girlier women in bobbed hair and tight little skirts smiled up at Linnea. One even reached up to straighten her tie. We were Caucasian giants in that jammed-up room. There were American pop posters of k.d. lang and Melissa Etheridge pinned to the walls. There was cigarette smog and a humidity of beer. There were the usual few staggering girls, the drunks we would run into in any dyke bar anywhere. And we found out the place wasn't really so crowded. On busy nights, an English-speaking German woman told us, the patrons had to hold their beers up over their heads, as if they were riding the rush-hour trains.

But we did not come to Japan to bask in the low light of a dyke bar. It was years since my last beer, and I hardly ever went to bars anymore.

What pulled us to this tavern was the instinct most gays and lesbians we know hone from the beginning, a longing for the incandescence of the rest, the family, the us. In recent years since Linnea and I have begun to travel together we have gone to new places and wondered—where would it be safe to kiss in this city? Then it's usually true that we end up saving our kisses for later and spend our hours in other parts of town, the Italian district of San Francisco, Chinatown in New York, never knowing where we might find that taste, that scent (the gnocchi at that Italian café in the Village, the waft from gold canisters of a tea room in Seattle) that will remind us of our own breathing, the life together we don't stop wanting.

One of the places we found that reminder of life in Japan was on a show stage very much like the ones in Vegas where feathers and smoke and costumes shiver under the follow spot. But this was no typical girly revue. The women of Takarazuka dress as Linnea often does—as cross-dressing lovers, as female gentlemen—and in Japan they are the heart-throbs of thousands.

We attended the show on a weekday afternoon and every seat was filled. The theater was plush and spangled, the lobby painted with murals of the top stars in full regalia. Their sequined costumes from previous shows were cocooned in Plexiglas display cases. The gift shop was packed with photographs of troupe members. Close-ups accentuated the slicked-back hair, the piercing stage gaze. Long shots were of a Fred-and-Ginger-style waltz. The romantic lead wore crisp white trousers and held her partner by the waist. The one in a billowing skirt swooned and backbended in her lover's grasp. We were two of only a few Westerners in the audience and the only ones we could be sure were lesbians, although there was a pair we wondered about. Seated a few rows in front of us was a young woman with her hair bobbed at the chin, a style we had noticed in the Shinjuku bar, and wearing a skirt that revealed a good portion of her thighs. She sat next to a stockier woman in loose trousers and with hair snipped off above the ears, the shortest hairstyle we had seen on a woman in Japan.

The rest of the velvet seats were filled with proper adolescent girls and middle-aged wives who showed no signs of late nights in their city's seedier districts. There were hardly any men, besides a few American pairs we figured to be gay. There were Linnea and me, my blue cotton dress damp from the heat of the train, Linnea's knees stiff from all our walking. But we forgot ourselves once the Takarazuka stars sashayed down the dappled runway in top hat and tails while the audience cried out.

Linnea and I didn't add our shouts to the choir, but we could understand the feeling. It was all music and giddy love and two women's bodies embracing. The guidebooks say nothing about Takarazuka and lesbians, and even our more savvy sources state that lesbianism was not what Takarazuka's creator had in mind. It was 1913 when the entrepreneur some call the "Japanese Ziegfeld" hired his first all-female revue to bring people to his faltering spa, a stop along his new railroad line. The story of the theater is common knowledge in Japan. The performers are called Takarasiennes, after Parisiennes, and the women of the troupe are selected by audition when they are still girls. They work their way up year by year, at first cleaning up after the others and eventually are sorted by height into intensive training in the male or female roles they will from then on maintain, even in their off-hours. The theater administrators don't talk about the scandals that have surfaced now and then over the years—lesbian love affairs among the ranks. They tell foreign interviewers that the Takarazuka training prepares the performers for marriage. Living as a man for all those years, they promise, will teach a bride to understand what her husband wants from his wife.

Yet whatever the intentions—of the theater, of any particular Takarasienne—it's impossible for Linnea and me to see anything but our sort of love on that star-studded stage, in ways we never do watching videos of the real Fred and Ginger, so gray compared to this big Busby Berkeley finish, this Las Vegas pizzazz of heavy headdresses and yellow-lit steps that climb all the way into heaven. Miki Maya was the star of our show, a two-parter. The first act was a stage remake of the James Dean version of *East of Eden*. The second was a Broadway-style extravaganza called *Dandyism*. It was a musical tribute (according to the English translation in the program) to the art of being a gentleman. Maya-san was flanked by a chorus of interchangeable knees and faces, and it was not girls in feathers who caused all the commotion. It was the cross-dressed heartthrob in a glitter jacket and creased pants, descending to the center stage to sing her solo surrounded by females in silver chiffon dresses.

These fans know Miki Maya is not an actual man. The performers make little effort to disguise their origins. These are not American drag kings who might pass on the street as the real thing. Although their hair is waxed back, their breasts flattened, the eyes of the male leads are painted with heavy theatrical fringe. Their lips are darkened with the reddest lipstick shades. The fans may not think of their love as lesbian but there is no doubt that the objects of their adoration are women.

Linnea and I stuck around after the show to watch the audience wait, in neat lines, at the stage door, always orderly, bearing boxes of sweets and wrapped packages and letters promising never-ending love to Miki and the others. Linnea and I sat on the curb of a street without cars, the pseudo-avenues once imagined by the impresario who transformed his failed resort into this family amusement park from which the theater gets its name. We watched as the actresses who played the girls stepped through the doors and the ones who waited applauded politely. But when a male player stepped out into the clinging evening, the women's voices rose again in bird cries of love. Moving clumps of bodies pushed toward their beloved's face. A few even chased the stars all the way off the theater grounds, outrageous behavior for a Japanese housewife.

Linnea and I had never seen anything like Takarazuka. Where else had we ever witnessed the romance between two women's bodies so projected and pantomimed? Our mouths hang open for hours. Our fingers are numb from the shock. I picture Linnea as the star of this show. I contemplate what I have in common with those Japanese housewives and teenagers. I imagine my back arched. My starry eyes lifted to my lover's face. Is my beloved a flat-chested goddess with 1,000 arms asunder? Is she a bejeweled heartthrob from the proscenium stage? All I can tell is that she is the one I will marry. So I fall back into her embrace. I cling to her there.

~

My little Polish grandma who so recently died did not speak highly of marriage. Her husband, my grandfather, was drunk through most of their married years and not a body anyone could cling to. But the other family matriarch, Grandma Rose, a golf-course retiree like my parents, has always told me that a woman needs a man to keep her from falling, despite the fact that she has lived on her own for twenty-five years, ever since her second husband passed away.

Once Grandma Rose bought me a pink velveteen hostess gown for Christmas and said, "Now you can get married." I suppose she meant I should find someone who would be the strong one as I held on, in my furry pink housecoat, in my feathered pink slippers. Not that Gram's life was anything like this. Her first husband, my father's dad, was a Croatian immigrant who she says was the best hoofer on the floor at the old Chicago Park District dances. He was an accounting clerk employed by a Chicago steel mill, and died suddenly while his children were still young. Her second husband had an executive post at a corporation in the days when men kept such jobs for life. He wore a tie. He brought home a paycheck. He bought her a three-bedroom rambler in which they kept separate bedrooms in a suburb south of Chicago, at the spot where the freeway bends east toward Indiana. I remember his gold retirement watch, glinting against his dark forearm hair.

Gram has always told me that the thing to do is to marry for that gold watch, as if she hadn't battled the rush-hour traffic all the way downtown to her own job every morning until she was in her sixties. As if she weren't up at dawn every day still, volunteering at the hospital, or dragging storm-torn branches around her blooming Florida yard. I see that she has done well on her husband's retirement. I imagine she would like to see me so settled.

I never got to observe Gram with her first husband, the one she loved to dance with. He was dead long before my father danced his first dance with the woman he would marry. I don't know if Gram swooned, if she clung. Perhaps if I did, I might know if she is talking about love as well as money. Would she listen if I tried to explain how I have found what I need? She knows about Linnea and me, but declined our invitation to dance at our wedding reception. I have rarely seen Gram dance at all, except with her sisters years ago at her own mother's eightieth birthday. She wore a powder blue suit. Her legs were so smooth in her Sunday hosiery. Her white hair was swooped up over her forehead. And I've seen her dance with my cousin Dino, who will foxtrot in public with anyone except his own true love. And I've seen her take to the floor with Linnea who dipped and twirled her across the floor of my brother's wedding hall.

I imagine Grandma Rose picking out that pretty pink robe. She must have stroked the polyester pile. She must have envisioned the life that would go along with it, a house with clean windows, morning coffee in a stainless-steel kitchen, a husband always there to catch his wife when she leaned too far back into the swell of the waltz. Linnea was one of so few at Paulie and Mitsuko's wedding who knew the right way to lead through a dip, so Gram ought to be able to see what I possess. Still, I am certain that she believes I am a sad case with no gold watches to inherit. Like her, I married the best hoofer in the joint, and have discovered since that a wife has so much more to do than keep herself from falling.

~

I am not sure what people, our neighbors for instance, assume about Linnea and me. Do they imagine us to be as odd as the images hanging on our dining-room walls, the framed posters of the Takarazuka shows? The women in our gallery embrace, one straight and strong, one limp and clinging, a pose so familiar to anyone who has ever seen a Hollywood musical, so strange to anyone who realizes that they have never before seen two women in a picture like this.

I can't tell what our neighbors notice about Linnea and me. Our good friends know something of what transpires beneath our surfaces and if we are going out, to a party, to dinner and a show, we will be sure to dress in a way that conveys our Fred-and-Ginger feeling for each other. But if we are just out to walk the dog or weed the garden or drop something off at the post office, we usually don't feel much like dressing for the show. Plain athletic shoes. T-shirts and jeans. None of this is much to go by, plus we are getting to that age in which, if you're a woman, nobody sees you anyway. We may look alike to them. Two white gals approaching forty, one graying, one with curious cat's-eye glasses.

When I sit on my front porch I nearly always notice the thirtyish woman who lives across the street from me. She has a stream of blond hair, some streaks of it nearly white, which she cut off at the shoulders this summer. A week later her young daughter had hers shorn as well, to the ears, and so I assume all that hair was giving them trouble. The mom wears black tights and a short black jumper every day to work and I envy the way she can twist her hair up into a bun with one hand, as Grandma

Rose can, and keep it there with a single bobby pin. It's the action of a woman who takes care of things. I wonder if she makes her black jumpers, just as she makes cut-outs for her front windows with her children, blossoms in the spring, snowflakes to celebrate winter. I know very little about her. She is a window dresser at a downtown department store. Her husband takes his time painting the house. She told Linnea that she loves Frank Sinatra.

She seems to be a wife my grandmothers would recognize, someone who understands what I am always reinventing, the job description, the ways a wife has to do her share of holding it all it place. But there is always so much more than I can spot from across the street. I am projecting, of course. Yet I do enjoy imagining such a life, filled with all the domestic attentions I would like to give Linnea, but never seem to have time for.

Who knows what impression my neighbors get from watching me? I am certain they don't see Fred Astaire's dance partner, no Mrs. cushy-robed-coffee-brewer here. But then most of them probably don't watch me at all. They are too busy with their children, or working out, or fixing up their houses. They are probably uninterested in what I am up to as I laze about in an oversized T-shirt and leggings, on the porch again, on the green leather lounger I dragged out from the living room, another book in my lap.

Most people I have come across, at least those who don't hang in the bohemian world, seem to think right away that there is something strange about me. I look put together in the wrong order. I once had a lover who pointed to posters of women wrapped in sheets running their fingers through bobbed hair, saying this is how you look. But she was a woman who liked me best in bed. When we stood up we fought. Linnea points to a different sort of portrait, a sculpture made from springs and old toothbrushes and bits of broken glass, stuff the artist must have found in the alley. As much as I would like to be photographable I really am better represented by things that rattle and catch odd angles of sun and are only lovely to a certain twist of eye. "There you are," Linnea will say, and we will laugh because it's so funny the way someone I have never met could build such a likeness.

I don't know what people see when they look at Linnea either, except

· 262 ·

they are always drawn to confide in her. If we are seated next to strangers at a restaurant that seats family-style, the man sitting next to her will nod at me, distant, stony, and I will be aloof, too. Then he will turn to Linnea and visibly loosen, telling her all about how he recently remarried, how he was learning to fly a plane, how he left his first marriage because there was no laughter but now he was laughing all the time. Linnea attracts people, in fact has trouble keeping them from hanging onto her as if they were drowning and she was the only boat.

When our young nieces visit for a week in the summer, we clear the dining-room table for art projects. When we play with clay we try to build a model of Auntie Linnea. I put together boxy shapes, a square head, a rectangular torso, a whirlpool of gray at the hairline. "Yes," they tell me. "It looks like her." She is a body you don't expect to tip over, as solid as a shipping crate.

So this may be what the neighbors see in the weeks before Linnea's and my wedding. Not Linnea's tumble and the way I am learning to hold on, but a good box. An assemblage of junk. A peculiar translation of husband and wife. If that is true, then they must assume, as Grandma Rose did of any husband, that Linnea is the one who carries me, all my rusty gears and bent fenders collected in her sturdy lap. But her box breaks down. My super glue surprises me and holds.

Heart Ground

Japanese students practicing English on the trains told us, "Ah, Nagasaki. Such a romantic city." Linnea and I were surprised to hear it. How could it be, we wondered, that a city we Americans ruined with the A-bomb could evoke such rhapsody? But then isn't it just like Americans to assume that the damage we caused, even fifty years after the fact, is another's defining moment? Besides, the bomb landed in a Nagasaki suburb, on what had been the biggest Catholic church in Asia. The city itself is built on a hillside, gardened and cobblestoned, and overlooks a swath of blue water and the slow wake of ocean liners. There was a time that Nagasaki was the only Japanese seaport open to the rest of the world, and so they have a Chinatown, and the shops sell Portuguese-inspired cakes flavored with green tea. At night the lights of the port glitter like a tossed fabric of sequins. It surprised us, but we had to agree. Nagasaki was a honeymoon city.

It was near the train station that we found the most curious Kannon, a great aluminum-cast sculpture. Kannon's hollow interior housed the Nagasaki Kannon Universal Temple. This Kannon had only two arms and appeared more female than male, although her draped chest was flat. She held one hand up in blessing, the other out toward the people. Three aluminum infants gathered at her feet with their arms stretched toward her. She was built in 1979, I read, which was, I recalled, one of my most drunken years. I am always fascinated to learn of what else was happening in the years when I was so far gone. We didn't find Kannon the first night. We retired early to our inn, and as it turned out this honeymoon city was the only one in Japan where Linnea and I spent our whole evening kissing. The next day it was so hot. My ankles were swollen from all the walking. We pulled our heavy limbs up the slippery stones of the streets and narrow-alley staircases until we saw Kannon's great metal head poking up over the shingled rooftops. We couldn't get close enough to see into her belly, but read that she has a Foucault Pendulum inside her body's cavity, swinging in tune to the Earth's turning.

Not visible, then visible again, Kannon's face rises from the center of city blocks where nothing happens but everyday living. (After the honeymoon there is another thing, eyes that have witnessed both the big bomb and the slow passage of ocean liners. Linnea and I touch each other in silence, the paper walls of the inn no sound barrier, the thin futon pallet barely cushion enough. The moon rinses us with light then is obscured by clouds.) Everyday the Kannon temple bell tolls at 11:02, exactly the minute the A-bomb erupted. Downtown, there is an outdoor escalator carrying tourists up the hill to a garden where a Scottish trader lived in a wood house with his Japanese wife. Puccini is piped in among the fountains and flowers, because a famous Japanese opera singer who portrayed Madame Butterfly once visited this hillside. On the outskirts of the city, on the morning before we had to get back on the train, we see Kannon's aluminum head popping up over the rooftops. As we get closer, we spot her bare toes balancing on a turtle's back. Light catches and sinks into her wide matte forehead. (All the avenues are blocked, the stairways too deep to maneuver. The Earth keeps inching around its axis. Oh tolling heart, how do we get to you?)

~

We went to Japan because we were new aunties. My brother and his wife's first child, a daughter, was conceived on their honeymoon in Greece and born just six months before we arrived. Linnea and I spent weekends on a futon in the tatami room of their tiny apartment, three stories up from the tight outer Tokyo streets that surrounded the Yokota Air Force base. When I met my new niece she was laughing, but once it stopped raining and the summer heat descended, as my brother warned us it would, the baby's teeth began to emerge through the red flesh of her gums. She started crying then, and kept crying for most of the time we spent with her.

Mitsuko was exhausted by the pregnancy, the birth, all that muggy wailing, and so whenever she noticed the aunties were safely ensconced in baby-sitting position, she fled from us, to the grocery store, or into any errand where she could find a couple hours' respite. She left us with a child who was smiling, but who could start howling at any moment. Once she started crying, I would walk her up and back across the tiny apartment, singing her off-key renditions of Steve Goodman songs I used to hear in the Chicago folk clubs. If that didn't quiet her down, I carried her out onto the balcony so she could howl out over Tokyo for a while. Her bellow mingled with the sounds of drummers rehearsing for an upcoming festival and megaphones advertising the merits of political candidates.

This baby wasn't the first niece of my marriage. Linnea's sister had her two girls. But this was the first niece of my blood. As much as my neck ached and my arms grew numb after only an hour of holding her, as much as I sweated and longed to join Linnea in a little midday nap, I was happy to be rhyming and swaying with this bawling little girl who bore the face of my brother and so too my face, but also the features of this country that seemed to me the other side of the mirror from my home.

I could see from this balcony the ripples of this never-ending city, popping and sparking across a hazy horizon. I felt time tolling along beneath us and could imagine her face lengthened into that of a teenager, and I wondered if she would come to howl at her mother the way I spent adolescence howling at mine, or if Mitsuko would always be able to calm her with whispery intimacies, the Japanese words that her daughter's all-American papa, despite his language study, might never completely share. Whether the baby was smiling or crying, I could make out a brown blaze in her gaze. In my own eye that kind of flickering had become, in the late days of my youth, a green sparking bonfire that nearly burned me down. My life was an experiment, far away from my family, while in that same year, on the other side of the mirror, in the country where my niece would one day be born, workers constructed a face of Kannon to peer out over the Nagasaki rooftops. Just like an American, I suppose, to imagine such a thing has anything to do with me, and yet the thought of it, my falling, a goddess rising, reverberates. It was only all these years later that I had begun to understand how far my bad old days were behind me, how capable I was, finally, of such a simple thing as holding a crying child of my family. I gazed out over the rooftops too, grasping my baby niece to my hip, watching for Mitsuko with her grocery basket, trying to convey some kind of comfort from that hot place in myself that had taken me so long to learn how to handle.

~

When the ministers and politicians tell us the natural movement of the Earth around its center dictates that we can't marry because our two female bodies together won't make a child, I have come to think of our nieces and nephews. Family is, after all, more than Mama and Papa and Baby makes three. The new generations of our family are so young now, and so much about them will change, but at this moment we have two girls, ages eight and six, one who loves to read, one who loves roller coasters, and another who is three now, lives overseas, loves big-budget musicals and her weekly ballet class. There are two baby boys now as well, one with a crew cut that makes him look just like his father, and another who has just learned to walk, baby Godzilla we are told, lurching from one side of the living room to the other, knocking over speakers and pulling things from shelves.

With all the talk among gays and lesbians about how to make family, it seems the most obvious is so often overlooked. Linnea and I have not poured through sperm-bank biographies, nor rescued abandoned babies from orphanages in China or Bosnia, nor borrowed sperm from a friend and squirted it between each other's open thighs with a turkey baster, nor gone out in search of a party partner and come home knocked up. We know of lesbians who have followed all of these routes and more, and we could yet choose the same, but so far we have not. I've sat up late with Mitsuko at my parents' house in Florida as she sorts and folds another day of baby clothes, the children finally asleep. She's had another child, a boy, since the air force moved my brother and his family from Tokyo to London. I am charmed as Mitsuko tells me how she feels her babies, her husband, herself are one breathing entity. Such expansion beyond the limits of the self, such multiplied living—as she speaks I think it's something I should want, something I do want. Then Mitsuko asks me if I will ever have a child, and I cringe, remembering how I feel whenever I am engulfed, the old fear that my body will be swallowed, and so I tell her no, I will never have children.

And yet the hours we spend with our sisters' and brothers' children, although not parenthood, is an expansion. Such as the time each summer when our nieces from Linnea's side come to stay with us. The older one has taken to roaming around our house, fingering our things, asking, "Why do you have a room that is just Elvis and a room that is just teapots and a room that is just leopard?" Some of our chorus have pointed out that these are questions that anyone with any sense might ask, but what we like about our niece's inquiries are the serious way she makes them. She is old enough now to notice we are not like her parents, or like the parents of her friends in the Wisconsin ex-urbs where she is about to enter third grade. She jumps into our laps and hugs us. Her long braid stirs up the dust. She whispers, *I love you*, into our ears, nods seriously when we ask her to tell us what she thinks of the novel it took hours for her to pick out at the funny city bookstore with the live cats and birds and even a rooster, a store where we are always sure to take her when she comes to see us.

Meanwhile Mitsuko's daughter is learning her words in both Japanese and English. This niece calls our names in hybrid syllables—*An Nay A, An Ba Ree*. The night before the last big family wedding she refused to go to bed, so Auntie Linnea and I stayed up late with her. We helped her play with crayons and stickers and bubbles and let her dress herself in my silk scarves. The next day she took the stage at her uncle Benny's nuptials, where she spun and twisted on the hand of the best man, her papa, as the lace-swathed bride stepped down the red-carpeted aisle. Then she spotted Linnea and me amidst a streak of cousins. She tugged on Papa's coat and pointed at us, surprised to see we were there, too. Then a reader quoted a passage about Adam and his rib and Linnea and I, listening, widened our eyes at each other, spun back to the outside again, to our roles as the other ones, the critics. This new sister-in-law, adored by my brother, her face round and pretty underneath a torrent of permed curls, was hardly a subset of any man. I had seen her quickly transmogrify, a hot white beacon, whenever anyone tried to take her over, and as someone who had spent so many years doing the same I had to empathize. So Linnea and I wondered, why did women who were so perfectly capable of loaning out ribs of their own still allow such things to be said at their weddings? But our inquisition was interrupted by the voice of our niece calling out to us from under the bare feet of the Baptist Jesus, *Anbaree, Annaya,* and we were returned, welcomed back to the family heart.

The View from Bohemia

When Linnea and I were married we made up different words for it, no imagery of self-immolation, no two bodies merged into one. We talked about rivers and shores, about meeting and bending and changing together, but never losing ourselves. What would a merged river and shore turn out to be? Just mud. That is not what we wanted.

But we were married in Las Vegas where the chapels run stock weddings on the hour. There were parts of the ritual we couldn't control. Take the photograph of Linnea and me lighting a Unity Candle. I look so much taller than Linnea because of the silver high-heeled sandals I am wearing. Her leopard-print tie matches the leopard scarf around my neck as we lean over the candle. Our individual wicks meet over a third while a chorus of four smiles over our shoulders. Peter's tie is a mosaic, varieties of animal print, and Paul wears a tawny-toned dress shirt. Chris accents with a long zebra-print jacket and Alissa sports a matching zebra tie. Linnea and I look centered, clear, so aware of what we are doing. In the photograph you can't tell how long it took me to decide on a dress, or what trouble we had over Linnea's necktie. You can't see that we stayed up all night to rewrite the candle-ceremony words then finally decided to ask the reverend visiting from the Las Vegas gay and lesbian church to read from our love letters rather than from the standard script—flames flickering alone now burning as one. And she did as we asked. But all you see in the photographs are the white flowers, the white candles, the common accoutrements of an American wedding. You have to look close to notice that the flames, while joined, still burned twice, possessing two tremulous points of flicker.

I'm not sure what people think when we pass around the pictures of our wedding. Linnea and I stand in a room surrounded by white pews, cupids with sneaky smiles, wedding blossom bric-a-brac. And we are dressed up in the sort of clothes men and women wear to their weddings. It must seem to some that we are trying to vanish into the mainstream, trying to be married in that way my brothers are married, the way our parents, our straight neighbors are married. It must look to others like a joke, a great perversion, two women dressed up as who they can never be to each other. Husband and Wife. What Linnea and I see are shining squares of all our jostling, all our laughing. Or rather, that is what we see now. The days leading up to our wedding were more confusing.

Imagine it. Two women who have, for who knows how long, changed places. One who says her light has gone out. Another who finally has all her own lamps on but doesn't know yet how to maneuver in the absence of her familiar shadows. Imagine that they know who they are to each other, and yet seek something more, a candle wick springing to fire beneath their palms, a light from the sky aglow under their own skin. Then imagine how that light seems to be visible but just out of their reach, a lit-up city across churning water. The city is the same one they had to leave in order find each other, but now they are homesick. How do they get back to it?

≈

The light from the other side might be from the sun, or a distant comet, or the molten glow of heavy industry, or a lighthouse beam in the fog, or a temple icon that captures the lamp of the day's last hours, or the Emerald City, or whatever it is they say Bernadette saw wavering in the caves of Lourdes, Moses saw ablaze on the mountainside. Or it may be just another created thing. A refracted reflection. A picture show.

Practically everyone has seen some version of the movie. My favorite is Gene Kelly and Leslie Caron in the ballet scene of *An American in Paris*, the sultry swell of Gershwin and the bodies rising into the sound, blue-feathered birds against a smoky sky. This is how it's supposed to feel to be in love. This is how it does feel to love Linnea, the same lyric, but in translation. I am the bare-shouldered woman in the cobalt blue skirt. Linnea is the man with the muscled thighs. It's easy as long as we choose a part and stick to it, harder when we try to see a woman in both of the roles. One keeps two feet on the ground. The other embraces with her thighs, backbends toward the floor. Who is the holder, who is the held? If we imagine two women in the ballet it's easier to admit that nobody knows for sure. It could be either one of us.

It is the thing between those two bodies—not the names of the embracers but the embrace itself, the choreography of love, so far beyond what is dangling or gathered between our thighs—that we wanted to illuminate at our wedding. I can't think of words bigger than this picture of the dancer's fluid hold, the partner's slide into arms that will not drop her. The picture of leaping into love, yes, but also how it feels to be in love still. The reason we decided to have a wedding was so simple. We wanted a word big enough to convey not so much who we are but rather what exists between us. All of our past, all of our future. The brassy trumpet glide of our love. The verdant stare of my dead cat. The way my dead grandmother pronounced her sentences. The way Linnea tears up when she looks at the curling photographs of Italian immigrants who remind her of the people on her mother's side. The vintage rediscoveries and the new constructions. We did not want a new word that we made up for the occasion, but an old one that everyone would understand.

But there is no word that *everyone* understands. Not really. Say marriage and automatically the old definitions come into play. One woman. One man.

So imagine again those two women, those lesbians who had been so happy in Bohemia but now ache for a familiar light on the other shore, that flickering screen, that molten machinery blaze, that industrial cityscape, the skyline of their birth. They wade into the river up to their knees, trying to trudge across the windy passage from their new home to the old one. The smell of city ice rides the breeze. Sharp gusts slap their exposed skin. Half-frozen water numbs their toes. They don't mean to escape to the other side. They want only to visit, for the holidays perhaps. I want to return to that old landscape triumphant, my beloved in tow, ready to shout, look, look, despite this long winter and all the grinding trouble of life I have found my one true thing, the ember from the center. Yet I find that the closer Linnea and I get to home the more ghostly we become. I hold Linnea's hand in mine as we wade deeper and notice we can see through our flesh and bones to the unreachable light on the other side.

~

Linnea and I hold onto each other, our fingers entwined. We ballet toward our wedding vows. One moment we are a dance of ghosts. The light from the other side pierces us. Then I look again and we are solid compositions. The weight of our limbs thumps against our own hard earth. Then it is the water and the distant light that is ghostly, forming fast rivers and industrial shadows across the open canvas of our skin.

It was in this solid form that we decided to have a wedding in Vegas. Such a strange thing, it made me laugh every time I thought of it. But we had decided to go ahead with it and so I did what I had to. I called the wedding chapel.

Cupid's was the name of the place we chose. We read about it in a Las Vegas guidebook. Sylvia, the woman who ran the place, was a hopeless romantic and just loved any sort of wedding. She was available for consultation at her 800 number, twenty-four hours a day. I was nervous when I dialed, half expecting the usual icy confusion I encountered in the outside world when I said the two words together. *Lesbian. Wedding.*

"Sure thing, honey," she said, in her gangster-doll voice. I imagined lightbulb bright hair. I imagined diamonds woven into her eyelashes. "Now is one of you," she asked, "a little bit more butch, one of you a little bit more femme?" I had been afraid that the phone line would shatter when I posed my question, but clearly she had done this before.

From here it should have been so easy. Make some plans. Bring nice clothes. Nothing fancy. Just run away to Las Vegas to get married. What I didn't foresee was that once I uttered the word—wedding—our plans would become a rough passage through rocky cascades, with me crazed, lashed to the raft and muttering into the whitecaps.

Imagine it, the rebel boho girl, trying to be a bride. My forehead was too hot. I was overcome with thirst, just as I had been the afternoon I watched my baby brother get married. I was reaching for a gleam I couldn't make out, a fire that flickered again whenever Linnea said, "Will you really marry me?" I wanted to collect her into my arms, the way Gene Kelly lifted Leslie Caron and held her to his heart as Gershwin's trumpet wailed, but my legs were so shaky. I felt more like a wife than a husband. I was beginning to understand a simple thing, that I had to be the strong one, the stable one for a while, but my first attempts were so uncertain.

My big confusion about our wedding started with Sylvia, and all of her talk. She sibulated in my ear, *Special Day. No other day like it. We'll sneak you in so Linnea doesn't see your dress. She must not see you until you walk down the aisle. Listen to me please. I know about Romance.* Somehow I knew every word she was going to say before the sentences slid into my ear and I became intoxicated.

It was as if every sketchy want, each scratch of the past few years coalesced into the picture Sylvia painted in my ear. I could see the outline of my own life just the way my mother, my aunts, my grandmothers had seen theirs, through the diamond eyes of a bride. Isn't that what I had wished for, the past, that history?

I saw her, Linnea's bride, refracted by the department-store mirrors as I tried on new dresses. I saw my long Slavic face and olive complexion, and my funky cat's-eye glasses and my dyed purple Doc Martens boots and my body no longer the smooth and skinny one I wore when Linnea fell in love with me. I tried on every special dress they had in my size and stared into the glass, envisioning Linnea's face at the other end of the chapel carpet, alight and waiting for my wedding-day promise. I wanted the moment Linnea spotted me to be indelible in her memory. I wanted our love to extinguish her need for any other fire. I wanted Linnea's sadness to pass, along with all of my endless questioning. I wanted a full spectrum of blessings to be laid upon our heads. I wanted the whole big myth of the American Wedding, with all it was supposed to bring to us. I trembled and choked with every new zipper, every clinging hem. I recalled Sylvia's whisper. What would it take, which dress, which bra, which shoes, to make me, a messy assemblage of a girl, into a diamond-eyed woman, not a shadow or a ghost, but something brighter, a slow-spinning hallucination that takes the shape of a bride?

∼

Oh my God, did you turn into a straight woman? I was eating breakfast at a Minneapolis dairy renovated into a retro-hip café, with Cy, a member of our chorus. We leaned over our plates, held lukewarm coffee cups in our hands as the sun warmed our necks and the shaky outdoor tables swayed a bit in the spring wind. Cy's shirt was speckled with latex pigment, the gold leaf he had painted his dining-room woodwork, and his boots were dusty with dried mud from his perennial garden. Trained for the theater, Cy loved a good farce, and so he screeched when I told him my story. How I went to the Mall of America to find a wedding dress. How I spent eight hours at that mall of malls. How I was sweating and crying before I got away. I wanted to surprise Linnea in new clothes, not white lace, it never got that bad, but I still wanted to be a vision Linnea would recognize but had never seen before.

It wasn't a straight woman I had become. God knows, if I were a straight woman anything like the one I used to be, I would have never gotten married at all. Or if I had, it would have been just the two of us, no witnesses, shouting our vows from the upper plateau of a red rock mountain. Or I would have gathered a circle of friends in the park and been married by the shouts of a chorus declaring us so. I would have rented a loft and asked our friends to paint our two bodies in all of their favorite shades. I would have done what straight friends of mine did, invited everyone over for a barbecue and surprised them with a poofy white dress, rings, a priest.

But it was a woman I married. It was Linnea. I recently met a woman who was so cynical about marriage. She's a boho sort of heterosexual who lives in Wisconsin, a Japanese immigrant whose acclimation to America occurred in a Midwestern college town. She left her husband for no good reason that I could make out except that she didn't want to be married anymore. "It's so funny," I told her, as we sipped tea in a sunny Minneapolis café, "to hear you talk so casually about wanting out of where I want in."

"But if I was in love with a woman for twelve years," she said, "I would want to marry her, too. You bet." Surly art-school kids with pierced lips and eyebrows delivered sandwiches to the tiny islands of tables around us. Afternoon light shifted through plate glass and outside the cars streamed to or from downtown. We finished our tea and laughed at our opposite affinities.

Yet other straight women and even my sister-in-law Mitsuko have gaped at me so when I have told them about my time of bride fever. I am, after all, the one they depend on to be different, the one they come to when they want to reject whatever is expected of them. *So have you become one of them,* they ask, meaning I suppose one of those women I knew growing up, a big-mouthed girl who could organize anything, a keg party, a junior-high reunion. She's the one whom no one could remember ever being a virgin and yet lies awake imagining her wedding day, her lithe body stepping down the cathedral carpet while the soloist sings a Carpenters' song. I never wanted any of her world. That's part of the reason I left the other side in the first place.

Come on now, I can hear the chorus hooting. *You couldn't have completely lost your way. It was, after all, Linnea you were marrying.* Of course. I didn't entirely misplace my mind. Most of the time I was my usual self with much more than usual to do, a wedding to plan. And yet there were those bubbles of time where I slipped from one universe into another. Hardly anyone knew it was happening. It was mostly in my head. Sylvia whispering, *I know about Romance.* Minutes illumined as the letters of a sacred text. Moments when I was so certain that it mattered what I wore, how my hair looked, what color I polished my nails. I was so afraid I might jinx our happiness if I did any of this wrong and then our wedding would not be one we wanted to remember. As if the heat that came on under Linnea's skin when she said, *will you really marry me?* had to do with the wedding instead of the marriage.

I returned from the mall with a new dress a color the saleslady called pistachio, a pale shimmer of silk with a minty green cast, with rhinestone buttons and a scalloped chiffon hem that fell just below the knee, and a silk leopard-print scarf the same shade that I imagined I would drape around my neck in just the way I had seen in the photographs of Marilyn Monroe when she married Joe DiMaggio. I came home with all of it wrapped up in opaque plastic so that Linnea couldn't see. It was more money than I had ever spent on clothes. I came home cradling my new dress in my arms and the first thing that happened was we had a fight. Linnea had been shopping, too, and had come home with an amber and brown leopard-print tie and a black Italian mobster shirt. Had I still planned to wear one of my collection of leopard-print dresses I would have loved what she picked out, but everything had changed.

"But you can't wear that," I told her. "We'll clash."

"But how can I match you if I can't see the dress?"

"But Sylvia said . . ." I choked. "You can't look at it."

"Then cut me off a little piece. Just a strip from the seam."

"You want me to snip from my designer dress? You want me to cut up my wedding clothes?"

We sat across from each other in our sunset-colored living room with our heads in our hands. *Oh my God,* the chorus howled. *What have you done?*

～

You fell for that? All the way through my bride time I could hear our chorus screaming at me from dry land. But it wasn't so much a stupid plummet into a river where I knew I didn't belong. It wasn't entirely that I wanted to fall in and see what would happen. Mostly it was the thing they say can trick even the best swimmers. Imagine those two women splashing along a treacherous shoreline. Imagine the one who had waded in the farthest, as she was so often prone to do, getting tripped up by the undercurrent. I was scared. My arms flailed. The muddy water carried me deeper.

You have to consider what swirled around me out there, as I was caught in the depths between beaches, ducking under the rudders of passing boats as I tried to consider all the churns and glitters of what it might mean to be a homosexual bride, a lesbian wife.

There was all the junk of the bridal industry that I didn't want, although I had to look it all over before I knew for sure. There were the reception candies and the tiny dried flowers to throw instead of rice. There were the live butterflies to let loose from the front steps of the church. There were the ice sculptures and the engraved matchbooks and the embalming services for the wedding bouquets. There was foundation makeup the bridal-fair salesman swore he could blend to perfectly match my complexion, the sugar flowers for the wedding cake, the diet powders they promised would make me lose weight before my big day, and the drawing for the honeymoon cruise that would surely fatten me up again.

I did want our wedding to be a showstopper, but not the kind you find at a bridal fair. I wanted some of the splendor of what floated by next, the Takarazuka shows that always ended in a wedding, a slow dance under a white spotlight, then a free-for-all tumble into a white tulled and bouquet-tossing finale. I wanted my cross-dressed groom at the center, stepping down the foot-lit stairway, her chorus, a cast of thousands, fanning out behind. I wanted the house lights up and I wanted to cling in Linnea's arms and I wanted the rest of the cast singing along, too, every mouth improvising on our melody. Without the chorus, there is no show, no wedding, just two women grappling alone under too much stage light, their embraces hollow on a vacant stage.

The faces of our crooners were reflected in the choppy waters. They were our friends, the ones we know well and also the others, the old lesbian world of wives and husbands that used to be, another history, the 1950s working-class-bar milieu when femmes wore beehives, butches pompadours. I have seen the photographs. The butches wore ties and slicked-back hair and when they laughed together I could spot the same softness I see today among Linnea's football-watching friends with puppyish grins, bashfulness visible just behind the eyes, an invitation to tease until they blush. Their femme wives are the ones with the attitude, tough hides under all that ratted-up hair, no fluff and perfumey passivity. Their femininity had hip and lip and fuck-you chin.

The waters were full of the faces of the ones that we remember, and also the ones we are related to. There were my parents who admitted they loved Linnea but who didn't understand what we meant by a wedding, and Linnea's sisters and brother who did, sighed *finally,* and sent us a basket of fruit and chocolate and bottles of bubbly. There were all our opinioned intimates who said, *what do you mean Las Vegas? We want to come to your wedding*. There were the laws that still said we couldn't marry and the TV sitcoms where the main character's lesbian sister gets married anyway.

I wasn't sure what to grab onto. Which image could float me back to hard ground? And what shore did I want? I might be the unemployed steelworker's wife. I might be the dancer in a blue net dress who ascends in her lover's balletic embrace. Or if not her, then the one who stays standing while her lover risks the leap and swoon. Or it could even be me who glimmers from the mountainside, like the statue of Kannon Linnea and I spotted from the window of a Japanese seaside inn. I might be a wife made up of all of this.

Or I might just be another Vegas bride. Ask the most seasoned members of our chorus, the ones who were there that day inside the shimmying walls of the chapel on Las Vegas Boulevard.

Ask Eduardo, the chapel camera man who photographed the whole affair and then asked us what was that song we danced to, real music he called it, Johnny Hartman's maple tones riding the smoky keen of Coltrane's sax.

Ask our Elvis, a Vegas wedding chapel veteran who pulled off a believable rendition of the King's side-burned and white jumpsuited years with a resonant voice and a crummy amplifier. The hair on his chest was exposed and there seemed to be a sock in his crotch as he stood between Linnea and me in the photo we used for our reception invite. He laughed when Linnea promised, "You're the only man who will ever come between us."

Ask Reverend Daphne who mispronounced some of the words of our wedding vows and slipped a *Lord Be with You* in at the end, even though we asked her to leave God out of it.

Ask Sylvia who watched on the office video monitor as she prepped the couple after us for their big day. Sylvia was not the blond bouffant showgirl as I had imagined, not the glittering goddess I talked to on the phone, but an ample redhead with a big laugh, no makeup, and comfortable shoes.

Ask the chatty limo driver who drove us to supper, or the waiter at Spago, a blond gay boy from Wisconsin who arranged for the kitchen to surprise us with a special wedding pastry, or ask the women in Minneapolis from the organic foods café who, later on, made the blueberry-tiered wedding cake for our backyard reception.

In the weeks before we went to Vegas, I thought I needed to know exactly what separates any two women from that faraway shore, that lit-up city in which our marriages never play the wide screen. All I was able to figure out was that this river seems as wide as a sea, and I am never going to make it all the way across to find out. I thought for a second that I was almost there, in the department-store mirror, watching myself dress up as an off-the-rack bride. Then I noticed how Linnea and I muttered and rocked, our heads in our hands, and I knew I had to turn back. I made a mistake. I don't want my brothers' weddings. I don't want to return to my old home. I don't have the strength to flail the rest of the way across, nor the time, and I would have to dump too much of the new stuff to make room for the old, and I still want to stay away as much as I want to return, so I can't make my arms and legs stroke in tandem. Meanwhile all that swirls around me in these depths is both knife-edged and spongy, dull and glinting. I want all of it, none of it. I will never be certain.

All I can do is stop motoring my arms around and drift back to the shore where I began. Where I rattle my bones back up onto the sand. Where Linnea is waiting, still as a beach agate. Flecks of compressed luster are visible in her eyes. I can see it. She cannot and she stares off into a skittering horizon. I forget at first how she needs me right now and I sob into the sand about how, from the telescopes of the other side, our marriage will always be sheer as Grandma Rose's dress-up stockings.

And so in the days before my wedding I cry about it. And then I don't. After all, it's not really sanctification that we need so much as muscle, and it's my turn to provide it. I nudge Linnea until she notices that I have returned and together we watch as clouds fill in the sky and then dissipate again. We do, after all, both prefer life on this side of the water. I dry myself off in the yellow sun and open air and remember to tighten my jaw, lead with my chin in the same posture, perhaps, that all wives should strive for.

Linnea and I are not ghosts in each other's eyes. Solidity flows back around our translucent bones and we respond once again to our old tune. And so I try on my wedding clothes. Linnea and I stand before the mirror of our cornflower blue bedroom that looks out over our south-side city alley. Her face reflects the sun seeping in our back window as she whispers, "It is the most beautiful dress." We laugh at the big deal I make out of things. Linnea will find a shirt that matches. We will go to fabric stores, buy a complementary leopard-print cloth, hire a team of seamstresses to make her the perfect tie. I will put on my pistachio dress and my silver bride shoes and Linnea will put on her suit and her two-tone wing tips. We will get married.

Where I Call Her Beloved

Linnea and I became so tired of waiting for our lives to arrive, exhausted by year after year of maps, wondering where Linnea's career might take us, to the blue ink of seasides, to the yellow densities of cities. It took us so long to see that we were already living, now, here in a place where we had lived, for years, where a home built itself around our feet.

Things started to change the summer before our wedding. There were more strings of nights full of watching the muscles in Linnea's face crumble, watching her eyes widen as if they might fill with water if only she would let them, watching her shoulders slacken as she clung to me.

She had no words to give me for what was churning through her then. The faces of students. Memories of hours pounding out a dissertation. The hug her usually brisk advisor gave her after the defense, welcoming her into a profession with no place for her. The dream of a life filled with musty books from the bottom shelf of the stacks. The shiver when her eyes fell across the words of what she had been searching for, or if not that, then a flash of something she didn't expect. Or the shift in a student's face, clouds racing off to the corners, the daystar emerging as something was learned. All of that and more of what I can't imagine whirlpooled through her eyes as I held her head in my lap, ran my hand through her agitated curls.

Then one night she whispered to me, "I need to do something . . . to get my mind off this. A little job. Maybe a convenience store."

I tried to imagine Linnea behind the counter of the gas station at the corner and all I could think of was the city news. All I could see was a twitching man with a stocking over his face, a sharp ring of fire my beloved can't avoid. People work their whole lives in these kind of places, I know. This was just another of my random blips, my worst day-dreams. But then sometimes the worst does happen. I read the paper. It's happened at least once a year on our side of the city alone. And it wasn't just me shaking my head. Almost everyone in the chorus said the same. *Let's think of something else.*

Which is just what I told her. We were driving south down Cedar Avenue toward home, past the oldest cemetery in the city, past the corner where prostitutes congregate, past the carpet store with the hand-scrawled sign offering Beanie Babies for sale. Not a convenience store, I said. No way.

"Then what do you expect me to do?"

"I don't know," I said with a long exhalation. "Be a bartender?"

Such a funny thing for me to say nearly a decade since my last drink. But all at once we could see the pressed white shirt, the sleek drop of the tie, the approachable face, the rattle of the martini shaker. We could even see what we could not possibly know yet, the way so many different people would come up her and say the same thing. *You're a real bartender. You're like the old-time bartender.* People our parents' age who remembered the days when martinis were king would say it. Young people who had only seen such a real bartender in the movies would say it. Linnea would smile, the golden light of the bar reflecting off her spectacles, a cocktail shaker rattling in each one of her thousands of arms.

Before and after our big Vegas wedding, we tried to focus on our every-day. The smoky tones of dusk as the dropping sun cut across our bed-room windows. The lavender petals of the purple coneflower growing back in our garden without bidding. Our dog Patsy sunning herself on the wide cement steps leading into our kitchen. By the time Linnea and I decided to get married our two remaining cats had adjusted to the ab-sence of old Artemis. Sometimes Linnea and I thought we saw the shadow of her familiar bones leaping from the kitchen floor to a sunny hot spot at the table's center.

When we walked down to the park to see Burnside-san, I asked

Linnea the same question I had been asking her for years now. What makes us married?

"It's just how I feel about us," she said, as we tossed a stick into the center of the green gully of grass. Pasty ran right past it. Now that she is over ten years old, she has trouble making out some of the details because a cataract she has had since she was a puppy clouds the light of her left eye.

"But *how* does it feel?" I asked, wanting more, wanting to touch it. Linnea stood still, thinking, watching the dog sniff around for her stick in the purpling greenery of a northern city at the end of summer. Linnea's jeans were snug and worn around her hips. At her waist was the wide black belt with the silver conchos that she made herself, and her faded denim shirt was tucked in. She's always so organized around the edges, even on a walk to the park. She was wearing new shoes, men's reinforced-toe work oxfords she bought for standing behind the bar. Her hair was as silver as the undersides of the scuttling clouds.

"It feels like a cup of tea with you at night," she said. "It feels like a motorcycle ride, in the evening, after it's been really hot."

"Yes," I say, looping my arm through her arm. On the way out of the park we nod to Burnside-san, a star of sun caught in his copper forehead.

~

And oh, how I would love to leave it on a simple glowing moment, the sun settling in, Patsy chomping on a stick as she ran back toward us, tossing it at our feet. A rosy spot to pause, within our everyday breathing.

But I can't stop there because it's not the way things are, just us, alone with our dog, no refrain from the chorus, neighbors hidden away in their houses, the light falling, the music fading.

Imagine, for instance, a stucco duplex at the far corner of our gardened-city avenue. Imagine another absentee landlord. Only one of his tenants is a legal adult without a police record. The rest are her children, young men their mother can't control, tens and twenties fan between their fingers. They fill their pockets with Baggies full of powder, pirouette their merchandise into the windows of passing cars. For months that house was a hub of trouble, little brothers and sisters with bruises on their faces, a volley of shots fired from a speeding automobile, and then a foot in a cast, an arm in a bandage and still, those greenbacks fluttering between their knuckles. Anyone could see what was going on. At the block-club meetings we heard our neighbors' stories. Some crouched behind curtains to watch the goings on. One found a bullet hole in the porch gutter. How much were we all going to lose? For a while it was the only thing the people on our block talked about. It took a SWAT team to break it up, crates of guns pulled out of the dining room, the family split up between jail, relatives, and slum lord properties on someone else's block. Once they were gone we could hear the frantic city birds chattering in the trees again and everyone went back to whatever they had been doing, but the world beyond our bedroom reverberates still.

Then imagine me once again trying to explain myself to my parents. Their daughter tells them she is going to Vegas to marry her longtime beloved, the one who over all these years they have come to love almost as much as they do their own, even though they can't bring themselves to say it. "Be sure to see the Country Western show at the Golden Nugget Casino," was all her mother can think to say.

I was visiting my parents on their golf course when I made the announcement, and my sister-in-law Mitsuko was there, too, with her babies, with her husband, my brother Paulie, on respite from his overseas air-force duties. We sat in the hot tub together as the sun set over the golf-course sod, so far from the industry-streaked skies where Paulie and I had grown up. The February breeze was rustling the green shrubbery. This new place was an oasis for my folks, the reward for a life teaching in the public schools that had become so confusing by the time they retired. South Side of Chicago demographics had changed. The white kids they were used to, children and grandchildren of the old neighborhoods with last names inherited from the east and south sides of Europe were a minority there now. As soon as they could they retired to Florida.

In the hot tub I rumbled on about Linnea's and my plans, telling my brother and sister-in-law all about the cheap airfare to Vegas, the little chapel just off the strip, the Elvis who would croon us into our future.

Paulie laughed and said, "I want to do it, too. Whattya say, Mitz? A vow renewal when we hit ten years? An Elvis ceremony?"

Mitsuko cocked her head in his direction, one ear distracted, listening for her napping children's cries. Her long hair was gathered up in a messy bun. The tendrils around her face were damp. Get married again? Elvis? She had told me more than once that she would never go through another American wedding. She was exhausted forever by the way her husband and his family let what seemed to her the simplest things volcano into such messy business. And I had come to see that although I still envied the extravaganza of her big day, the family life she shared with my brother was not exactly what I would choose. She was always tensed for a child's wail; they would have to wait all those years for another uninterrupted conversation. Linnea's and my life probably looks too arid to them with so much talking, no little breathing subsets of ourselves to keep safe. What to us is pigment and viscosity must to them look dull.

Mitsuko and my brother embrace their life with the same fervor that I embrace mine with Linnea. I have observed the looks on their faces when they watch their daughter in a room full of four-year-olds in powder blue tutus tumbling through a rehearsal of "Dance of the Sugar Plum Fairies," or as they hold their baby son by the hands as he takes his first few steps. For them all the sacrifices are worth it. Linnea and I would rather remain doting aunties, the eccentric lesbian relatives, the ones unencumbered enough to send our nieces and nephews artsy books and tickets to the theater.

Before Mitsuko married my brother I had hoped she would be the sister I never had. What I got was the common bond of the sister-in-law, a family relationship to a female of my generation, albeit a woman very different than me. But before the children called for her again, Mitsuko found words to tell me she understood some of what Linnea and I wanted from our wedding, which was the other thing she and Paulie possessed. A place in the family story.

Paulie screwed his long face into a knot when I told him what little our mother had to say about my wedding. "Should I tell them again?" I asked him. He thought for a moment, with his eyes closed, his chin underwater as the hot-tub jets spouted and gurgled around his floating head. The sky, always so blue here, began to dim indigo over our heads. "Once more," he said.

So I did tell them. Once more. In the family room of their little A-frame that looked out over twelve feet of blue-tiled pool and the variegated shrubbery of their yard and beyond that a green isthmus crawling with the white-canopied roofs of golf carts. That swimming pool was exactly the sort I used to make believe I could see out my bedroom window when I was a girl, when the real view was smoggy Halsted Avenue, clogged with semis, and a field of power lines with an abandoned factory at the center. The presence of a real pool in the yard made me jittery. How did my mother bridge the distance between then and now? Her eyes skittered when I told her about the wedding. Clouds moved in over her new retirement glow. I suppose my news wasn't what the golf-course-community newsletter was looking for. The muscles of my father's face told me less. His long Slavic nose, his elongated cheeks could have been a mirror of my own. "Don't miss the light show at Caesar's Palace," he said.

Imagine, please, that it doesn't end here, and yet know that the daughter feels it has all ground to a halt and wonders why she decided to reach beyond her own body, her beloved's body. She flies away, back to the snow, unable to think of a way to bring it up again.

Then imagine the one she is to marry, the woman who used to be a professor, now a part-time teacher and a full-time bartender. *The real thing,* her bar customers keep telling her. Better times approach, but only in fits and starts. There are fine moments when she is working at either one of her jobs. A sea of student faces is attached to her words. Another circle of faces across the curved surface of the bar asks her to make them something new, or even amazingly, thanks her when she cuts them off.

Then she came home. Not all the time, but often, she stared as if the floors were windows. She left little notes to herself scattered around the house, instructions she never managed to follow. Her hair was almost as gray as her grandmother's. When we went out to dinner, I had to remind her of what she liked to eat. "This will be what it's like when you're old," I told her, and we both laughed at our shared picture of her as ancient Uncle Linnea in baggy pants and red suspenders, a cloud of white hair

under a baseball cap. Other times it wasn't so funny. She couldn't remember things I told her last year, last week, yesterday. Once I went
away for a few days. When I telephoned she tried to speak to me but
couldn't find any words.

∾

Looking back over it now I have to say, it was always the chorus who
muscled us through. The ones who called to make sure we got home in
the lightning storm. The ones who brought us gold- or silver-flecked
Madonnas from all over the world. The ones who brought pumpkin pie,
apple pie, Rice Krispie bars molded into the mathematical π, to the party
dubbed Night of a Thousand Pies. The ones who came to my sobriety
parties. The ones who helped pay for the Turkey Day bird. The ones who
sang at our Karaoke Thanksgiving. The ones who took us out for a meal.
The ones we ate with every Sunday. The ones who hoisted our king-
sized mattress over the second-story bedroom deck when we couldn't fit
it up the inside stairs.

Alissa goes fishing with Linnea every June. Our pal Cy, who adores
fabric almost as much as he loves an art-film matinee, was the one who
restored our wagon-wheel couch and found the material to recover my
leopard-print chair. My beloved's old friend Therese, her jitterbug partner from their Gay Nineties days, took Linnea to breakfast during her
worst hours, told her she had to stop being the girl-scout leader for a
while. Years back, the morning after I tried drinking again, the same
Chris who would stand up at our wedding gave me phone numbers she
hoped I would call. Lucinda, who used to build theater sets, lives a few
blocks away in her rebuilt HUD house and watches Patsy when we go
out of town. Peter and Paul come by to feed the cats and keep a key for
when we lock ourselves out. The day I bought my wedding dress, Ellen
and Robin materialized in Nordstrom's shoe department around an
obelisk of hip-hop boots, sat still as I pulled all that pistachio silk out of
my bag and held it against my chest, picked out strappy silver shoes for
me, then lent me their cell phone so I could call home. Linnea's motor-
cyle crony Peg, whom she's known since she was twenty, gave her the
St. John's Wort capsules that helped put syllables back under her tongue.

There was the fellow femme friend who drove downtown with me to check out the scary Bridal Fair. There was Linnea's college roommate who drove in from Moorhead to help us assemble the storm-sogged reception canopies. There was the one who made all the wedding-party coffee. The one who dubbed the Vegas video. There were the ones who gave us yellow iris bulbs and lilac bushes to plant in our garden, the ones who showed up at our reception in a sheer leopard-print dressing jacket or a tawny spotted miniskirt, the ones who held on tight to each other and danced across the wedding-party lawn. There were the ones who came back and the ones who went away. There were the ones dead before they should have been, men younger than we are now. (The one who scared the dog when he came to our Christmas party in a red *That Girl* wig. The one from among my ex-alcoholics, who laughed so hard when I told of my last time—vodka in macrobiotic tea.) Some of the chorus we have known forever, some for not so long. Some of them asked us to be in their weddings. Some of them made dinner for our families the night before our reception. Some of them carried our bags in Vegas. Some of them pored over the pictures later. Some of them toasted us in our backyard. Their long-stemmed and booze-less glasses raised. Their arms long stalks of living light.

⁓

Does it matter that Linnea's and my names are not listed in any of the official annals of union? I don't know. It's true that I chafe against all our invisibilities.

When we traveled in Japan on our own, away from Paulie and Mitsuko and our new niece, we seemed to be nothing but anonymous Caucasians in the eyes of the Japanese people all around us in the stations, in the streets, slipping silver yen into the slots of the street-side tea-dispensing machines. From my anonymity I watched the exquisite difference of each face in the crowd, especially on the trains, even among the schoolchildren who all dressed the same, blue skirts or trousers, white shirts. One girl's face was round, her bangs shorn short. A smile rippled behind her eyes even when the train lurched and her knees bent as she held onto the silver bar that ran the length of the commuter car. Another girl had long tresses, lightened red, a trend we noticed among a certain Slacker set. This girl had a narrow face and a permanent pout to her lips as she pulled her hair over her shoulder and fingered her split ends.

Linnea and I were bigger than everyone around us, and paler. If anyone understood the words we spoke to each other, they didn't let on. In the beginning there was a free feeling about it, not just that no one knew us, but rather that no one could guess who we were to each other. Sisters, they may have assumed, or cousins, if they bothered to look, which mostly it seemed they did not. At home our ghosting is of a different variety. Our love is not always visible but our bodies are flags. Gangster wannabe kids in the park have screamed that a good fuck would cure us. Middle-class heterosexual husbands and wives have seen us seated at the bed and breakfast table and moved to the farthest seat they could find. Friends of my brothers have stared at us as if trying to get us in focus. I have been tempted to snap my fingers in their faces, just in case they have fallen into an accidental trance.

In Japan, we were at first exhilarated by this escape from recognition. I understood how it must have felt in the big American cities in the 1950s, when homosexuality was automatically a secret-society membership. I understood why my cousin Dino wants to bring female dates to his straight brother's weddings.

But in Japan, after a few weeks, I was tired of it. I missed our community chorus. I missed my part in other choruses. I began to have trouble seeing myself in the mirror, or even in Linnea's dark eyes. If we are not seen, there is always a danger that we will cease to see ourselves. It might be the only reason it does matter, in the end, that we are not allowed to be legally bound.

So in the meantime, Linnea and I give each other wedding rings to remind us that any sanctity we hold has been bestowed to us by ourselves. The new rings are white gold with a green garnet stone, green for the resilience of life. We wear our rings on the fourth finger of the left hand, the married finger, a location from which it was once believed a nerve flowed directly to the heart.

∾

Imagine how we cried, Linnea and I, at our Sin City wedding, while Elvis swiveled and Reverend Daphne swayed in her long white robe. We never imagined a minister at our wedding, but Daphne was part of the gay commitment ceremony package. With a name like Daphne we were hoping for a drag queen, but at least she was a lesbian. We never dreamed our Elvis would sound so much like the real thing, or that we wouldn't care that the passing trucks caused our little wedding chapel to quake, or that I would have been nervous as a bride, so wooden and aware of my legs and arms. Imagine the high beam of Linnea's face, not just that afternoon but the whole time we were in Vegas, and how the six of us looked there among the flowered archways. Imagine the sharp jackets. The animal-print ties. The attendant of honor's red Liz Taylor dress and black pearls. The groom's mobster shoes. The bride's strappy silver heels that I heard from one of our nieces later were the same shoes her wedding-day Barbie wears. Linnea's and my carefully composed words of promise sounded like funny folderol in this tacky chapel, and so imagine how we laughed, as Elvis daydreamed between songs, as the camera flash streaked our faces, as we honeymooned in Vegas with our friends, and then came home to talk about it.

The last time our six- and eight-year-old nieces camped out at our house was only a couple weeks after they had been to our wedding reception. The older one stood on the stairway leading from the leopard library to the upstairs landing. It was the same stairway where her little sister, just the summer before, broke into laughter when she said, "Auntie Linnea, do you remember when I thought you were a boy?"

Now her big sister, the one with so many questions about our house, was staring at the framed show posters we have hanging where others would put family portraits. They are the Takarasiennes in various stages of embrace. "What is the story of these pictures?" she asked me.

I paused for a moment. Then I just told her. They were actresses. From Japan. Some of them dress like women and some like men. The story of their shows is how they love each other. I paused again before I added, "Like Auntie Linnea and me."

Our young niece was recently back from swimming. She had just brushed her long brown and blond hair that hung loose down to the middle of her thighs. It rippled in the evening light as she nodded, interested, clouds scuttling to the far reaches of her gaze.

∾

At our wedding reception we filled our little plot of land with nieces whose hair swung to the back of their knees, with the starry-eyed chorus in shorts or in fancy clothes, pretty sisters in sundresses who clung to their good-looking beaux, a baby nephew with a new coif, a new sister-in-law with a torrent of hair the same shade as her copper-colored jumpsuit, children and grown-ups, some pregnant ladies, other people's grandmothers, one brother in a tidy summer short-sleeved shirt tuning up his usual singing tribute, one brother with his bare-breasted biker tattoos unveiled, one mother who didn't cover the tattooed peacock on her shoulder, another mother who wore white summer linen, one father who parked himself in front of the boho jazz quartet and muttered to anyone who would listen how it had always been his dream, a bebop band in the backyard.

The day started out with monsoon rains but was sunny by the time our friends and family arrived. We had a visit from an Elvis impersonator who wasn't as good-looking as the one in Vegas. We had a long table of Chinese food and pasta salad and bread and a healthy maple-syrup cake for me and a nasty chocolate number with a frosting Elvis swiveling before a Las Vegas skyline for Linnea and cases of sparkling water and juices for the toasts. Linnea's students poured drinks and kept all the platters full.

Linnea and I wore clothes we had worn before, a leopard-print dress, a leopard-spotted shirt, sandals and shoes the same sunset shade of suede. Our nieces danced with Elvis. Linnea's Italian lesbians danced with each other. On their own our guests gathered in circles, with old friends, with strangers. My gay ex-alcoholics sat with our Christian missionary neighbors. Peter wore a hot pink dress shirt and a rhinestone bracelet and hung out with my mother and father. Linnea's new employers were there, three sisters, a grandmother, a six-month-old baby from the restaurant where Linnea and I used to talk it all through over sweltering bowls of Chinese noodles and soup. Linnea was their bar manager now, had even invented for them a signature martini. Their gift was a red lacquer plaque from China with gold-plated characters of their wish for us. Double Happiness.

My parents, who had no words for us in the past managed somehow to find them in time. I can't say how or why, but they chose to traverse the bridge over that windy channel to where their strange daughter resides. Were we solid bodies or did we flicker in their gaze? I can't say for sure. I only know that along with cards and checks from a few aunts and uncles and even a nice note from my cousin Antony's third wife, our best surprise was that my mother spilled blueberry-cake frosting on her white skirt and then complained as if it were any old wedding. For other people's mothers, this might not be proof of improvement, but for my mother and me it was the thing that set the Earth turning again. Ever since she loves to talk about it—how our food could have been warmer and how good the band was and how mad she is that Dino didn't show and how clean they kept their beautiful house, those nice boys who came with us to Vegas.

Paulie and Mitsuko and their babies toasted us with tea cups from a video they sent from overseas. Peter in pink toasted for the chorus with sweet words that made Linnea's sister cry. Linnea's mother Toni saluted us for her side of the family, my father and Benny spoke for mine, stepping up before the multitudes as the chorus roared. There were over 100 people there. It seemed like 1,001. Glasses raised. Voices gathered. A thick wood of family. A golden prairie of smiling faces. All due respect to Reverend Daphne, but it was the chorus who married us.

～

So, are we married? Can we call this marriage? Will we let those words fall forth from our lips, for better or worse? You bet.

But I knew that a long time ago. There was that summer afternoon at our old apartment a few blocks from the freeway's constant clamor. I sat on the pebbled steps that led up to the sloped side porch, watching the day's late light play over my knees, when a grinning fellow walked by on his way to the bus stop. He pulled his shoulders back when he saw me there.

"Ooooh baby, you are beautiful," he sang.

We both knew he was full of shit, and the sun was still pulsing, and it wasn't too hot, so we laughed about it together.

"You married, baby?" he asked, the sun at his back.

"Yeah," I answered, without hesitation. "I sure am." I could feel Linnea behind me, in the apartment, watching the news or scratching the dog between the ears or working on the saddle bags she was making for her motorcycle. The guy walked away then, shaking his head as the sun broke apart over the freeway.

These summer days, if I sit on my front porch swing with a cup of tea as the sun slants toward evening, I can see Linnea out in front. Her new project is her truck, too old to be pretty in the way it was meant to be. There are people in our city who hold parades, every summer, a cavalcade of cars with interesting stuff glued to the roofs, hoods, fenders, and, whatever else she does—as a teacher, a scholar, a martini-maker—Linnea intends to join them next year. She cements dice and cocktail shakers, ice buckets and luck-be-a-lady Madonnas onto every open surface. She made Styrofoam olives for the radio antennae, found Plexiglas martini glasses for the roof, shellacked photos of Sinatra around the gas cap where she carefully stenciled, "fueled by Frank," even painted a replica of the old Las Vegas Sands' marquee on the back hatch. Her truck has become the cluttered canvas of her passage into who-knows-what sort of life.

A life with me. The planet inches forward around its axis and on the other side of the globe a pendulum swings in tandem inside the aluminum breast of a holy protector's body. Halfway between, there's an English cathedral where Our Lady of Canterbury has heard my plea for our continued safe passage and in Chicago the icon of Our Lady of Cicero, teardrop stains marking her painted cheeks, seemed to be listening when I asked for the same. On our side of the world the tiger lilies are blooming. My old cat Arte feeds her ashes to the trees. My beloved polishes the faces of dice lined up along her silver door handles. She starts the engine and the cocktail shaker jiggles and we laugh and mutter *ridiculous*. Her face is bright as the lamps around a baseball diamond, as the neon pulse of Vegas that is visible, we have read, from as far away as the moon. Later we will walk Patsy to see old Mr. Burnside glint across the park's green gully, grinning like a guy who just lined up all the cherries on his slot machine.

Later still, we will touch in the white light of the moon, under the yellow lanterns of the south side, atop our king-sized bed on a simple frame, under the skylights that we had to replace after they cracked in the last hailstorm. We will probably hear those neighborhood kids who mess around at night in the alley, a little crew of tough girls in basketball shoes whose hair is pulled tight off their faces. They have nothing to do but hang out under the alley lamp and scratch their names into our garage paint. From the street we will hear the clank and grind of the city and in our chests we will hear the murmur of the chorus and in our ears we will recognize each other as we whisper, *You are my beloved.* Linnea's words, my words, are silent in each other's mouths as the world inches around on its axis, while we are still together.

ACKNOWLEDGMENTS

There are so many who deserve thanks for their role in the creation of this book. I owe much to Bertha, my long time writer's group, especially current members Judith Katz, Morgan Grayce Willow, and Ellen Lansky, as well as Lynette D'Amico and Susan Rothbaum who were there at the start of this project. Mary Petrie was a savvy reader of early drafts, and I am indebted to Pamela Fletcher, Judith Niemi, Cheri Register, Patrice Koelsch, Beryl Singleton Bissel, and especially Scott Sanders for their commentary midway. I also want to thank everyone at Graywolf for their attention to detail, and their extraordinary affability.

The Minnesota State Arts Board, the Dayton Hudson, General Mills, and Jerome Foundations, the Loft Literary Center and the eminently generous McKnight and Bush Foundations administrated and/or funded the fellowships which allowed me the money and time I needed to research and write this book. A week-long retreat early on at Norcroft and a priceless month near the end at Hedgebrook allowed me the solitude and focus this work required. I am grateful to all the contest judges, and to the benefactors of the foundations, as well as to the countless people who maintain these invaluable institutions.

I referred to many sources as I was asking the questions that move through this book. Many thanks to the Lesbian Herstory Archives in Brooklyn, the James C. Hormel Gay and Lesbian Center at the San Francisco Public Library, and the Minnesota History Room at the Minneapolis Public Library. I also read numerous books and articles and viewed videos related to my subject, and several were crucial to my focus and ideas. The sources which had the biggest impact were:

Darlinghissima: Letters to a Friend by Janet Flanner, thirty years of personal letters written by the *New Yorker* commentator to her beloved, edited with commentary by Natalia Danesi Murray.

The Essential Guide to Lesbian and Gay Weddings by Tess Ayers and Paul Brown.

Same-Sex Marriage: Pro and Con, edited by Andrew Sullivan.

Takarazuka: Sexual Politics and Popular Culture in Modern Japan by Jennifer Robertson.

Dream Girls, a video documentary about the all-female Takarazuka Revue, directed by Kim Longinotto and Jano Williams.

"Sheila Dances with Sheila" by Lois Weaver in *Butch/Femme: Inside Lesbian Gender,* edited by Sally R. Munt.

"Get Married? Yes, but Not by the State" by Alisa Solomon and "Hidden Hitchings." The Ambivalent History of Same-Sex Unions" by Jonathan Ned Katz. Both published as a part of "The Great Gay Marriage Debate" in *The Village Voice,* 9 January 1996.

Personal thanks go to my friends and family for putting up with a creative nonfiction writer in their midst. I extend my deepest acknowledgment, ardor, respect, and friendship to Linnea Stenson, my one and only love, for her responses to my daily pages and for everything else— our past, our present, our future.

Barrie Jean Borich is the winner of many literary awards and the author of *Restoring the Color of Roses* (Firebrand), a memoir set in the Calumet region of Chicago where she grew up. Today she lives with her beloved, Linnea Stenson, in Minneapolis, Minnesota, and teaches at Hamline University and Minneapolis College of Art and Design.

Visit the author's web site at: www.BarrieJeanBorich.net

The type has been set in Weiss Antiqua, a typeface designed by Emil Rudolf Weiss (1875-1942), a German poet, painter, calligrapher and type designer. This font was cut by Louis Hoell and issued by the Bauer Foundry, Frankfurt.

This book was designed by Wendy Holdman and set in type by Stanton Publication Services, Inc., and manufactured by Maple-Vail Book Manufacturing on acid-free paper.

Graywolf Press is dedicated to the creation and promotion of thoughtful and imaginative contemporary literature essential to a vital and diverse culture. For further information, visit us online at: www.graywolfpress.org.

Other Graywolf titles you might enjoy are:

Graywolf Forum Three: The Business of Memory, edited by Charles Baxter

Nola: A Memoir of Faith, Art, and Madness by Robin Hemley

North Enough: AIDS and Other Clear-Cuts by Jan Zita Grover

A Four-Sided Bed by Elizabeth Searle

The Risk of His Music by Peter Weltner

The Graywolf Silver Anthology